LOVE, DRUGS, ART, RELIGION

Love, Drugs, Art, Religion

The Pains and Consolations of Existence

BRIAN R. CLACK
University of San Diego, USA

ASHGATE

Published by
Ashgate Publishing Limited
Wey Court East
Union Road
Farnham
Surrey, GU9 7PT
England

Ashgate Publishing Company
110 Cherry Street
Suite 3-1
Burlington, VT 05401-3818
USA

www.ashgate.com

British Library Cataloguing in Publication Data
A catalogue record for this book is available from the British Library

The Library of Congress Cataloging-in-Publication Data has been applied for.

ISBN 9781409406754 (hbk)
ISBN 9781409406761 (pbk)
ISBN 9781409406778 (ebk-PDF)

Printed in the United Kingdom by Henry Ling Limited,
at the Dorset Press, Dorchester, DT1 1HD

Truly the light is sweet, and a pleasant thing is it for the eyes to behold the sun. But if a man live many years, and rejoice in them all; yet let him remember the days of darkness, for they shall be many.
Ecclesiastes 11:7–8

I'm a pessimist, in that I know it's not going to end well.
Scott Walker

Contents

List of Figures

Preface

In different circumstances, the natural home for this book would lie within the literature of the philosophy of religion. Indeed, it is primarily intended as a contribution to the understanding of the formation, nature and meaning of religious belief, and conceives religion to be a human phenomenon generated by the stresses and vicissitudes of human life. Historically, this contextualizing of religion within the troubling conditions of our existence has occupied a considerable portion of the activity of those philosophers turning their attention to religion. One might naturally think here of the work of Hume, of Feuerbach, and (in a very different manner) of Wittgenstein. Projects of that nature are, however, only infrequently found in contemporary philosophy of religion, which, despite its many admirable qualities, has a tendency to proceed as though religious doctrines and beliefs had a life entirely independent of the human beings who formulated them. The project of this book, contrariwise, is to think about religion completely as a phenomenon – as an efflux, even – of human life and its ineluctable difficulties. The inspiration for the book comes from the ever-pregnant work of Sigmund Freud, and particularly his suggestion, in *Civilization and Its Discontents*, that life is so unbearably difficult for human beings that we require something akin to palliative treatment, and that as a consequence certain strategies of coping and consolation have assumed a treasured status within human life and society. Religion is here conceived as one such 'palliative measure', and it takes its place alongside three others: intoxicants, art and sexual love. One of my principal aims, therefore, is to attempt to illuminate the character (and the possibilities) of religion by considering it within this context of palliation. But the other palliative measures previously mentioned are also given individual attention, and their role in the alleviation of suffering assessed. The project of the book is thus somewhat expansive and ambitious: it constitutes an investigation into the perennial difficulties of the human condition and the strategies we employ simply to stop ourselves from falling apart and collapsing under the weight of existence.

H.E. Baber, a dear colleague of mine at the University of San Diego, has suggested to me that this book constitutes something like 'a compendium of reflections by the usual suspects' (Freud, Schopenhauer, and so on). There is some truth in that. I sometimes think of this book as being, in part, just such a compendium, a collection of ideas harvested from (or inspired by) thinkers with whom I feel a temperamental affinity. My hope is that the utilization of these ideas might throw some light on the conditions of human life out of which religious phenomena – and the other palliative measures – have arisen. Some of those conditions (the inescapability of suffering, our sense of smallness and insignificance in the face of a universe unimaginably old and vast) are so central to the human experience, and our typical responses to anxieties of those kinds (for example, seeking solace in love or in drugs) so well known, that one might think this subject barely requires the sustained treatment it receives in the pages to follow. *There needs no ghost, my lord, risen from the grave to tell us this.* Against that suspicion, however, two things should be noted. First, and as Wittgenstein reminds us, many things often need to be drawn to our attention despite their being – indeed, *due* to their being – always before our eyes: like Poe's purloined letter, the answer to many questions about religion might lie directly in front of us, in the painful and anxiety-ridden nature of human existence. And secondly, if these features of life are indeed so familiar as not to require delineation, then one can only wonder why philosophy of religion proceeds as it typically does, examining the questions raised by religious belief in isolation from these burning and perennial problems.

In the course of this book, I quote from two different editions of *Civilization and Its Discontents*: Joan Riviere's original translation from 1930, and the version contained within James Strachey's *Standard Edition of the Complete Psychological Works of Sigmund Freud*. The Riviere translation is utilized only in the chapter on love (since I have a preference for her rendering of Freud's thoughts on that matter), but to avoid any confusion the initials J.R. are included in the footnoted references to that translation, thereby distinguishing it clearly from the more frequently cited version drawn from the *Standard Edition*. Grateful acknowledgment is given to W.W. Norton & Company for permission to quote from James Strachey's translations of both *Civilization and Its Discontents* and *The Future of an Illusion*; material from the *Standard Edition of the Complete Psychological Works of Sigmund Freud*, translated and edited by James Strachey, and published by the Hogarth Press, is reprinted by permission of The Random House Group Limited and the Marsh Agency Limited on behalf of Sigmund Freud Copyrights. The lines from Ovid's 'The Cures for Love' and the excerpts from the poetry of Giacomo Leopardi are both reproduced by permission of Oxford University Press. Every attempt has been made to trace copyright holders. The author and the publishers would like to apologize in advance for any inadvertent use of copyright material.

Some of the material included in this book has previously appeared in article form. These articles are: '"At Home in the Uncanny": Freud's Account of *das Unheimliche* in the Context of His Theory of Religious Belief', *Religion*, 38/3 (2008), pp. 250–58; and 'Religious Belief and the Disregard of Reality', in Joseph Carlisle, James C. Carter and Daniel Whistler (eds), *Moral Powers, Fragile Beliefs* (New York: Continuum, 2011), pp. 261–87. I am grateful to the editors and publishers concerned for permission to use this material.

Words of gratitude are owed to many people. I want, first of all, to thank Sarah Lloyd and David Shervington at Ashgate for their patience and efficiency. Of all my publications, this book is the most personal thing I have written and it is fitting that I should express heartfelt thanks to all those who have given me the support and the encouragement requisite for its completion and to those whose reflections have made this book better than it would otherwise have been (all its faults, of course, remain my own responsibility). Accordingly, I would like to thank my parents, Alan Clack and Ann Clack, for their unwavering love, and a host of others whose names here can only be listed but whose qualities are so deeply appreciated: John Adshead, Michael Agnew, Justin Bergh, Keith Bernstein, Michael Brearley, Beverley Clack, Adam Clayton, Jason Crum, Liz Edwards, Michelle Grier, Michelle Heidt, Jonathan Herapath, Lawrence Hinman, Patrick Hurley, Alison McKendrick, Mike Onofrio, Amanda Petersen, Linda Peterson, David Phillips, Gaby Rodriguez, Lisa Smith, Celia Stringer and Lori Watson. Finally, more than thanks are due to Nicole Lively, who provided for me an environment of love and happiness which allowed the thoughts found within these pages to be given expression. To her I dedicate this book.

B.R.C.
San Diego, November 2013

Chapter 1
'Life, as we find it, is too hard for us ...'

Man that is born of a woman hath but a short time to live, and is full of misery.

The Book of Common Prayer

William Paley's *Natural Theology*, first published in 1802, is remembered principally for an analogy drawn by the author between the world and a watch, an analogy intended to demonstrate the existence of God. The marks of contrivance so apparent in the structure of a watch (its complexity and intricacy, the interconnectedness of its parts) will lead any investigator – even one heretofore incognizant of watches and clocks – to conclude that it was put together for some purpose, put together by some intelligent designer. Since the world exhibits those self-same features demanding explanation in terms of a designer (complexity, intricacy, purposive interconnectedness), with the only difference being that of magnitude, the contrivances of nature far surpassing the contrivances of human creativity, one must concede the existence of a Creator of the world. Thus runs the familiar argument from design. There is no shortage of defenders of this kind of argument, but an intense assault upon its foundations (aimed variously by David Hume, Immanuel Kant and the Darwinian tradition) has probably undermined its effectiveness. But my intention in raising the case of Paley here has not to do with that issue. Rather, I wish to bring to prominence an aspect of Paley's thought bearing on the vital matter of what attitude a person should take towards this world.

A standard criticism of the design argument concerns the restrictions on any conclusion that may be drawn from an observation of complexity and order in nature. Hume pointedly advanced such a criticism thus: 'If the cause be known only by the effect, we never ought to ascribe to it any qualities, beyond what are precisely requisite to produce the effect.'[1] For instance, if only one side of a set of scales is visible and it can be seen that an object weighing ten ounces is outweighed by something on the other (hidden) side, the only conclusion legitimately to be drawn concerning the hidden object is that it is heavier than ten ounces. Anything more would be mere speculation. The application of this insight to the question of design is straightforward. One might, perhaps, be justified in inferring that some designer is responsible for the order detected in nature, but nothing more substantial can be said of that being than that it is a designer. From this data alone, it cannot be said that the designer possesses omnipotence, omniscience or any of the long etcetera of attributes traditionally ascribed to the deity. To flesh out the

---

[1]   David Hume, *Enquiries Concerning Human Understanding and Concerning the Principles of Morals* (Oxford, 1975), p. 136.

bare idea of a designer with such a set of attributes would go well beyond the evidence at hand, and can merely be an exercise in 'exaggeration and flattery'.[2]

This is not a conclusion Paley is willing to embrace, for certain features of the world warrant conclusions about the nature of the deity and the attributes properly and not arbitrarily predicated of him. One such attribute is *goodness*. Of course, those sympathetic to Hume will hold that the character of the world – even if this character supported the idea of design – can not support or ground any doctrine regarding divine benevolence, since the prevalence of pain and suffering must put a halt to any speculation that the creator of the universe is loving and cares about the well-being of the world's inhabitants. The evidence would better warrant a conclusion that the designer is malevolent or (at best) indifferent to suffering. Paley does not share such qualms. An objective evaluation, stripped of affected melancholy, should reveal the truly felicitous character of nature. In giving Paley's view of this matter I am now no longer concerned with this as data marshalled in support of the doctrine of divine benevolence. It is the view of life contained in his words that will itself be our focus of attention.

> It is a happy world after all. The air, the earth, the water, teem with delighted existence. In a spring noon, or a summer evening, on whichever side I turn my eyes, myriads of happy beings crowd upon my view. 'The insect youth are on the wing.' Swarms of new-born *flies* are trying their pinions in the air. Their sportive motions, their wanton mazes, their gratuitous activity, their continual change of place without use or purpose, testify their joy, and exultation they feel in their lately discovered faculties. A *bee* amongst the flowers in spring, is one of cheerfullest objects that can be looked upon. Its life appears to be all enjoyment: so busy, and so pleased ... If we look to what the *waters* produce, shoals of the fry of fish frequent the margins of rivers, of lakes, and of the sea itself. These are so happy, that they know not what to do with themselves. Their attitudes, their vivacity; their leaps out of the water, their frolics in it, (which I have noticed a thousand times with equal attention and amusement,) all conduce to show their excess of spirits, and are simply the effects of that excess.[3]

Paley continues in this vein for a good number of pages, detailing a picture of the blissful harmony of existence. This picture encompasses the entirety of being, applying to both human and nonhuman, young and old: 'Happiness is found with the purring cat, no less than with the playful kitten; in the arm-chair of dozing age, as well as in either the sprightliness of the dance, or the animation of the chase.'[4] Though inflated and evidently whimsical, Paley's depiction nonetheless occupies a place in a widely accepted view of life, which shall here be called *existential felicity*. Such a view of things has historically found expression in manifold ways,

---

[2] Ibid., p. 137.
[3] William Paley, *Natural Theology* (London, 1838), pp. 278–9.
[4] Ibid., p. 280.

from the judgement of the Creator on his work ('God saw that it was good') to the United States Declaration of Independence, in which 'pursuit of happiness' is regarded as an unalienable right. So here we encounter a perspective on things enshrined alike in theological doctrines, political documents, and the outlook of countless individuals: the world is good, life is a blessing, and the conditions for happiness are built into the very fabric of existence.

But what if that view is wrong? What if it is not merely an exaggeration but an error to declare the world a place conducive to happiness? What kind of lives could human beings then be expected to lead? What strategies need be employed simply to cope?

A great many writers have drawn attention to the deficiencies of a view of existence such as that expounded by Paley, highlighting instead how physical and mental suffering undermines and outbalances the fleeting pleasures offered by life. Such attacks on existential felicity have been most strongly (though by no means exclusively) advanced by that tradition of thought known as *pessimism*, a tradition counting among its principal figures such writers as Jean-Jacques Rousseau, Giacomo Leopardi, Arthur Schopenhauer, Thomas Hardy and Sigmund Freud.[5] Indeed, Freud's widely-read book *Civilization and Its Discontents* occupies a central place in the canon of pessimistic literature, and within its pages we find a most explicit negation of existential felicity: 'One feels inclined to say that the intention that man should be "happy" is not included in the plan of "Creation".'[6] Our attention must thus turn to the range of features that might plausibly be held to work against the very possibility of human happiness. We will start with an element of our condition that even the most optimistic of individuals will need to acknowledge: suffering.

---

[5]   The nature of pessimism has been anatomized well by Joshua Foa Dienstag in his book *Pessimism: Philosophy, Ethic, Spirit*, the influence of which on the presentation of ideas in this first chapter is a large one. One of the issues broached by Dienstag concerns the unpopularity in our time of any thought with a pessimistic tone. At least in the United States, 'it is enough to label an idea (or a person) "pessimistic" in order to be allowed to dismiss it (or him) without further discussion as irrational, emotional, indefensible or, worst of all, unpatriotic' (Joshua Foa Dienstag, *Pessimism: Philosophy, Ethic, Spirit* (Princeton, NJ, 2006), p. ix). Yet as Dienstag appropriately notes, despite the abuse and scorn poured upon pessimistic writers, they 'keep appearing – and this should not be surprising since the world keeps delivering bad news' (ibid., p. x).

[6]   Sigmund Freud, *Civilization and Its Discontents*, in *The Standard Edition of the Complete Psychological Works of Sigmund Freud* (24 vols, London, 1953–74) (hereafter S.E.), vol. XXI, p. 76. Freud's remark echoes a thought offered by Rousseau in *Reveries of the Solitary Walker*: 'Happiness is a lasting state which does not seem to be made for man in this world' (Jean-Jacques Rousseau, *Reveries of the Solitary Walker* (Harmondsworth, 1979), p. 137).

A Blighted Star, Not Sound

Early on in Hardy's novel *Tess of the d'Urbervilles*, the young Tess Durbeyfield converses with her brother Abraham about the starry skies above them. Abraham persistently requests answers from his older sister about these twinklers, how far away they are, and whether God lives on the other side of them.

> 'Did you say the stars were worlds, Tess?'
> 'Yes.'
> 'All like ours?'
> 'I don't know; but I think so. They sometimes seem to be like the apples on our stubbard-tree. Most of them splendid and sound – a few blighted.'
> 'Which do we live on – a splendid one or a blighted one?'
> 'A blighted one.'
> ''Tis very unlucky that we didn't pitch on a sound one, when there were so many more of 'em!'
> 'Yes.'[7]

At the root of Tess's judgement that our world is 'a blighted star, and not a sound one'[8] is a recognition, from her own experience, of the troubles afflicting human beings. She refers to her father's drunkenness and her mother's seemingly endless domestic toil, though in the context of the novel as a whole, this blighted state of things can be seen to refer to something more terrible: the extraordinary sufferings she is fated to endure.

It would seem therefore to be the phenomena of suffering and pain which principally mark our world out as being of the blighted variety, and this is a view forcefully expressed also by Hume. In the *Dialogues Concerning Natural Religion*, 'the whole earth' is depicted as 'cursed and polluted':

> A perpetual war is kindled amongst all living creatures. Necessity, hunger, want stimulate the strong and courageous; fear, anxiety, terror agitate the weak and infirm. The first entrance into life gives anguish to the new-born infant and to its wretched parent; weakness, impotence, distress attend each stage of that life, and it is, at last, finished in agony and horror.[9]

Here Hume recounts how suffering permeates the entire span of an individual's life, every moment from birth to death being accompanied by pains of distinctive kinds. Each pain a person experiences can be seen to stem from one of a number of sources, and these sources are classified by Freud in a clear threefold schema. Let us then return to *Civilization and Its Discontents*, the book in which this schema is advanced.

---

[7] Thomas Hardy, *Tess of the d'Urbervilles* (Oxford, 2005), p. 37.

[8] Ibid., p. 39.

[9] David Hume, *Dialogues Concerning Natural Religion* (New York, 1948), p. 62.

Freud's isolation of the three directions whence suffering may arise is framed by a contrast he draws between the exacting conditions required for the sensation of happiness and the ease, on the other hand, with which unhappiness is experienced. Our individual lives, after their own fashion, constitute evidence to support this judgement. Happy experiences – a dinner party, a vacation, a wedding – require much planning (and money), whereas it takes no such exertion to experience the misery of a disease or an illness, and death may be brought about by something as small as 'a hair, a fly, an insect'.[10] Freud, however, alerts our attention to something else. Intense enjoyment, he says, can be derived only from a contrast, and not from a steady state of things, for happiness comes from the 'satisfaction of needs which have been dammed up to a high degree, and it is from its nature only possible as an episodic phenomenon'.[11] One may here think of the enjoyment of eating after a day without food, or the intensity of an orgasm following a period of sexual abstinence and frustration. Any prolonged experience, contrariwise, can only bring mild contentment, irritation even, and he reminds us of Goethe's remark that 'nothing is harder to bear than a succession of fair days'.[12] The contrast of happy experiences with painful ones is therefore acute. While our possibilities of happiness are restricted by our very constitution (since those possibilities depend on a contrast with dissatisfaction, and cannot long be extended), unhappiness would appear to be far less difficult to experience:

> We are threatened with suffering from three directions: from our own body, which is doomed to decay and dissolution and which cannot even do without pain and anxiety as warning signals; from the external world, which may rage against us with overwhelming and merciless forces of destruction; and finally from our relations to other men.[13]

It will be illuminating to pause and reflect on these three sources, indicating how each undermines the prospects for happiness.

A person may count herself fortunate if in the course of her life she has avoided being harmed by other people and by ferocious forces of nature, but a human body is an essentially transient and evanescent structure, destined to fall apart as the years pass and life rolls creakily to its inevitable conclusion. Primitive humans, it has been conjectured, had no conception of a natural death, imagining that all individuals possessed a natural immortality and would never die unless their lives were cut short prematurely by violence or sorcery.[14] We, of course, now know

---

[10]   David Hume, 'Of Suicide', in *Essays: Moral, Political, and Literary* (Indianapolis, IN, 1985), p. 583.

[11]   Freud, *Civilization and Its Discontents*, p. 76.

[12]   Ibid., n. 1.

[13]   Ibid., p. 77.

[14]   See J.G. Frazer, *The Belief in Immortality and the Worship of the Dead* (London, 1913), p. 59, and John Hick, *Death and Eternal Life* (London, 1976), pp. 56–7.

better. As Midas Dekkers reminds us, the cause of death ultimately lies within: 'We're not made very well: we wear out; any fool can see that.'[15] Not only does the process of bodily dilapidation remind us starkly of where we are ultimately headed, thereby filling our minds with all manner of fears, but it also brings with it pains both emotional and physical. We may sadly rue the loss of our looks and think longingly of days before the arrival of thinning hair and sagging skin. Nor are the pains of decrepitude merely those of vanity. One's body aches more as it ages, the suppleness of the joints deteriorates, and the dreadful suffering brought inter alia by arthritis, osteoporosis or senility can horribly afflict a person.

> The doctors leave, the pains return,
> My body is nothing but veins, skin and bone.
> Sitting is a sufferance, lying down a torment.
> My very thighs need crutches.
> What price fame, honours, youth, and art?
> When this hour comes all is smoke and fog.
> It is an agony bent on killing us.[16]

And as though the torments of the body occasioned by inevitable internal processes were not enough, pains are also visited upon us both by the impersonal forces of the natural world and by other people, the second and third sources of suffering respectively.

The suffering inflicted upon people by the natural world is familiar enough, and the scope of these forces has been perfectly articulated by Freud himself. In *The Future of an Illusion* he notes how one of the principal functions of civilization is to defend us against nature, which threatens coldly and relentlessly to destroy us. And civilization has indeed been successful in this task, and not to an insignificant degree. Medical advances have provided us with treatments and cures for many hitherto remorseless diseases; focused improvements in architecture and engineering have been effective in lessening the damage to buildings wrought by earthquakes; technological innovations allow now for early warning of the arrival of hurricanes, thus permitting evacuations of affected populations; and so on.

> But no one is under the illusion that nature has already been vanquished; and few dare hope that she will ever be entirely subjected to man. There are the elements, which seem to mock at all human control: the earth, which quakes and is torn apart and buries all human life and its works; water, which deluges and drowns everything in a turmoil; storms, which blow everything before them; there are diseases, which we have only recently recognized as attacks by other organisms;

---

[15] Midas Dekkers, *The Way of All Flesh* (London, 2000), p. 80.
[16] Andreas Gryphius, 'To Himself', quoted in Umberto Eco, *On Ugliness* (London, 2007), p. 177.

and finally there is the painful riddle of death, against which no medicine has yet been found, nor probably will be.[17]

It is hard to deny the truth of this point. However much our technology brilliantly protects us from some of nature's threats, there will always be some more powerful force demonstrating to us our insurmountable helplessness.

While it certainly is the collective energies and co-operative projects of human beings that have scored some victories over impersonal natural forces, our relations with other people are nonetheless not unproblematic. These others may increase and augment our sufferings in two ways: passively, by an unwillingness to provide assistance; and actively, by the infliction of mental and physical pain. Hardy memorably gives expression to the passivity aspect in *Jude the Obscure* when he tells of the youthful Jude Fawley's despair at his prospects of ever learning Latin and entering the university town of Christminster. Mortified that there 'were no brains in his head equal to this business', Jude's sadness engulfs him. He might have been comforted by the consoling words of another coming along the way where he sat. 'But nobody did come, because nobody does.'[18] With these seven devastating words Hardy voices the fundamental loneliness of suffering and the futility of hoping for consolation from uncaring others. It is, of course, an exaggerated picture. Yet real life not infrequently provides terrible instances of support for Hardy's judgement. The dreadful case immediately brought to mind is that of Kitty Genovese, stabbed to death over a half-hour period while 38 of her respectable, law-abiding neighbours stood idly by, failing even to call the police, still less intervene in the assault.[19] 'I was tired' was one neighbour's excuse. No generalizations should be extrapolated either from a case like this or from the fictional narrative given by Hardy, of course, but it is clear that the unwillingness to assist others (as manifested, for example, in apathy regarding the problems of poverty, homelessness and injustice) adds considerably to the sufferings of the world.

As if passivity and neglect in the face of suffering were not enough, human beings seem to make an active contribution as well, positively adding to the sum total of the world's pains. This is a familiar – and an undeniable – observation. Here, for example, is Hume:

> This very society by which we surmount those wild beasts, our natural enemies, what new enemies does it not raise to us? What woe and misery does it not occasion? Man is the greatest enemy of man. Oppression, injustice, contempt, contumely, violence, sedition, war, calumny, treachery, fraud – by these they mutually torment each other, and they would soon dissolve that society which

---

[17]   Sigmund Freud, *The Future of an Illusion*, S.E. vol. XXI, pp. 15–16.

[18]   Thomas Hardy, *Jude the Obscure* (Oxford, 2002), p. 25.

[19]   Martin Gansberg, 'Moral Cowardice', in Louis Pojman and Lewis Vaughn (eds), *The Moral Life* (New York, 2011), pp. 487–91.

they had formed were it not for the dread of still greater ills which must attend their separation.[20]

The theme is continued in similar terms by Freud himself:

> [M]en are not gentle creatures who want to be loved, and who at the most can defend themselves if they are attacked; they are, on the contrary, creatures among whose instinctual endowments is to be reckoned a powerful share of aggressiveness. As a result, their neighbour is for them not only a potential helper or sexual object, but also someone who tempts them to satisfy their aggressiveness on him, to exploit his capacity for work without compensation, to use him sexually without his consent, to seize his possessions, to humiliate him, to cause him pain, to torture and to kill him. *Homo homini lupus*. Who, in the face of all his experience of life and of history, will have the courage to dispute this assertion?[21]

Sadly, no concrete examples are required to fill out and substantiate this description. We know these things all too well. While one may primarily think of the horrors of war and violence in this context, it contributes to the brilliance of Schopenhauer's excoriation of man – a being described by him, following Gobineau, as '*l'animal méchant par excellence*'[22] – that he draws to our attention the ubiquitous petty cruelties of everyday life: casual mistreatment of animals, malicious gossip, slander, *schadenfreude*, the list goes on. The recognition that people both endure (as victims) terrible sufferings and inflict (as perpetrators) awful pains on others informs one of Schopenhauer's harshest denunciations of existence: 'For the world is Hell, and men are on the one hand the tormented souls and on the other the devils in it.'[23]

Although it would be foolish to understate these points (man does indeed frequently reveal himself to be 'a hideous wild beast'[24]), the capacity of our fellow humans to provide love, pleasure and consolation to us should not lightly be disregarded. A sober and balanced account of the problems of life must therefore preserve the fundamentally *mixed* character of our experience of others: we are certainly threatened by the cruelty and violence of our fellow human beings, and yet also depend on other people both to ameliorate the pains we endure and to diminish (and maybe even annihilate) the loneliness we so anxiously fear. It was indeed Schopenhauer himself who provided a most fitting fable for our ambivalent condition vis-à-vis other people, his celebrated fable of the porcupines:

---

[20]   Hume, *Dialogues*, p. 63.

[21]   Freud, *Civilization*, p. 111.

[22]   Arthur Schopenhauer, *Parerga and Paralipomena* (2 vols, Oxford, 1974), vol. 2, p. 214.

[23]   Arthur Schopenhauer, *Essays and Aphorisms* (Harmondsworth, 1970), p. 48.

[24]   Schopenhauer, *Parerga*, vol. 2, p. 211.

One cold winter's day, a number of porcupines huddled together quite closely in order through their mutual warmth to prevent themselves from being frozen. But they soon felt the effect of their quills on one another, which made them again move apart. Now when the need for warmth once more brought them together, the drawback of the quills was repeated so that they were tossed between two evils, until they had discovered the proper distance from which they could best tolerate one another.[25]

On this view, our need for community with others springs from factors causing us discomfort (loneliness, monotony and pain), but our encounters with our fellows do not bring unbridled happiness, since the 'many unpleasant and repulsive qualities' of people produce in us distinctive pains of their own variety. Our attitude towards others of our kind must therefore be one of deep ambivalence.

Historical Disappointment

In one of the most inspiring passages of his writing, John Stuart Mill declared that '[a]ll the grand sources ... of human suffering are in a great degree, many of them entirely, conquerable by human care and effort'.[26] The problem of poverty, for example, may be 'completely extinguishable by the wisdom of society', while disease ('that most intractable of enemies') may be 'indefinitely reduced' by the progress of science and by good physical education. The removal of the sources of suffering is a 'grievously slow' process, and 'many generations will perish in the breach before the conquest is completed', but we should rally ourselves collectively and gain enjoyment and fulfilment from knowing both that the lives of future generations will be enriched by our efforts and that history is, as it were, on our side: our species is fighting a war against suffering, a war that is eminently winnable.

Though this rallying cry for collective human action is undeniably laudable, no pessimist will read Mill's words without wincing at their relentlessly upbeat tone. Two things may especially jar: the confidence that the sources of suffering are largely conquerable; and the view that one can be optimistic that the onward course of history promises happier days ahead. From what has already gone before, it should be clear that those of a pessimistic persuasion would reject the claim that suffering is a function merely of our current inability to conquer its sources. Suffering, according to the pessimist, is a permanent (rather than merely a temporary) feature of the human condition; after all, the nature of those three sources of suffering outlined above

---

[25]   Ibid., pp. 651–2; and see Freud's allusion to this in *Group Psychology and the Analysis of the Ego*, S.E. vol. XVIII, p. 101.

[26]   John Stuart Mill, *Utilitarianism* (London, 1864), p. 22.

would appear to give them a perennial, unconquerable quality.[27] Schopenhauer further supports this picture of suffering's non-contingent persistence by arguing that pain and evil possess a positive reality lacked by experiences of happiness and pleasure. 'I know of no greater absurdity', he writes, 'than that of most metaphysical systems which declare evil to be something negative; whereas it is precisely that which is positive and makes itself felt.'[28] On this analysis (essentially a reversal of the picture of suffering bequeathed to us by St Augustine, in which evil is conceived simply as an absence or privation of good), *pain* is that which is actually experienced; hence *pain* is real and positive. Happiness, on the other hand, consists merely in the state of being (at least temporarily) free from pain: happiness is therefore what is negative, the absence of pain. For example, we are aware of unpleasant sensations – hunger or thirst, say – but we are not aware of their absence. I might naturally think, 'I am really thirsty', or 'I am awfully hungry', but I don't find myself possessed by the feeling of *not* being thirsty or hungry. Indeed, I'll only ever say 'I am not thirsty' if provoked – say, by someone asking me whether I want a drink. Likewise, I become aware of a pain in my foot; but I never just find myself thinking, 'Oh, my foot feels really nice today' (or if that thought ever were to occur, it could only be as one following a period of prior discomfort, an expression of *relief from pain*). To summarize, 'We feel pain, but not painlessness; care, but not freedom from care', one especially sad consequence of this being that 'we do not become conscious of the three greatest blessings of life as such, namely health, youth, and freedom, as long as we possess them, but only after we have lost them; for they too are negations'.[29] For Schopenhauer and thinkers of his ilk, therefore, suffering is no temporary aberration, but rather an essential and unalterable characteristic of existence.

The notion of progress in history is likewise derided by the pessimistic tradition.[30] The pessimist is not committed to holding a picture of historical decline

---

[27] About this Freud is adamant, at least with regard to the first two sources of suffering he describes: 'We shall never completely master nature; and our bodily organism, itself a part of that nature, will always remain a transient structure with a limited capacity for adaptation and achievement' (Freud, *Civilization*, p. 86). No paralysing effect ought to flow from this recognition. Even though suffering cannot ever be fully removed, 'we can mitigate some' – and we should indeed aim at so doing – but the optimism of Mill's vision of the future is likely to result in disappointment.

[28] Schopenhauer, *Parerga*, vol. 2, pp. 291–2.

[29] Arthur Schopenhauer, *The World as Will and Representation* (2 vols, New York, 1969), vol. 2, p. 575. Most poignantly, perhaps: 'We notice that certain days of our life were happy only after they have made room for unhappy ones' (ibid.).

[30] Just as a belief in historical progress is seen by the pessimist as not sufficiently grounded, so on a more individual level hope for the improvement of one's own condition seems not to be borne out by the experience of one's past: 'Ask yourself, ask any of your acquaintance, whether they would live over again the last ten or twenty years of their life. No! but the next twenty, they say, will be better' (Hume, *Dialogues*, pp. 65–6). Nietzsche discusses this also, commenting that, for those with this hopeful perspective on the past and future, 'happiness lies behind the hill they are advancing towards' (Friedrich

(though such accounts were advanced by Rousseau and – in a very different form – by Oswald Spengler in *The Decline of the West*); rather, doubt is simply to be cast on the idea either that progress has occurred, or that any instances of progress are not counterbalanced by corresponding costs, or that those instances of apparent progress may really contribute to the elimination of suffering. Doubts of this kind are expressed in *Civilization and Its Discontents*. The driving question of that book is why so many people have taken up an attitude of hostility toward civilization. Such an attitude is especially strange to understand given civilization's role in acting as our principal bulwark against the threats posed by nature. Should one not be grateful rather than hostile? Freud surveys a number of elements contributing to this hostility (knowledge of the apparently happier lives of members of preliterate societies, the role of civilized morality in the development of neurotic disorders, and so on), before reaching 'an added factor of disappointment',[31] that factor of principal concern to us here. One cannot fail to be impressed by the extraordinary advances in science, technology and medicine, but these do not appear to have made humanity any happier. Indeed, any step taken forward seems counteracted by a parallel rearward move. Freud notes that the apparent gains in happiness resulting from technological advances (such as improvements in telecommunications that allow us to remain in contact with loved ones living hundreds of miles away, increased life expectancy, and so on) are actually in the nature of 'cheap pleasure' (like the pleasure resulting, he says, from putting a bare leg out of the bedclothes on a cold night and then pulling it back in again). It is true that technological advances have made it easier to speak with those separated from us, but it was a comparable advance that made long-distance travel possible in the first place, thereby facilitating the departure of our loved ones. It is, again, an undeniable truth that life expectancy has increased, but 'what good to us is a long life if it is difficult and barren of joys, and if it is so full of misery that we can only welcome death as a deliverer?'[32] The suspicion active in thoughts such as these would seem

---

Nietzsche, 'On the Uses and Disadvantages of History for Life', in *Untimely Meditations* (Cambridge, 1997), p. 65).

[31]   Freud, *Civilization*, p. 87.

[32]   Ibid., p. 88. One might also bring Freud's thoughts into connection with some remarks made by Ludwig Wittgenstein (and recounted by Rush Rhees) concerning conceptions of progress and decline: 'when there is a change in the conditions in which people live, we may call it progress because it opens up new opportunities. But in the course of this change, opportunities which were there before may be lost. In one way it was progress, in another it was decline. A historical change may be progress and also be ruin. There is no method of weighing one against the other to justify you in speaking of "progress on the whole".' Wittgenstein gave the example of the mining of iron and coal: this makes it possible for industry to develop yet scars a landscape with slag-heaps and machinery. Objecting to this, Benjamin Farrington said that even with all the ugly side-effects of civilization, he would still 'rather live as we do now than have to live as the caveman did'. Wittgenstein's response: 'Yes of course you would. But would the caveman?' (Rush Rhees, 'Postscript', in Rush Rhees (ed.), *Recollections of Wittgenstein* (Oxford, 1984), p. 201. It is also in

to be that overall levels of happiness and unhappiness remain relatively unaffected by historical changes and technological innovations. Disappointment thus ensues. We expect from all this effort and energy some kind of enhancement of happiness, and yet our sadness continues unabated.

A Maniac Scattering Dust

Pain is not the exclusive preserve of human beings, of course, for nonhuman animals are immersed in lives of excruciating suffering too. Schopenhauer dwells on this at length, describing how one sees in the condition of animals 'only momentary gratification, fleeting pleasure conditioned by wants, much and long suffering, constant struggle, *bellum omnium*, everything a hunter and everything hunted, pressure, want, need, and anxiety, shrieking and howling; and this goes on *in saecula saeculorum*, or until once again the crust of the planet breaks'.[33] A graphic example is then supplied to illustrate the claim:

> Junghuhn relates that in Java he saw an immense field entirely covered with skeletons, and took it to be a battle-field. However, they were nothing but skeletons of large turtles five feet long, three feet broad, and of equal height. These turtles come this way from the sea, in order to lay their eggs, and are then seized by wild dogs; with their united strength, these dogs lay them on their backs, tear open their lower armour, the small scales of the belly, and devour them alive. But then a tiger often pounces on the dogs. Now all this misery is repeated thousands and thousands of times, year in year out.[34]

Not only do human beings share in this constant and violent struggle (a person 'discovers adversaries everywhere, lives in continual conflict and dies with sword in hand'[35]), but our condition is also arguably worse due to the added element of *time-consciousness*. An animal, Schopenhauer claims, is more content with its life than a human ever is, simply because 'its consciousness is restricted to what is clearly evident and thus to the present moment: the animal is the present incarnate'.[36] Existing unhistorically and without a sense of time, the animal is

---

this context worthy of note that Freud and Wittgenstein shared an admiration for Johann Nestroy's dictum that 'It is in the nature of every advance, that it appears much greater than it actually is', Freud quoting this on two occasions (in *The Question of Lay Analysis*, S.E. vol. XX, p. 193, and later in 'Analysis Terminable and Interminable', S.E. vol. XXIII, p. 228), and Wittgenstein employing it as the motto for his *Philosophical Investigations* (Oxford, 1953), p. viii.

[33]   Schopenhauer, *World*, vol. 2, p. 354.
[34]   Ibid.
[35]   Schopenhauer, *Essays and Aphorisms*, p. 42.
[36]   Ibid., p. 45; see also Nietzsche, 'Uses and Disadvantages', pp. 60–62.

insulated against some of the most unbearable pains and anxieties with which humans must deal, namely those concerning the past and the future.

These anxieties are perhaps most poignantly depicted by Rousseau in his *Discourse on the Origin of Inequality*. Rousseau here attempts to describe the origin and nature of the time-burdened character of the human condition, setting it into a larger narrative of decline, one in which the original idyllic condition of human beings was disturbed by two catastrophic developments: the institution of private property, which set formerly pacific humans at variance with one another; and the emergence of time-consciousness from a previously atemporal animalistic understanding, which annihilated humanity's prior peace of mind. Rousseau begins by speculating about what mental processes and what kind of understanding human beings in the original condition would have had. These, he concludes, would have been entirely centred on *the present*, the *now*:

> Let us conclude that, wandering in the forests, without industry, without speech, without dwelling, without war, without relationships, with no need for his fellow men, and correspondingly with no desire to do them harm, perhaps never even recognizing any of them individually, savage man, subject to few passions and self-sufficient, had only the sentiments and enlightenment appropriate to that state; he felt only his true needs, took notice of only what he believed he had an interest in seeing; and that his intelligence made no more progress than his vanity. If by chance he made some discovery, he was all the less able to communicate it to others because he did not even know his own children. Art perished with its inventor. There was neither education nor progress; generations were multiplied to no purpose. Since each one always began from the same point, centuries went by with all the crudeness of the first ages; the species was already old, and man remained ever a child.[37]

Some passion – some emotion or other – always drives knowledge, according to Rousseau, and in this original condition the limited desires of human beings would have correspondingly entailed a limited amount and scope of knowledge:

> We seek to know only because we desire to find enjoyment; and it is impossible to conceive why someone who had neither desires nor fears would go to the bother of reasoning ... His [that is, the savage man's] desires do not go beyond his physical needs. The only goods he knows in the universe are food, a woman and rest; the only evils he fears are pain and hunger. I say pain and not death because an animal will never know what it is to die; and knowledge of death and its terrors is one of the first acquisitions that man has made in withdrawing from the animal condition ... His soul, agitated by nothing, is given over to the single feeling of his own present existence, without any idea of the future, however

---

[37]   Jean-Jacques Rousseau, 'Discourse on the Origin and Foundations of Inequality Among Men', in *The Basic Political Writings* (Indianapolis, IN, 1987), p. 57.

near it may be, and his projects, as limited as his views, hardly extend to the end of the day.[38]

The departure of our species from its previously entirely animal constitution is something typically seen as an advance, enabling the emergence of abstract thought, speculation and discovery, yet Rousseau is keen here to highlight the detrimental effects of this departure on our sense of contentment. These effects flow from the loss of a present-centred existence. An animal can form no concept of past or future; it responds to stimuli in the present in a routine and automatic way, but is unable to form plans or hopes about the future, and can have no regrets about the past. To be human, on the other hand, is to live with a linear sense of time. This produces possibilities of sadness and terror unimaginable to the animal. We regret the loss of our past (the happy days of our childhood, lost loves, ecstatic moments now gone), and we fear what awaits us in the future (principally: death and its terrors). Emerged from this prior animal condition, our apparently advanced state, our seemingly brilliant capacity to *reflect*, to *understand*, to *know*, has brought with it only discontent and anxiety: 'Reflection … causes [man] to regret past benefits and keeps him from enjoying the present: it shows him a happy future that his imagination might seduce and his desires torment him, and an unhappy future that he might experience it in anticipation.'[39] The timelessness of animal existence – and, by extension, the timelessness of the original human condition – is a paradise, but it is something we have left behind and can never recover.

One need not accept Rousseau's panegyric to our earliest ancestors and their pacific condition in order to find this account compelling. The crucial elements are simple and twofold: firstly, that the capacity for reflection, far from being an unalloyed triumph or a cause for self-congratulation, emerged merely from certain natural exigencies; and, secondly, that time-consciousness is the cause of dreadful sorrows mercifully absent from the lives of animals. Both of these elements are explored (without, characteristically, an upbeat view of our ancestors' mode of life) by Schopenhauer. The natural world, he contends, exhibits four distinct categories of thing: inanimate matter, plants, animals and humans.[40] The more advanced elements in this hierarchy build upon, and emerge from, those preceding them according to certain needs necessitating development. In the case of the emergence of animals from plant life, the necessitating factor was mobility (an organism of a certain level of complexity will need to move around to meet the demands of nourishment and reproduction), while the emergence of the rational intellect (that which is commonly deemed to distinguish the human from the animal) is likewise driven by considerations of survival, the task being that of forming a more-or-less accurate picture of the environment, its patterns and predictable cycles, so as to meet the

---

[38]   Ibid., p. 46.

[39]   Jean-Jacques Rousseau, 'Preface to *Narcissus*', in *The Discourses and Other Early Political Writings* (Cambridge, 1997), p. 102.

[40]   See Schopenhauer, *World*, vol. 1, pp. 153–61.

pressing needs of the organism. This goes some way to explaining why the intellect, conceived physiologically as the function of a 'pulpy mass in the skull',[41] goes so badly astray when engaged in rarefied metaphysical or theological speculation: 'destined exclusively for practical ends',[42] the mind is simply not equipped, nor is it its task, to go beyond the realm of empirical experience. This unreliability of the mind, at least whenever engaged in non-practical tasks, is to be contrasted with the efficiency of the non-conscious processes of the body, such as the healing of wounds and instinctual acts of one kind or another. Compared with these animal processes, the operations of the intellect are 'mere botching and bungling',[43] and reveal the mind to be of a secondary nature, not the essence of the human at all. And, of course, in addition to being something of a ham-fisted tool, the intellect has given us those aforementioned things about which no animal need worry: the experiences of loss, anxiety, boredom, and countless other sorrows generated by our apprehension of the passing of time. One might be prepared, in the face of this, to entertain the idea that the emergence of mind might be some kind of evolutionary error; put another way, 'Consciousness is nature's nightmare'.[44]

Just as it is consciousness of time which introduces all sorts of sorrows into a life, so the *effects* of time would appear to threaten all that a person may find significant: 'Time is that by virtue of which everything becomes nothingness in our hands and loses all real value.'[45] This topic requires no introduction. Indeed, the nullifying quality of time is a staple of the wisdom of all cultures. In classical mythology, Cronus (or Saturn) – later conflated with Chronos, the personification of time – devours the children he has sired, and in Goya's gruesome depiction of this scene (Figure 1.1) the babies of the original story are replaced with a grown adult body, the result being that we recognize ourselves and our fate: time creates us simply to destroy. 'Hour glasses', Lichtenberg notes, 'remind us, not only of how time flies, but at the same time of the dust into which we shall one day decay.'[46] The theme is mined in Biblical literature: Genesis proclaims boldly our dual origin and fate ('dust thou art, and unto dust shalt thou return'[47]), while the author of Ecclesiastes sees the meaning-threatening nature of this return. 'All go unto one place, all are of the dust, and all turn to dust again';[48] yet if this is so, to what avail our tasks, goals and achievements, what matters it if one is successful or wise, for 'there is no remembrance of the wise than of the fool for ever; seeing that which now is, in the days to come shall be forgotten. And how dieth the wise

[41] Ibid., vol. 2, p. 273.
[42] Ibid., p. 286.
[43] Ibid., p. 269.
[44] E.M. Cioran, *Tears and Saints* (Chicago, IL, 1998), p. 102.
[45] Schopenhauer, *Essays and Aphorisms*, p. 51.
[46] Georg Christoph Lichtenberg, *Aphorisms* (London, 1990), p. 42.
[47] Genesis 3:19.
[48] Ecclesiastes 3:20.

Figure 1.1   Francisco Goya, *Saturn Devouring His Son*, 146 × 83 cm, oil on
                canvas, circa 1819–23, Museo del Prado, Madrid (Getty Images /
                Hulton Fine Art Collection)

man? as the fool.'[49] All, hence, is vanity and futility. Each one of our cherished
projects – our creative enterprises, moral endeavours and loving relationships –
will come to an end when we die and will in time be entirely forgotten, while the
collective projects of our species will likewise one day be wiped away by the death

---

[49]   Ecclesiastes 2:16.

of our planet: 'all things our race has known / Time likewise bears away.'[50] Since things happen just once, are brief and doomed to destruction, they might as well not have happened at all: *'Einmal ist keinmal.'*[51]

These themes of the dust-destined fate of humans and the ephemeral (and accordingly futile) nature of existence find their way into Freud's thought, too. In one of his more well-known pieces of self-analysis, Freud relays a dream in which, in search of pudding, he enters a kitchen, finding there three women, one of whom is twisting something about in her hand, as though she were making dumplings. Freud's associations lead him to a memory from his childhood:

> When I was six years old and was given my first lessons by my mother, I was expected to believe that we were all made of earth and must therefore return to earth. This did not suit me and I expressed doubts of the doctrine. My mother thereupon rubbed the palms of her hands together – just as she did in making dumplings, except that there was no dough between them – and showed me the blackish scales of *epidermis* produced by the friction as a proof that we were made of earth. My astonishment at this ocular demonstration knew no bounds and I acquiesced in the belief which I was later to hear expressed in the words: *'Du bist der Natur einen Tod schuldig'.*[52]

The analysis of this dream leads Freud ultimately to the thought that 'life is short and death inevitable'.[53] As we will later see, Freud does not himself draw a conclusion of futility from the evanescent character of life, but he does sympathetically consider just such a diagnosis. In 'On Transience', Freud recounts a summer walk he undertook with a poet who, though appreciating the beauty of the countryside could take no pleasure in it: 'He was disturbed by the thought that all this beauty was fated to extinction, that it would vanish when winter came, like all human beauty and all the beauty and splendour that men have created or may create.'[54] It is the undeniable fact of transience that may be felt to strip everything of its worth and life of its joy: the face that is beautiful today in time will be wizened, and all things are doomed to the same fate.[55] When placed in the context

[50] Giacomo Leopardi, 'The Evening after the Holy Day', in *Selected Prose and Poetry* (London, 1966), p. 217.

[51] Milan Kundera, *The Unbearable Lightness of Being* (New York, 1999), p. 8: 'What happens but once, says the German adage, might as well not have happened at all.'

[52] Sigmund Freud, *The Interpretation of Dreams* (First Part), S.E. vol. IV, p. 205. The words in German mean 'Thou owest Nature a death', an imperfect recollection of a line from Shakespeare's *Henry IV Part One*: 'Why, thou owest God a death' (Act V, Scene I).

[53] Ibid., p. 207.

[54] Sigmund Freud, 'On Transience', S.E. vol. XIV, p. 305. Freud's response to the poet's despair will be addressed in the final chapter of this book.

[55] Leopardi's poem 'On the Portrait of a Beautiful Lady' addresses this painful truth. Reflecting on the image of a woman carved on her sepulchral monument, the poet notes

of an extraordinarily long temporal process, our brief lives, fated to dusty decay along with all else in this fleeting world, assume, it would appear, an unmistakable character of futility.

Impersonal Monsters, Namely, Immensities

Reflection upon our immersion in an infinitely long temporal process is capable of producing within us the painful feeling of our own insignificance. This is the case also when one's attention turns to the spatial immensity of the universe, its vastness contrasting with the trifling size of individual human lives. The anxieties ensuing from this contrast are perfectly expressed by Pascal:

> When I consider the short span of my life absorbed into the preceding and subsequent eternity, *memoria hospitis unius diei praetereuntis* [like the memory of a one-day guest (Wisd. 5:15)], the small space which I fill and even can see, swallowed up in the infinite immensity of spaces of which I know nothing and which knows nothing of me, I am terrified, and surprised to find myself here rather than there, for there is no reason why it should be here rather than there, why now rather than then. Who put me here? On whose orders and on whose decision have this place and this time been allotted to me?[56]

In part, Pascal's fears concern the arbitrariness of our position in this enormously old and inconceivably large universe: thrown into this world, we had no say on where and when we were born, and our self-determination is therefore severely compromised. But most terrifying of all is our *smallness*, for in comparison with the universe, each one of us is barely a speck, hardly more than a nothing. This objective assessment of our near-nothingness stands in opposition to the subjective feeling of our existential centrality, and the casualty of this contradiction is surely clear: our narcissistic sense of importance must be jettisoned.

In his strangely abstract novel *Two on a Tower*, Hardy sets the ill-fated love story of Lady Viviette Constantine and the young Swithin St Cleeve against the backdrop of vast and merciless impersonal forces, St Cleeve's researches into astronomy functioning as the perfect means to underscore the smallness and insignificance of all human endeavour. Lady Constantine visits St Cleeve on a starlit night and he shows her the heavens, as she had desired, but is keen to stress how, of all the sciences, astronomy 'deserves the character of the terrible'. This is because 'the actual sky is a horror', full of 'horrid monsters ... waiting to be

---

the features which, in her lifetime, must have made men breathless (her delightful mouth, neck and breast): 'But now you are no more than dirt and bones, / And now a thing of stone / Must hide the sad, malignant spectacle' (Leopardi, *Selected Prose and Poetry*, p. 283).

[56]   Blaise Pascal, *Pensées* (Oxford, 1999), p. 26 (§102).

discovered by any moderately penetrating mind'. And what kind of monsters are these?

> 'Impersonal monsters, namely, Immensities. Until a person has thought out the stars and their interspaces, he has hardly learnt that there are things much more terrible than monsters of shape, namely, monsters of magnitude without known shape. Such monsters are the voids and waste places of the sky.'[57]

Viviette is overpowered by such thoughts ('It makes me feel that it is not worth while to live; it quite annihilates me'), and she advises St Cleeve that astronomy is an unwise study for him, since it makes one 'feel human insignificance too plainly'. Under the weight of the stars, the two lovers 'more and more felt the contrast between their own tiny magnitudes and those among which they had recklessly plunged, till they were oppressed with the presence of a vastness they could not cope with even as an idea, and which hung about them like a nightmare'.[58]

The smallness of our lives (and the corresponding threat of insignificance) is not merely a device poetically employed by brooding philosophers and novelists, of course. For it is undeniably the case that the human species (and each of one us to an even more striking degree) is an infinitesimally small and short-lived part of an incomparably older and larger universe, and any attempt to make sense of our existence cannot ignore this disquieting fact without surrendering its claim on our interest and assent. When our little fleshy lives are placed in this astronomic context, we seem compelled to give up that grandiose sense of our special status in the universe and admit the full extent of our insignificance.[59]

It is but a short step from this judgement regarding insignificance to one asserting that our existence is purposeless. Freud suspects that the question of the purpose of human life deserves to be dismissed altogether, arising as it does from 'human presumptuousness'.[60] Nobody, after all, talks about the purpose of animal lives, which seem purely to be immersed in the endless *bellum omnium* spoken of by Schopenhauer, and once we have dropped our fond hopes for our own unique status, we can clearly see how human beings are just as much a part of the aimless struggle which appears to be the true nature of all existence. This is depicted vividly by Hume:

> Look round this universe. What an immense profusion of beings, animated and organized, sensible and active! You admire this prodigious variety and fecundity.

---

[57]   Thomas Hardy, *Two on a Tower* (London, 1999), p. 29. Towards the end of the novel, St Cleeve is still oppressed by these waste places, and is struck by 'the ghostly finger of limitless vacancy' (p. 250). Pascal once again comes to mind: 'The eternal silence of these infinite spaces terrifies me' (Pascal, *Pensées*, p. 73 (§233)).

[58]   Hardy, *Two on a Tower*, pp. 29, 28, 57–8, respectively.

[59]   See Freud, *Future*, p. 49.

[60]   Freud, *Civilization*, p. 75.

But inspect a little more narrowly these living existences, the only beings worth regarding. How hostile and destructive to each other! How insufficient all of them for their own happiness! How contemptible or odious to the spectator! The whole presents nothing but the idea of a blind nature, impregnated by a great vivifying principle, and pouring forth from her lap, without discernment or parental care, her maimed and abortive children![61]

Again, it was Schopenhauer who most systematically advanced a view of existence as a blind, aimless natural process, and who drew from it a conclusion of complete purposelessness. About this more needs to be said, since details of this view of life will emerge again in the pages to follow.

Though accepting the distinction drawn by Kant between *phenomena* (the world of appearances) and *noumena* (things as they are in themselves), Schopenhauer rejected the conclusion that noumenal reality was radically unknowable. A diagnosis of unknowability follows only if one thinks of the individual purely as a knowing subject (a conception witheringly described as 'a winged cherub without a body').[62] But the human being is not simply an observer of the world, but is also rooted in that world, and is thus both a knowing subject and an object among others. Each person's body, moreover, is capable of being known by him or her in two very different ways: it is given as an object to be perceived and considered; but is also given in an entirely different way, namely as that which can be known to everyone with immediacy.[63] In other words, I can experience myself, indirectly, *from the outside*, namely as a body of a certain height, weight and structure, a thing to be experienced by means of my organs of perception; I can also, however, experience myself, directly, *from the inside*, with an immediacy not shared by perception. This dual manner of knowing reflects the twofold character of the knower as both phenomenal and noumenal, as belonging both to the world of appearances and to that of things-in-themselves. The key, therefore, to knowledge of the innermost nature of things lies in our immediate grasp of our own essential being, which Schopenhauer denotes by the word 'will'. Actions of the body, he maintains, are physical manifestations of the will; indeed, the body itself just *is* will (more concretely, perhaps, a will-to-live), both conscious willing and non-conscious willing (the latter seen, for instance, in the beating of the heart and the arousal of the sexual organs) constituting our very essence. Our innermost nature identified as will, Schopenhauer extends his analysis beyond human nature to see in animal lives, and even in impersonal forces such as gravity, the same manifestation of will, recognized here as the essential nature of the world.

Armed with this insight drawn initially from the apprehension of our own innermost nature, one might see in the natural world confirmation of the claim that all things are manifestations of a will-to-live. For what does one see when

---

[61]   Hume, *Dialogues*, pp. 78–9.

[62]   Schopenhauer, *World*, vol. 1, p. 99.

[63]   See ibid., p. 100.

one looks at nature? One sees plants of the most extraordinary diversity breaking through the hard ground, establishing themselves and clinging to life in the most adverse conditions; while animals also, engaged in the perennial struggle for existence and reproduction, exhibit all the marks of this will to live, everything pressing towards existence. From this flows a diagnosis of purposelessness. The lack of purpose can be seen most clearly in the lives of non-human animals, which arise in vast numbers, and live often very brief lives, the reproductive task seeming to be the sole aim. Consider, for instance, the life of the ground mole.[64] This small mammal spends its life burrowing underground, expending great amounts of energy in search of a worm, which, once consumed, will provide the mole with enough strength and energy to continue digging for another worm, a process that goes on for the duration of the animal's life. If the mole is fortunate enough to escape capture by one of its many predators, which will tear it apart and eat it, it may find itself a mate and together they will produce a new generation of moles, some of which will die before reaching maturity, the others destined to spend their lives digging in the earth for worms, seeking mates thereby to continue the whole pathetic cycle, powered purely by the will to live. It is hard to detect any purpose beyond reproduction in the life of the poor ground mole, and – presumptuousness eschewed – the same might reasonably be said of human life too. It may seem that human existence has a greater significance, since we are immersed in cultural achievements (such as poetry, music, political structures and religious systems), but by any objective assessment the function of a human being seems only to be reproduction after its kind, the individual existing as a mere link in a chain, goaded on blindly to continue the life of our species until nature has finally done with us.[65] Not only, therefore, do our lives contain unbearable sufferings, but these sufferings seem entirely in vain, our brief lives without purpose or significance.

Some Kind of Mistake

As if it were not bad enough that our existence is plagued with suffering (arising from numerous and inescapable sources) and haunted by perennial anxieties concerning time and insignificance, the human condition is made even worse by the fact that we expect things to be better than they are, that we expect our lives to be happy. There is, in other words, a clash between the way the world is and the way we want and expect it to be, a clash between actuality and desire. It is for

---

[64] I owe the outlines of this case to Richard Taylor's essay 'Arthur Schopenhauer', in Ninian Smart, John Clayton, Patrick Sherry and Steven T. Katz (eds), *Nineteenth Century Religious Thought in the West* (3 vols, Cambridge, 1985), vol. 1, pp. 157–80.

[65] '[T]he individual has for nature only an indirect value, in so far as it is a means for maintaining the species. Apart from this, its existence is a matter of indifference to nature; in fact, nature herself leads it to destruction as soon as it ceases to be fit for that purpose' (Schopenhauer, *World*, vol. 2, p. 351).

this reason that Schopenhauer holds that, the longer one lives, the more one sees that life 'on the whole … is a disappointment, nay a cheat': 'If two men who were friends in youth meet in old age after the lapse of an entire generation, the principal feeling the sight of one another, linked as it is with recollections of earlier years, will arouse in both will be one of total disappointment with the whole of life, which once lay so fair before them in the rosy dawn of youth, promised so much and performed so little.'[66] Joshua Dienstag aptly describes this aforementioned clash as an 'ontological misalignment between human beings and the world they inhabit',[67] suffering and (at best) disappointment arising from the poor fit between human hopes and goals on the one hand and the consistently hope-thwarting nature of our world on the other. Dienstag attributes this disappointment, at least in part, to 'the false optimism that predominates in modern society',[68] though we should properly see it as something less historically contingent and more of an abiding consequence of our psychological constitution.[69] The enduring character of this misalignment is brought out by Leopardi in his 'Dialogue between Nature and an Icelander'. The Icelander bewails the natural sufferings afflicting humanity, documenting those factors we have already had cause to dwell upon, before noting the irony that Nature has instilled in human beings an insatiable craving for pleasure that can never be satisfied by the world and its processes. Nature's response – 'Did you perhaps imagine that the world was made for your benefit?'[70] – illustrates the great fault of existential felicity: our desire for happiness is thwarted by the universe's cold indifference. Thoughts akin to these animate also Schopenhauer's memorable summary of our condition: 'Human life must be some kind of mistake.'[71] The mistake in question here concerns the contradiction between the essence of the human being as a desiring creature and the unsatisfiability of its desires: 'man is a compound of needs and necessities hard to satisfy; and … even when they are

---

[66]   Schopenhauer, *Essays and Aphorisms*, p. 47.

[67]   Dienstag, *Pessimism*, p. 33.

[68]   Ibid.

[69]   Though our desire here is to downplay the role of modern optimism in the production of disappointment, Dienstag is certainly right to draw our attention to how suffering is exacerbated by optimism. Optimism leads us to think that life is going to be rosy (it won't be), while an education – particularly an American one – which leads young people to think of success as being totally within their control, and which teaches them that anything is possible in life, is egregiously guilty in this regard. As Freud noted, decades ago, 'In sending the young out into life with such a false psychological orientation, education is behaving as though one were to equip people starting on a Polar expedition with summer clothing and maps of the Italian lakes' (Freud, *Civilization*, p. 134, n. 1).

[70]   Giacomo Leopardi, quoted in Dienstag, *Pessimism*, p. 34.

[71]   Arthur Schopenhauer, *Studies in Pessimism* (London, 1893), p. 37.

satisfied all he obtains is a state of painlessness, where nothing remains to him but abandonment to boredom.'[72]

The terms of ontological misalignment formulated by Freud in *Civilization and Its Discontents*, the way in which he, like Schopenhauer, sees the human species as something akin to an error, centre upon the primacy of the 'pleasure principle' in the mental apparatus. This principle denotes the mind's overarching tendency to seek pleasure and to draw back from any event that might cause pain; it also indicates that the primary unit of the mind (more specifically, the unconscious mind) is the *wish*. Such thoughts come famously to the fore in Freud's theory of dream interpretation: once analysed, a dream reveals itself to be the disguised fulfilment of a wish.[73] For Freud, this was the clue to understanding one characteristic element of the unconscious: it consists, he contends, not of depictions of reality, nor of reasonable beliefs, but of wishes and desires. The human person should not then be regarded as the rational being so admired within the Western philosophical tradition, but rather as a desire-driven creature keen to encounter the world as he or she wants it to be, rather than as how it really is.

It is, moreover, the pleasure principle that determines what people demand of life and wish to achieve in it: 'they strive after happiness; they want to become happy and to remain so.'[74] And it is here that Freud's diagnosis of ontological misalignment makes itself felt:

> As we see, what decides the purpose of life is simply the programme of the pleasure principle. This principle dominates the operation of the mental apparatus from the start. There can be no doubt about its efficacy, and yet its programme is at loggerheads with the whole world, with the macrocosm as much as with the microcosm. There is no possibility at all of its being carried through; all the regulations of the universe run counter to it.[75]

Happiness, Freud thus contends, is not a possibility for human beings, and this is particularly painful since happiness is what we want most of all. As a result of this jarring contradiction between desire and actuality, the human species has the character merely of an error.

Given this understanding of the erroneous nature of human existence, death (the prospect of which so terrifies the human mind) appears as something else altogether: the rectification of a mistake. Schopenhauer again:

---

[72]   Ibid, pp. 37–8. One further example of this ontological misalignment is famously to be found in *The Myth of Sisyphus*, in which Camus contrasts the human needs for happiness and reason with 'the unreasonable silence of the world' (Albert Camus, *The Myth of Sisyphus* (Harmondsworth, 1975), p. 32): a diagnosis of life's absurdity flows precisely from this clash.

[73]   See Freud, *Interpretation*, especially pp. 122–33.

[74]   Freud, *Civilization*, p. 76.

[75]   Ibid.

Awakened to life out of the night of unconsciousness, the will finds itself as an individual in an endless and boundless world, among innumerable individuals, all striving, suffering, and erring; and, as if through a troubled dream, it hurries back to the old unconsciousness.[76]

Comparable thoughts are articulated in *Beyond the Pleasure Principle*, in which Freud sketches a speculative view of the origin and aim of organic life. When external forces affected an organism and made it more complex, the organism's internal forces (namely, its instincts) tried to bring it back to its former, simpler stage of development, and ultimately to the original inorganic state in which it was blissfully undisturbed by stimuli. 'The aim of all life', Freud famously writes, 'is death'; living substance undertaking 'ever more complicated *détours* before reaching its aim of death'.[77] As with Schopenhauer's analysis of the situation (in which 'the world on all sides is bankrupt, and … life is a business that does not cover the costs'),[78] Freud's view is that existence is a painful undertaking (at the very least, an 'inconvenience', as Cioran called it) and that each individual life ultimately yearns for the peace of death. The fear of death might thus be mitigated, for once life is recognized in these terms – as a painful error – one might say to the dying individual: 'You are ceasing to be something which you would have done better never to become.'[79]

The pessimistic themes spelled out thus far – the pain of existence, the blighted nature of the world, the insignificance of all human striving, the emptiness of life, and the release offered by death – are summated with great economy by Leopardi:

Now be for ever still,
Weary my heart. For the last cheat is dead,
I thought eternal. Dead. For us, I know
Not only the dear hope
Of being deluded gone, but the desire.
Rest still for ever. You
Have beaten long enough. And to no purpose
Were all your strivings; earth not worth your sighs.
Boredom and bitterness
Is life; and the rest, nothing; the world is dirt.
Lie quiet now. Despair
For the last time. Fate granted our kind

---

[76]   Schopenhauer, *World*, vol. 2, p. 573.
[77]   Sigmund Freud, *Beyond the Pleasure Principle*, S.E. vol. XVIII, pp. 38–9.
[78]   Schopenhauer, *World*, vol. 2, p. 574.
[79]   Ibid., p. 501. The lesson was not lost on Hardy who, depicting Jude Fawley's compassionate nature, says that 'he was the sort of man who was born to ache a good deal before the fall of the curtain upon his unnecessary life should signify that all was well with him again' (Hardy, *Jude the Obscure*, p. 11).

Only to die. And now you may despise
Yourself, nature, the brute
Power which, hidden, ordains the common doom,
And all the immeasurable emptiness of things.[80]

The Idea of a Palliative

The account of human life outlined above is extreme, overstated even in its unremitting bleakness, but one need not accept all of these details in order to reject the notion of existential felicity. The most disheartening element of the pessimistic picture – namely, that our lives are insignificant and devoid of purpose – might quite properly be questioned. Our lives do at least appear (even if only at times) to be touched by some kind of purpose (even if only those purposes that we have ourselves constructed and authored), while it is at least possible that, on a larger, more cosmic scale, there is some kind of purpose to existence, a purpose that might, of course, forever be hidden from us. Less vulnerable to serious questioning is the emphasis placed by the pessimist on the full extent of suffering. Given even an approximate grasp of the pains and sorrows experienced by sentient entities during their brief lives – 'the sum total of distress, pain and suffering of every kind which the sun shines upon in its course'[81] – one will surely be astounded by the optimistic soundings of one such as Paley, for whom 'the common course of things is in favour of happiness; that happiness is the rule; misery the exception'.[82] One might be inclined at this juncture to question the basis of Paley's calculation, but that is not our task here. For the purposes of the project of this book, all that needs to be accepted (and who could possibly deny this?) is that, for the vast majority of human beings, life is an extraordinarily difficult undertaking, full of sensations of pain, anxiety, fear and loss, which prove often to be overwhelming.

It is an appreciation of this painful and anxiety-ridden character of existence that provides the context for Freud's account of the strategies commonly employed to soften, and to cope with, life's difficulties. A crucial passage – the inspiration for the present work – succinctly states Freud's position:

> Life, as we find it, is too hard for us; it brings us too many pains, disappointments and impossible tasks. In order to bear it we cannot dispense with palliative measures. 'We cannot do without auxiliary constructions', as Theodor Fontane tells us. There are perhaps three such measures: powerful deflections, which cause us to make light of our misery; substitutive satisfactions, which diminish

---

[80]   Leopardi, 'To Himself', in *Selected Prose and Poetry*, p. 281.
[81]   Schopenhauer, *Essays and Aphorisms*, p. 47.
[82]   Paley, *Natural Theology*, p. 282.

it; and intoxicating substances, which make us insensitive to it. Something of the kind is indispensable.[83]

Each of these three measures is given further comment. Freud tells us that 'Voltaire has deflections in mind when he ends *Candide* with the advice to cultivate one's garden'.[84] The words Voltaire uses in this piece of advice are: 'Let us work without reasoning, … it is the only way to make life endurable.'[85] It is important to note, however, that for Freud these deflections need not always be 'without reasoning', since he lists 'scientific activity' as an example of a deflective activity. The idea seems simply to be that engagement with a practical task can serve to deflect one from dwelling too much upon misery.[86] Such an engagement may even instil one's life with a felt sense of significance. Regarding substitutive satisfactions, Freud provides the example of art. Such satisfactions are 'illusions in contrast with reality, but they are none the less psychically effective, thanks to the role which phantasy has assumed in mental life'.[87] No more will be said of art here, since an entire later chapter is devoted to the subject. The same is true of the third group of palliative measures Freud mentions: intoxicating substances, which 'influence our body and alter its chemistry'.[88]

It is important to understand what Freud is doing when he claims that certain cultural phenomena function as measures palliating our desperate condition. The notion he advances has certain connections with – though must also clearly be distinguished from – the idea of a 'distraction' as put forward both by Pascal and by Woody Allen. The vision of life (or at least of a life without God) expounded by Pascal in his *Pensées* marches closely with the pessimistic diagnosis outlined above: a human life is pathetically small in comparison with the universe ('an imperceptible speck in nature's ample bosom'[89]), and is headed inevitably towards an end that is terrifying and painful: 'The last act is bloody, however wonderful the rest of the play. At the end, earth is thrown on the head, and that is the last of it.'[90] Memorable in its bleakness is Pascal's image of the human condition: 'Imagine a number of men in chains, all condemned to death, some of whom every day are slaughtered in full view of the others. Those who remain see their own condition in that of their fellows, and looking at each other in pain and without hope, await

---

[83]   Freud, *Civilization*, p. 75.

[84]   Ibid.

[85]   Voltaire, *Candide* (Bloomington, IN, 1961), p. 101.

[86]   One might bring to mind here Robert Burton's advice concerning the avoidance of melancholy: 'Be not solitary, be not idle' (Robert Burton, *The Anatomy of Melancholy* (New York, 1948), p. 970).

[87]   Freud, *Civilization*, p. 75.

[88]   Ibid.

[89]   Pascal, *Pensées*, p. 66 (§230).

[90]   Ibid., p. 59 (§197).

their turn!'[91] Pascal's contention is that the standard method of coping with our wretched state is simply not to think about it at all, and instead to fill our lives with distractions, diversions of one kind or another, gaming and hunting, noise and bustle. Anything will suffice, so long as it allows us not to think too much. Sitting quietly in one's room is awful, since our thoughts will tend to drift towards an exploration of both our insignificance and our mortality. So desperate is our condition that 'nothing can console us when we think about it closely'.[92] The value of distractions in the economy of life is thus clear: their function is to screen off the terrible reality of existence by providing an alternative to thought. Indeed, it is the ubiquitous presence of distractions that gives the fullest proof of the unhappiness of the human condition: 'If our condition were truly happy, we should not have to divert ourselves from thinking about it.'[93] The observation is a pertinent one: if life was as blessed as the proponents of existential felicity would have us believe, then sitting alone in a room and simply thinking would be a source of delight rather than of melancholy. That it typically proves to be the latter is instructive.

Those self-same themes just noted are subjected to sustained investigation in the movies of Woody Allen. Here we find particularly evocative depictions of the suffering of existence (life, we are told in *Annie Hall*, being divided equally between 'the horrible and miserable') and of the world's ephemeral and transient character ('it's all random, radiating aimlessly out of nothing, and eventually vanishing forever'[94]), while the anticipation of the horrors of death is never far away ('Do you realize what a thread we're hanging by?'[95]). As in Pascal's account, these potentially overwhelming features are dealt with by way of distraction. In *Manhattan*, Allen's character Isaac considers an 'idea for a short story about people in Manhattan who are constantly creating these real unnecessary neurotic problems for themselves 'cause it keeps them from dealing with the more unsolvable, terrifying problems about the universe'. Here, one's own individual difficulties (regarding career, relationships and so on) are screens invented to mask more appalling problems. Allen's emphasis upon the necessity of distractions is clearly present in *September*, when the character of Lane contemplates suicide, and is talked out of that course of action by her friend Stephanie:

STEPHANIE: Now give me those pills. Tomorrow will come and you'll find some distractions. You'll get rid of this place, you'll move back to the city, you'll

---

[91]   Ibid., p. 168 (§686). A comparable image advanced by Schopenhauer is noteworthy: 'We are like lambs playing in the field, while the butcher eyes them and selects first one and then another' (Schopenhauer, *Parerga*, vol. 2, p. 292).

[92]   Pascal, *Pensées*, p. 45 (§168).

[93]   Ibid., p. 26 (§104).

[94]   From *September*, quoted in Mark T. Conrad, 'God, Suicide, and the Meaning of Life in the Films of Woody Allen', in Mark T. Conrad and Aeon J. Skoble (eds), *Woody Allen and Philosophy* (Chicago, IL, 2004), p. 9.

[95]   From *Hannah and Her Sisters*, quoted in Conrad, 'God', p. 8.

work, you'll fall in love, and maybe it'll work out, and maybe it won't, but you'll
find a million petty things to keep you going, and distractions to keep you from
focusing on –
LANE: On the truth.[96]

On this view, our mode of life is largely *evasive*. As in Plato's famous allegory,
we reside in a cave of shadows, those enthralling shadows serving to distract us
from – and, indeed, blind us to – the evanescence and terrors of life.

Allen is helpful, too, in providing us with a prime example of a distraction
commonly employed by people: sports. Just as Pascal, three centuries earlier, had
seen gaming and hunting as principal forms of distracting activity, so Allen sees
the contemporary obsession with sports to be the result of a need to 'create a fake
world for ourselves' in contrast to the indifferent reality of things:

> They create a world of football, for example. You get lost in that world and
> you care about meaningless things. Who scores the most points, etc. People get
> caught up in it, and others make a lot of money with it. People by the thousands
> watch it, thinking it's very important who wins. But, in fact, if you step back for
> a second, it's utterly unimportant who wins. It means nothing.[97]

This example neatly exposes what both Allen and Pascal see as the weakness of
these distractions: a painful engagement with reality is diverted, but only at the
cost of superficiality. Wrestling with existential problems may be dreadful, and yet
it should not be avoided. It is inevitable, after all, that these matters will one day
catch up with us: 'We run carelessly over the precipice after having put something
in front of us to prevent us seeing it.'[98]

If Freud's idea of a 'palliative measure' were reducible simply to that of a
'distraction' then it would barely demand our sustained attention. But when
he speaks of the character of those strategies utilized to mitigate, in one way
or another, the difficulties of life, he seems to have things more varied and
multilayered in mind. What, therefore, is meant by a palliative measure? Taking
our cue from the field of medicine, we may say that a palliative is something that
relieves without curing, and that the provision of palliative care has the function
of alleviating the symptoms of a far-advanced, serious or life-threatening disease

---

[96]   *September*, quoted in Conrad, 'God', pp. 19–20.

[97]   Woody Allen, in Stig Björkman (ed.), *Woody Allen on Woody Allen* (New
York, 1995), p. 225.

[98]   Pascal, *Pensées*, p. 59 (§198). A significant passage from Tennessee Williams might
also be noted in this context: 'Fear and evasion are the two little beasts that chase each other's
tails in the revolving wire-cage of our nervous world. They distract us from feeling too much
about things. Time rushes toward us with its hospital tray of infinitely varied narcotics, even
while it is preparing for its inevitably fatal operation' (Tennessee Williams, 'The Timeless
World of a Play', in *New Selected Essays: Where I Live* (New York, 2009), p. 61.

without dealing with the underlying cause.[99] Such a system of care does not consist merely of one technique, but rather employs a range of methods appropriate for addressing the physical, psychological, social and existential concerns arising from severe, curative-unresponsive illness.[100] Freud's extension of the concept of a palliative from this medical field into the total arena of human existence would appear to encapsulate two basic insights. Firstly, life is not only a difficult but also a hopeless and a terminal condition; and secondly, in order to alleviate its pains we need recourse to a number of tools designed for that very task and provided to us by civilization. The function of a cultural palliative – such as art or intoxicating substances – is to provide such temporary relief. And just as palliative care in the medical field utilizes a range of techniques, so we may need access to a range of cultural palliative measures, rather than employing a single one (drugs, for instance) as the sole source of relief. Nor need a palliative measure be regarded as an unequivocally beneficent thing, since it is possible that hazardous side effects flow from aspects of such care.[101]

It is clear from the foregoing that a palliative differs substantially from a mere distraction. Medical palliative care does not simply *distract* patients from their suffering, after all. Nor is the effect sought purely anaesthetic (though pain control is, of course, an important element here). The typically stated aim, rather, is to enhance quality of life in the most trying of circumstances. The same things, *mutatis mutandis*, may be said of the palliative measures alluded to in *Civilization and Its Discontents*. While there may be a temptation to see something derogatory in labelling a certain cultural phenomenon as a palliative, such a temptation would arise from a confused equation of a palliative with an analgesic. To neutralize this equation, one need only remind oneself of the many functions of medical

---

[99] 'The word "palliative" derives from the Latin *pallium*, a cloak. Palliation means cloaking over, not addressing the underlying cause but ameliorating the effects' (Christina Faull, 'The History and Principles of Palliative Care', in Christina Faull, Yvonne Carter and Richard Woof (eds), *Handbook of Palliative Care* (Oxford, 1998), p. 1). See also Derek Doyle, Geoffrey Hanks and Neil MacDonald, 'Introduction', in Derek Doyle, Geoffrey Hanks and Neil MacDonald (eds), *The Oxford Textbook of Palliative Medicine* (Oxford, 1999), pp. 3–10. Fiona Randall and R.S. Downie provide a blunt definition: 'Palliative care is the care of patients whose disease is incurable and is expected to cause death within the foreseeable future' (Fiona Randall and R.S. Downie, *The Philosophy of Palliative Care: Critique and Reconstruction* (Oxford, 2006), p. 224).

[100] See Doyle et al, 'Introduction', p. 3; and Linda L. Emmanuel, 'Comprehensive Assessment', in Linda L. Emmanuel and S. Lawrence Librach (eds), *Palliative Care* (Philadelphia, PA, 2007), pp. 27–41.

[101] In the medical field, these hazards most commonly concern the use of painkillers and opioids (see Karen Forbes and Christina Faull, 'The Principles of Pain Management', in Christina Faull, Yvonne Carter and Richard Woof (eds), *Handbook of Palliative Care* (Oxford, 1998), pp. 122–3), though Randall and Downie have highlighted a wide range of further problematic aspects of palliative care as generally undertaken (Randall and Downie, *Philosophy*, passim).

palliative care and its role not just in pain-alleviation but also in other quality of life issues, such as the psychological and the spiritual.[102] Aware of these potential misunderstandings, one may even prefer to utilize the alternative term Freud uses for cultural palliatives, a term carrying less baggage: *auxiliary constructions*. This concept, he tells us, he has taken from Fontane. The crucial passage occurs in the novel *Effi Briest*, in which Wüllersdorf gives the following piece of advice to the anguished Baron von Instetten:

> 'There are plenty of people who see things just as we do, and one of them, who didn't have his troubles to seek, once said to me, "You know Wüllersdorf, you can't get through life without auxiliary structures". The man who said that was a master builder, so he should know. And he was right to put it like that. Not a day passes when I'm not reminded of those "auxiliary structures".'[103]

This brings into prominence the central function of the measures and strategies we will be exploring in this book: the role of an auxiliary structure is to provide additional help, to hold something up, to stop it from collapsing. Fontane's building metaphor helps to bring out that feature. With this in mind, we can define a palliative measure as *any activity or belief (or set of beliefs) having as its function (or among its principal functions) the non-curative mitigation of the suffering characteristic of the human condition and the attempted provision of such assistance as is indispensable for an endurable existence*. It is not necessary that the person using such a measure is aware that its function is a palliative one; indeed, in certain cases (though by no means in all), realization that the measure is palliative may lead to its abandonment. In what follows, the terms 'palliative measure' and 'auxiliary structure' will be used interchangeably.

We might also define a palliative measure in terms of what the idea for us denotes. Freud has, albeit rather abstractly, given us just such an initial denotation: powerful deflections; substitutive satisfactions; intoxicating substances. This abstraction is subsequently further fleshed out. He suggests that there are four principal strategies employed in the alleviation of existential suffering: intoxication; religious belief; enjoyment of art; and sexual love.[104] This suggestion, accordingly, provides us with the plan of this book. In the next chapter, the subject of drugs and intoxication will be addressed. It will be followed by a discussion of the palliative role of religious belief, itself not infrequently likened to a narcotic. Two further chapters will address art and love respectively. The initial chapter on religion will be a hostile one, largely defending the psychoanalytic claim that religious

---

[102] See Melissa Hart, 'Spiritual Care', in Linda L. Emmanuel and S. Lawrence Librach (eds), *Palliative Care* (Philadelphia, PA, 2007), pp. 524–39, and the criticisms of such an approach in Randall and Downie, *Philosophy*, especially pp. 25–51.

[103] Theodor Fontane, *Effi Briest* (London, 2000), p. 212.

[104] See Freud, *Civilization*, pp. 78–85. The details of his comments on each of these palliatives will be described in subsequent chapters.

belief is an infantile illusion. But that will not be our last word on religion. A final chapter will return to the subject, seeking to advance a conception of religious belief as a non-illusory palliative. In this regard, religion will be seen to mirror the dual nature of the other auxiliaries: as we will see, though each of these exhibits escapist forms, those manifestations are neither the limit nor the sole varieties. The book as a whole aims to advance a view of the difficulty of human life and the measures we employ simply to get us through it. Such palliatives are, as Freud tells us, indispensable. To exploit a phrase from St Paul, without them we would be of all men most miserable.

Chapter 2

The First Palliative: Intoxicants

People who say you shouldn't take drugs should try living inside my head for
a day.

Sebastian Horsley

Our initial investigation into the nature of a palliative revealed that such a measure
has as its function some mitigation of the suffering characteristic of the human
condition. It is natural and fitting that the use of drugs and intoxicants should occupy
a place within this sphere, since the concept of a palliative measure is rooted in an
analogy with the treatment of incurable illnesses, and drugs (principally opioids) are
the mainstay of pain management in end-of-life care. Not only have drugs proven
to be an effective weapon in the medical fight against physical pain, but they have
also been utilized by countless generations of men and women keen to lessen, alter
or for a while forget the troubling existential aspects of their real lives. This much
is well known. Realization of the lure of intoxication in times of difficulty is part
of humanity's collective understanding of our condition, and is aptly expressed in
Wilhelm Busch's words, quoted by Freud in *Civilization and Its Discontents*: '*Wer
Sorgen hat, hat auch Likör.*'[1] The range of substances employed is vast and their
effects widely diverse. Such diversity poses problems for the task of definition. If
one includes all drugs – those used for the treatment of disease as well as those used
for recreational purposes – then we should broadly define a drug as any substance
introduced into the body which either alters normal bodily function so as to treat,
cure or prevent a disease or else alters or augments a physical or mental state. The
aim of altering one's mental state (the principal focus of this chapter) is served
by all those substances that are psychoactive in character, a psychoactive drug
being one that 'alter[s] the state of consciousness of the user'.[2] In his discussion
of palliative measures, Freud prefers to employ the term 'intoxicating substances'
to refer to these agents. This is in some ways preferable (since the word 'drug'
has so many negative connotations associated with it), but we will here need to
operate with a broad understanding of 'intoxication', and define an intoxicating
substance as one that produces either excitement or stupefaction in the user. These
effects may be mild or intense, depending upon the substance and/or its dose. Our

---

[1]   'He who has cares also has liquor.' Wilhelm Busch, quoted in Sigmund Freud,
Civilization and Its Discontents, in *The Standard Edition of the Complete Psychological
Works of Sigmund Freud* (24 vols, London, 1953–74) (hereafter S.E.), vol. XXI, p. 75, n. 2.

[2]   Richard Rudgley, *The Encyclopedia of Psychoactive Substances* (London, 1998),
p. xi.

aim in this chapter will be to secure an understanding of the role of intoxication in the struggle against the pervasive existential pain and dissatisfaction previously documented. We will start, naturally, with Freud's own account of the palliative character of these substances.[3]

Freud and Intoxication

The thoughts of the inventor of psychoanalysis will be worth listening to in any discussion about drugs and intoxicants, since Freud – occasionally enthusiastic about cocaine and catastrophically dependent upon tobacco – must have known their various effects well. Freud's inability to give up (or even curtail) his smoking habits led ultimately, of course, to a protracted and horrendously painful death, and his correspondence reveals the full and amorous extent of his relationship with cigars and the unhappiness he endured during the brief periods in which health concerns necessitated attempts to abstain. In a letter to his friend Wilhelm Fliess, dated 2 June 1894, Freud speaks of life being 'unbearable' without cigars, and of 'the horrible misery of abstinence' which has left him 'completely incapable of working, a beaten man'.[4] Forty years later, when the effects of cancer, multiple surgeries and badly-fitting prostheses had severely limited his ability to smoke, he wrote to Arnold Zweig with the same complaint, bewailing how work was impossible for him in a period of self-denial: 'I cannot say that much is happening in my world. Since I have not been able to smoke freely, I no longer wish to write.'[5] From the extensive ruminations on smoking in his correspondence, it can be gleaned that abstinence robbed Freud of those benefits of nicotine beloved by smokers: its calming and its stimulating effects, its (albeit mild) amelioration of anxiety and its ability to increase attention and concentration. For Freud – engaged in a monumentally large outpouring of work and (at least in the 1880s and '90s) prone to anxiety – abstaining from smoking proved to be an impossible undertaking. For our purposes here, concerned as we are with the palliative employment of intoxicants, Freud's relationship with nicotine constitutes a fitting vignette, illustrating as it does the important role an intoxicant might come to perform in an individual's attempt to mitigate the pains and anxieties of life.

Freud's chronic dependency upon nicotine rather gives the lie to Ernest Jones' confident judgement regarding the so-called 'cocaine episode', the judgement,

---

[3]   Since the concern of this book is centred upon strategies employed to ameliorate existential pain and suffering, the use of drugs as a possible tool in an investigation into the hidden nature of reality (the kind of investigation most famously undertaken by Aldous Huxley in *The Doors of Perception* and *Heaven and Hell*, for example) will here be ignored.

[4]   Letter to Wilhelm Fliess (2 June 1894), in J.M. Masson (ed.), *The Complete Letters of Sigmund Freud to Wilhelm Fliess 1887–1904* (Cambridge, MA, 1985), p. 84.

[5]   Letter to Arnold Zweig (2 May 1935), in Ernst L. Freud (ed.), *The Letters of Sigmund Freud and Arnold Zweig* (New York, 1970), p. 106.

namely, that 'it needs a special disposition to develop a drug addiction, and fortunately Freud did not possess that'.[6] Much of what is written about this episode in Freud's life is wild and sensationalist,[7] and it is thankfully no part of the task of this book to articulate an opinion concerning the extent of his use of cocaine. It will be sufficient merely to note briefly the benefits he thought might flow from this 'magical substance'.[8] Keen to make a name for himself in medicine, Freud undertook in 1884 an investigation into the physiological effects of cocaine. The results of his studies saw light in a series of publications beginning with *Über Coca*. Freud initially there describes the nature of the coca plant (from which the alkaloid cocaine is derived) and the history and use of coca leaves in South America. The Peruvians, he tells us, regarded the coca plant as a divine gift, 'which satiates the hungry, strengthens the weak, and causes them to forget their misfortune'.[9] The potential clinical benefits of cocaine for the treatment of a range of disorders are subsequently enumerated. These include cachexia, disturbances of the digestive function and asthma, while cocaine's effectiveness both as an aphrodisiac and as a weapon against morphine and alcohol addiction is proclaimed. The list expands still further in subsequent papers, letters and pieces of personal advice, Freud recommending cocaine as an effective treatment for hydrophobia, seasickness and even diabetes. At the very end of *Über Coca* Freud mentions, almost as an afterthought, that cocaine might also be employed as a local anaesthetic. Spurred on by this suggestion, it was Carl Koller, rather than Freud himself, who demonstrated the effectiveness of the drug's anaesthetizing properties for diseases of the eye, and was lauded as the discoverer of local anaesthesia by cocaine.

Freud (at least at times) appears to have been irked by Koller's glory, blaming his duties towards his fiancée and his own laziness for this lost chance at clinical fame. The truth of the matter seems, however, to be that cocaine's anaesthetizing qualities were foreign to Freud's interests, and that he was, as Jones rightly notes, 'far more interested in its internal use than in any external application'.[10] Indeed, Freud writes most animatedly about cocaine when discussing its influence on the general mood, its lifting of depression and production of vivacity. It was these features that characterized Freud's own first use of the substance: 'He immediately tried the effect of a twentieth of a gramme; he found it turned the bad mood he was in into cheerfulness and gave him the feeling of having dined well "so that there is nothing at all one need bother about".'[11] These effects are detailed in *Über*

---

[6]   Ernest Jones, *Sigmund Freud: Life and Work* (3 vols, London, 1953–57), vol. 1, p. 89.

[7]   See Howard Markel, *An Anatomy of Addiction: Sigmund Freud, William Halsted, and the Miracle Drug Cocaine* (New York, 2011) for a good, sober account.

[8]   Letter to Martha Bernays (2 June 1884), quoted in Jones, *Sigmund Freud*, vol. 1, p. 93: 'I am just now busy collecting literature for a song of praise to this magical substance.'

[9]   Sigmund Freud, 'Über Coca', in *Cocaine Papers* (New York, 1974), p. 50.

[10]   Jones, *Sigmund Freud*, vol. 1, p. 92. See also Max Schur, *Freud: Living and Dying* (New York, 1972), p. 29, where the same point is made.

[11]   Jones, *Sigmund Freud*, vol. 1, p. 88.

Coca: cocaine produces 'a sudden exhilaration and feeling of lightness',[12] and has 'a wonderful stimulating effect' in which 'long-lasting, intensive mental or physical work can be performed without fatigue'.[13] The mood induced by cocaine, Freud suggests, is 'due not so much to direct stimulation as to the disappearance of elements of one's general state of well-being which cause depression'.[14] The promise of cocaine in this regard was, for Freud, extraordinary, since it seemed fitted to fill a lacuna in the pharmacological treatment of mental disorders: 'Psychiatry is rich in drugs that can subdue over-stimulated nervous activity but deficient in agents that can heighten the performance of the depressed nervous system.'[15] To Freud, cocaine seemed a perfect candidate to address that deficiency, and he employed it in his own battle against depression in the 1880s, writing that even a small dose of cocaine 'lifted me to the heights in a wonderful fashion'.[16] For our purposes we can disregard the shortcomings of Freud's overly enthusiastic declaration of cocaine's medicinal and psychiatric value. The significant element is Freud's recognition of the role of an intoxicating substance in the lifting of woe, a theme to which he returns in *Civilization and Its Discontents*.

Having outlined the sources of suffering (the body, the external world, other people) and the ontological misalignment undermining the very possibility of happiness, Freud notes that, under the pressure of these conditions, people come to moderate their claims to happiness and think themselves happy merely if substantial unhappiness has been avoided and suffering survived. In short, 'the task of avoiding suffering pushes that of obtaining pleasure into the background'.[17] Various strategies exist for this purpose. One can turn away from contact with other people, so as to escape from the pain that may attend interpersonal relations, or one might, in co-operation with others, take the fight to nature, thereby working to improve conditions for humanity. However, 'the most interesting methods of

---

[12] Freud, 'Über Coca', p. 58.

[13] Ibid., p. 60.

[14] Ibid.

[15] Sigmund Freud, 'On the General Effect of Cocaine', in *Cocaine Papers* (New York, 1974), p. 116.

[16] Letter to Martha Bernays (2 June 1884), quoted in Jones, *Sigmund Freud*, vol. 1, p. 93. Jones' description of Freud's mental and emotional condition during the years of the cocaine episode is worthy of quotation: 'For many years he suffered from periodic depressions and fatigue or apathy, neurotic symptoms which later took the form of anxiety attacks before being dispelled by his own analysis. These neurotic reactions were exacerbated by the turmoil of his love affair, with its lengthy privation and other difficulties. In the summer of 1884 in particular he was in a state of great agitation before the approaching visit to his betrothed, and by no means only because of the uncertainty about its being possible. Cocaine calmed the agitation and dispelled the depression. Moreover it gave him an unwonted sense of energy and vigour' (Jones, *Sigmund Freud*, vol. 1, pp. 92–3).

[17] Freud, *Civilization*, p. 77.

averting suffering are those which seek to influence our own organism'.[18] It is in this context that Freud proceeds to discuss the place of intoxication in human life, a context operating with an exclusively physicalist conception of suffering: 'In the last analysis, all suffering is nothing else than sensation; it only exists in so far as we feel it, and we only feel it in consequence of certain ways in which our organism is regulated.'[19] This point needs to be stressed: if suffering is ultimately a matter of physical sensations, then certain chemical agents might be effectively utilized so as to alter and regulate a person's receptivity to those sensations, thereby diminishing or eliminating suffering.

Freud's words on the role of intoxication deserve being quoted at length and will serve as the basis for the discussion to follow:

> The crudest, but also the most effective among these methods of influence is the chemical one – intoxication. I do not think that anyone completely understands its mechanism, but it is a fact that there are foreign substances which, when present in the blood or tissues, directly cause us pleasurable sensations; and they also so alter the conditions governing our sensibility that we become incapable of receiving unpleasurable impulses. The two effects not only occur simultaneously, but seem to be intimately bound up with each other … The service rendered by intoxicating media in the struggle for happiness and in keeping misery at a distance is so highly prized as a benefit that individuals and peoples alike have given them an established place in the economics of their libido. We owe to such media not merely the immediate yield of pleasure, but also a greatly desired degree of independence from the external world. For one knows that, with the help of this 'drowner of cares' one can at any time withdraw from the pressure of reality and find refuge in a world of one's own with better conditions of sensibility. As is well known, it is precisely this property of intoxicants which also determines their danger and their injuriousness. They are responsible, in certain circumstances, for the useless waste of a large quota of energy which might have been employed for the improvement of the human lot.[20]

A main concern in this chapter will be to explore the manner in which intoxication allows a person to 'withdraw from the pressure of reality', thereby gaining 'a degree of independence from the external world'. To this we should immediately turn.

---

[18] Ibid., p. 78.

[19] Ibid.

[20] Ibid. Since Freud wrote these words, the mechanism by which drugs affect the central nervous system has become less opaque. For clear and concise accounts of this mechanism, see Leslie Iverson, *Drugs* (Oxford, 2001), pp. 20–36, and Cynthia Kuhn, Scott Swartzwelder and Wilkie Wilson, *Buzzed* (New York, 2003), pp. 233–58.

Withdrawal from Reality: Narcosis

It is not too difficult to specify the factors informing a person's desire to withdraw (at least on occasion) from the pressures of reality. The world, after all, has the capacity to inflict agonizing pains and gnawing anxieties upon an individual, and there is nothing more natural than wishing to withdraw from all or some of that. So ubiquitous are these painful pressures that we might tentatively explore an analogy for the human condition drawn from a central concept within palliative medicine, the concept of *total pain*. Cicely Saunders, the founder of the hospice movement, advanced this concept as a way of articulating the immense complexity of the pain experienced by the terminally ill and it highlights the physical, emotional, social and spiritual elements informing the patient's suffering.[21] Without claiming that the pains and anxieties of a (healthy) person's life approximate to the excruciating suffering of the terminally ill, it can be said that the idea of 'total pain' provides a fair indication of the range of the torments afflicting all people. Distress ensues from physical discomfort, from psychological phenomena (such as anxiety, sadness and a sense of actual or impending loss), from the difficulties of social and interpersonal relations, and from spiritual (or existential) worries (concerning, for example, the direction, meaning and significance of life). And with this analogy also we can begin to see the role that intoxicants might assume in a person's struggle with these elements of pain. Against the prevailing opinion that pain-relieving opiates were dangerous and to be used sparingly (and even then only in cases where pain was absolutely intolerable), Saunders demonstrated that an opiate such as morphine was vital in the battle against pain and that it could be used effectively to relieve the suffering of those with advanced cancer.[22] The use of painkillers subsequently became a vital element of palliative medicine. Hence, just as the total pain experienced during a terminal illness is relieved by opiates and analgesics, so intoxicating substances constitute (at least one part of) a strategy undertaken by most people in their struggle against unhappiness and distress.

Plainly, intoxicants vary markedly in their effects. If one's desire is to escape the painful pressures of reality, then taking recourse in either *narcotics* or *depressants* would seem to be the natural means of withdrawing from an overly stimulating world.[23] A word is in order concerning these two types of substances. The very meaning of the term 'narcotic' is in particular danger of

---

[21]   See Thomas Dormandy, *The Worst of Evils* (New Haven, CT, 2006), pp. 497–8, and Karen Forbes and Christina Faull, 'The Principles of Pain Management', in Christina Faull, Yvonne Carter and Richard Woof (eds), *Handbook of Palliative Care* (Oxford, 1998), pp. 99–133.

[22]   See Dormandy, *Worst of Evils*, pp. 493–7.

[23]   In what follows, I adhere to the six-fold pharmacological taxonomy (narcotics, depressants, stimulants, hallucinogens, marijuana, and other mood- and performance-enhancing drugs (e.g. antidepressants, steroids)) outlined in Charles Faupel, Alan Horowitz and Greg Weaver, *The Sociology of American Drug Use* (Oxford, 2010), pp. 66–106. On the

being misunderstood (since it is not infrequently employed to refer to all illegal drugs), so it should here clearly be demarcated. Consistent with its etymological origin in the Greek word *narkotikos* – 'benumbing' – the word 'narcotic' refers strictly to those substances possessing analgesic and soporific effects, and which depress the activity of the central nervous system. Narcotic substances are those derived from the opium poppy plant or else synthesized with a similar chemical structure. Accordingly, narcotics can also be referred to as *opiates*. The category encompasses natural narcotics (opium, morphine and codeine), semisynthetic narcotics (heroin, dihydromorphone, oxycodone) and synthetic narcotics (opioids such as methadone and fentanyl). These substances are especially suited to the palliative task allocated to intoxicants by Freud, since they possess an unparalleled capacity to dull pain, making the user 'beautifully indifferent to it'.[24] The analgesic effects of opiates (mirroring the activity of endorphins, the body's own naturally occurring painkillers) are coupled with a marked euphoric effect, variously described as a 'warm feeling', being 'at peace with the world', or (more objectively) as 'a subjective state of well-being produced by the patient's dramatic release from pain and the anxieties and tensions accompanying it'.[25] It is easy to see how opiates progressed from being a medical treatment for pain to being a favoured route out of personal misery. Indeed, some users may have begun their habit after being administered opiates during an illness and recognizing their beneficial effect. These narcotics provide, Howard Markel tells us, 'a first-class, high-speed ticket to temporary oblivion', in which 'the opiate-dominated mind is embraced in a silky, dreamy envelope of comfort that promises escape from the hardships, stresses, and trials of daily life'.[26]

The power of narcotics in the struggle against the vicissitudes of existence has earned them a place, not merely in the lives of countless people, but in the productions of the literary mind. In *The Odyssey*, for example, Homer provides us with a classic description of the indifference to suffering brought about by opiates:

> Then a new thought came to Zeus-born Helen; into the bowl that their wine was drawn from she threw a drug that dispelled all grief and anger and banished remembrance of every trouble. Once it was mingled in the wine-bowl, any man who drank it down would never on that same day let a tear fall down his cheeks, no, not if his father and mother had died, or if his brother or his own son were slain with the sword before his eyes.[27]

---

specific nature of marijuana as a palliative, see Brian R. Clack, 'Cannabis and the Human Condition', in Dale Jacquette (ed.), *Cannabis* (Oxford, 2010), pp. 90–99.

[24]   Markel, *Anatomy*, p. 256, quoting Friedrich Sertürner, the discoverer of morphine.

[25]   Faupel et al., *Sociology*, p. 74.

[26]   Markel, *Anatomy*, p. 73.

[27]   Homer, *The Odyssey* (Oxford, 1980), p. 40.

Likewise, the effects of the fictitious intoxicant *soma*, so central to the plot of Huxley's *Brave New World*, bear a clear resemblance to the workings of the narcotics previously described. Lightening glumness and dispelling any dreadful thought, a '*soma*-holiday' transports users to 'an infinitely friendly world', erecting 'a quite impenetrable wall between the actual universe and their minds'.[28] A most alluring feature of soma lies in its capacity to make a person forget, forget their troubles, their more morbid thoughts, their own self even: 'I drink to my annihilation.'[29] Here we find, of course, the great attraction of narcosis to those for whom existence has proved too hard to bear. If narcotics can raise an 'impenetrable wall' between the user and the real world, then life's difficulties can (at least temporarily) be forgotten and one's memories, regrets and thwarted desires for a while erased.

The desire to forget has also historically been served by the consumption of alcohol. Louis Lewin reports the response of a Guatemalan, asked why he drank so much aguardiente (a strongly alcoholic beverage): '"A man must sometimes *zafarse de su memoria*," i.e. take a rest from memory.'[30] Moreover, no less a text than the Bible itself recommends inebriation as a palliative treatment for sorrow and an eraser of painful memories:

> Give strong drink unto him that is ready to perish,
> and wine unto those that be of heavy hearts.
> Let him drink, and forget his poverty,
> and remember his misery no more.[31]

In the taxonomy of intoxicating substances, alcohol belongs in the category of depressants, along with barbiturates (utilized most commonly to induce sleep), sedatives and tranquilizers (including such widely-consumed benzodiazepines as Valium and Xanax). As with narcotics, depressants are utilized to reduce the activity of the central nervous system, and result in relaxation, lowered awareness, decreased inhibition and drowsiness. As we will shortly see, given his account of the workings and purpose of the mental apparatus, the excitation-reducing qualities of narcotic and depressant substances are perfectly suited to occupy a privileged position in Freud's view of the appeal of intoxication.

This picture of the allure of intoxication sits well with the view of the three sources of suffering laid out by Freud. Intoxicants of one kind or another are utilized to mitigate the pains flowing from bodily ailments, from the external world, and from our relations with other people (unrequited or broken love, for example). In such a way, the use of intoxicating substances is enacted against the backdrop of the ontological misalignment between self and world discussed in

---

[28]   Aldous Huxley, *Brave New World* (London, 1977), p. 70.
[29]   Ibid., p. 72.
[30]   Louis Lewin, *Phantastica* (Rochester, VT, 1998), p. 3.
[31]   Proverbs 31:6–7.

the previous chapter. Our hopes and desires are not met by the world in which we find ourselves, and narcotics or depressants can bring about a temporary sense of independence from that disappointing, thwarting world: 'The man who sees his pursuit of happiness come to nothing … can still find consolation in the yield of pleasure of chronic intoxication.'[32]

Thus far, little mention has been made of the sufferings stemming from within a person's own *mind*, but these too are not infrequently countered by means of intoxication. The principal phenomenon of note here is that of self-criticism or conscience. This issue was the focus of a probing essay by Leo Tolstoy which (once stripped of its moralistic tone) bears a noteworthy resemblance to Freud's thinking on this matter. In 'Why Do Men Stupefy Themselves?', Tolstoy explores the possible reasons for the use of patently harmful intoxicants such as alcohol, tobacco, morphine and hashish. Dismissing the reasons given by users themselves – one smokes in order 'to be cheerful', or to 'to while away the time', or because 'it's pleasant' – Tolstoy detects a more powerful cause motivating the desire for stupefaction: 'Not in the taste, nor in any pleasure, recreation, or mirth they afford, lies the cause of the world-wide consumption of hashish, opium, wine, and tobacco, but simply in man's need to hide from himself the demands of conscience.'[33] The theoretical structure for this claim lies in Tolstoy's conception of the human person as consisting of two distinct parts: a blind, animalistic part, which eats, drinks, rests and propagates; and an observing, spiritual part that appraises the activity of the animal part. So long as one's animal activities coincide with the path dictated by the observing part of the self (coincide, that is, with the voice of conscience), mental harmony ensues; a painful dissonance occurs, however, whenever the spiritual and the animal are not in agreement. Human life, he says, consists therefore in '(1) bringing one's activities into harmony with conscience, or (2) hiding from one's self the indications of conscience in order to be able to continue to live as before'.[34] Evidently, the first course of action – moral enlightenment – is the noblest way to proceed, and yet many people opt for the second. To this end, external and internal methods of screening from oneself the demands of conscience are available. The external method consists in the kinds of diversions we surveyed in the preceding chapter (games, amusements and so on), while the internal method relies on 'obstructing the organ of attention itself', 'darkening conscience itself by poisoning the brain with stupefying substances'.[35] Here one might say that, just as intoxicating substances raise a wall against the external world, so they can also be employed to raise a wall against the moral world, the world of conscience, duty and responsibility. Tolstoy proceeds to note how moral judgements wax and wane according to one's state of drunkenness: when sober, a man is ashamed to steal,

---

[32]   Freud, *Civilization*, p. 84.
[33]   Leo Tolstoy, 'Why Do Men Stupefy Themselves?', in *Essays and Letters* (London, 1911), pp. 19–20.
[34]   Ibid., p. 18.
[35]   Ibid., p. 19.

kill or visit a prostitute, a sense of shame that vanishes in the state of intoxication. This is the case not merely when the intoxicant is alcohol or opium, for tobacco, Tolstoy complains, is just as efficient in darkening the voice of conscience. He recounts the case of a man who could complete the half-accomplished task of murdering his mistress only after pausing to steady his nerves with a cigarette, noting that 'any smoker may detect in himself the same definite desire to stupefy himself with tobacco at certain, specially difficult, moments'.[36] Tolstoy's account is useful in highlighting the painful internal pressures a person seeks to avoid by way of intoxication, and Freud in his own way pursues this line also when he explores the strenuous demands placed upon the individual by that psychic agency which serves as his correlate for conscience: the *super-ego*.

A constant theme within Freud's changing models of the human mind is that the mental apparatus exists in a condition of conflict with itself and that this conflict is the source of a range of phenomena including slips of the tongue and neurotic illnesses. One conspicuous indicator of this conflicted condition is the presence of the kind of observing agency we saw mentioned by Tolstoy. Freud himself speaks of a certain type of neurotic who complains of being observed and who hears this observing person reporting the outcome of their observation: 'now he's going to say this, now he's dressing to go out', and so on.[37] Not wishing to confine this phenomenon merely to those who suffer from delusions, Freud contends that 'in each of us there is present ... an agency like this which observes and threatens to punish'.[38] This agency – the super-ego – takes its place in Freud's final account of the mind alongside the *ego* (the representative of reason, common sense and the demands of external reality) and the *id* (the 'dark, inaccessible part of the personality', in which are located the 'seething excitations'[39] of instinctual life). In his most significant foray into moral theory, Freud argues that the sense of conscience is by no means innate within human beings, but arises when the voice of parental authority (in other words, external restraint) becomes internalized and 'observes, directs and threatens the ego in exactly the same way as earlier the parents did with the child'.[40] This is not the place for a full investigation into Freud's account of the origins and nature of conscience and morality. Our purposes are served rather by noting the torment ensuing when the super-ego becomes an overly punishing force. The super-ego, Freud contends, 'manifests itself essentially as a sense of guilt (or rather, as self-criticism – for the sense of guilt is the perception in the ego answering to this criticism)',[41] and behaves in an extraordinarily harsh manner towards the poor ego, which struggles to maintain its

---

[36]   Ibid., p. 24.

[37]   Sigmund Freud, *New Introductory Lectures on Psycho-Analysis*, S.E. vol. XXII, p. 59.

[38]   Ibid.

[39]   Ibid., p. 73.

[40]   Ibid., p. 62.

[41]   Sigmund Freud, *The Ego and the Id*, S.E. vol. XIX, p. 53.

sense of worth against the severest admonitions. This can result in depression and 'interminable self-torment'.[42] Seen in this light the ego becomes 'a poor creature'[43] menaced by dangers both without (the external world) and within (the super-ego's severity, for example).

Such ideas provide the context for a sketch of the usefulness of intoxication in the fight against a certain kind of internal mental torment. If one's sense of worth is undermined by the severity of a self-criticizing agency, then one might seek out ways in which the activities of that agency might be moderated and constrained. Just as the condition of sleep ushers in (on the Freudian interpretation) a weakening of the powers of the censoring agency of the mind, thereby permitting the emergence in dreams of repressed mental contents,[44] so the condition of intoxication might serve 'to revise the superego and make it milder, less harsh in its judgements, and so more bearable'.[45] A mark of this might be the relaxed inhibitions accompanying (for example) consumption of alcohol, an indicator, indeed, that the user has gained independence from those forces, both internal and external, which have weighed so heavily upon that person's life. Otto Fenichel has explained this well. The elation provided by alcohol stems from 'the fact that inhibitions and limiting considerations of reality are removed from consciousness before the instinctual impulses are',[46] the result being that checks on activity lose a degree of their power: the obstacles placed in one's path by the external world seem smaller and more negotiable, while that element of the psychic personality that inhibits action by criticizing and engendering a sense of embarrassment becomes temporarily suspended. Inebriation occupies therefore an important role in a person's struggle with the inhibiting and sometimes painfully judgemental character of the super-ego, appropriately regarded here as that 'part of the mind that is soluble in alcohol'.[47]

Another Side: The Dull Routine of Existence

It may seem that Freud is operating with a one-sided and unbalanced view of drug-use here. His emphasis upon intoxication as a refuge from life's troubles may make it appear as though drugs were sought out merely for their sedative or narcotic properties. But this is surely false. Not all drugs reduce the activity of

---

[42]   Ibid., p. 54. See also 'Mourning and Melancholia', in which Freud's explanation of depression lays emphasis upon the (as yet unidentified) super-ego's role in bringing about 'an extraordinary diminution in [the melancholic's] self-regard, an impoverishment of his ego on a grand scale' (Sigmund Freud, 'Mourning and Melancholia', S.E. vol. XIV, p. 246).

[43]   Freud, *Ego*, p. 56.

[44]   See Sigmund Freud, *The Interpretation of Dreams* (Second Part), S.E. vol. V, p. 526.

[45]   Mark Edmundson, *The Death of Sigmund Freud* (New York, 2007), p. 99.

[46]   Otto Fenichel, *The Psychoanalytic Theory of Neurosis* (London, 1955), p. 379.

[47]   Ibid.

the central nervous system; and for every sedative there is a stimulant; for every person seeking anxiety-reduction by means of a Valium or a Quaalude we can find another using psilocybin or LSD to achieve a hallucinogenic state, another in search of the stimulation and energy promised by coffee or amphetamines, and so on. Of course, Freud does allow for the possibility that drugs might do something other than sedate, might do something other than have a merely tranquilizing function: recall his observation that intoxicants are used, not just for the removal of unpleasant sensations, but also for the production of pleasant ones. Nevertheless, the general thrust of Freud's psychological theorizing is to emphasize precisely the reduction of unwanted stimuli rather than the quest for new stimulation. According to his principle of *psychic inertia*, first advanced in the early 'Project for a Scientific Psychology', the mind seeks, as far as possible, to eliminate all tension within it.[48] By the time he came to write *Beyond the Pleasure Principle*, Freud was contending that the 'dominating tendency of mental life, and perhaps of nervous life in general, is the effort to reduce, to keep constant or to remove internal tension due to stimuli'.[49] He referred to this as the 'Nirvana principle' and saw it as indicative of a *death instinct* within the human being, an instinct that aims 'to conduct the restlessness of life into the stability of the inorganic state'.[50] This undeniably leaves its mark on his account of the motivations for drug use, for from the principle of psychic inertia it is easy to move to the conviction that the great appeal of drugs lies in their promise to deliver a state of sensationless Nirvana, temporarily to annihilate the user, thereby removing all the painful tensions and stimuli of existence.

Freud's emphasis on the desire to dispose of stimulation and excitement may justifiably be regarded as a weakness in his theory of the mind and its workings. At the very least it requires amending. His view, as we have seen, is that human beings seek mental tranquillity and regard powerful emotions as undesirable intrusions which need quickly to be discharged, thus producing a state of quietude: '*Protection against* stimuli is an almost more important function for the living organism than *reception of* stimuli.'[51] In this scheme of things there is an emphasis on 'stimulus overload' but little or no place for what psychiatrist Anthony Storr has called 'stimulus hunger', the need human beings have to seek out stimuli when they find themselves in a tedious or monotonous environment, a reality which can be demonstrated by observation of (for example) prisoners who have spent considerable periods of time in solitary confinement: stimulus hunger occurs in such a condition and the individual involved will engage in strenuous mental activities in order to excite his or her mind and avoid sinking into despair.[52] Freud, however, does not seem to recognize that tedium may result from a lack of excitation.

48   See Sigmund Freud, 'Project for a Scientific Psychology', S.E. vol. I, pp. 296–8.
49   Sigmund Freud, *Beyond the Pleasure Principle*, S.E. vol. XVIII, pp. 55–6.
50   Sigmund Freud, 'The Economic Problem of Masochism', S.E. vol. XIX, p. 160.
51   Sigmund Freud, *Beyond*, p. 27.
52   Anthony Storr, *Music and the Mind* (London, 1997), p. 28.

That boredom is a psychological problem so entirely ignored by Freud is strange, though not totally unexpected, given his account of the economics of the mental apparatus.[53] This need not undermine an account of intoxicating substances that lays its stress upon their palliative role. To salvage this, we need only supplement Freud's account of the problems of human existence with Schopenhauer's compatible pessimistic contentions, outlined in the previous chapter. Suffering, to recapitulate, is due to the contradiction between the essence of the human being as a willing, desiring creature and the unsatisfiability of those desires; in short, suffering results when a desire remains unfulfilled. One should, however, be under no illusion that happiness would result from the fulfilment of *all* of one's desires. This is because satisfaction of desire leads not to happiness and contentment, but rather to boredom, which is itself just another species of suffering. This point is brought out clearly by Schopenhauer in a passage that begins by referencing something we also had reason earlier to consider: the 'unquenchable thirst' of willing (or striving) as the essence of the human being. The basis of all willing, he contends, is a sense of need or lack, and is therefore by its very nature painful:

> If, on the other hand, it lacks objects of willing, because it is at once deprived of them again by too easy a satisfaction, a fearful emptiness and boredom come over it; in other words, its being and its existence itself become an intolerable burden for it … This has been expressed very quaintly by saying that, after man had placed all pains and torments in hell, there was nothing left for heaven but boredom.[54]

The unsatisfactory nature of the human condition is not, on this view, solely due to pain and the overwhelming stresses of existence (stimulus overload) but also to the vacuity of the state of boredom (stimulus hunger). Human life swings back and forth between these two poles. Schopenhauer is not short of further representations of this twofold condition of suffering. For example, all people recognize the agonizing pains caused by such things as hunger and unrequited or thwarted love. But imagine the alternative. 'Suppose the human race were removed to Utopia where everything grew automatically and pigeons flew about ready roasted; where

---

[53] In the standard edition of Freud's works there are only three references to boredom: *all* of these occur within Josef Breuer's solo contributions to the co-authored *Studies on Hysteria*, S.E. vol. II.

[54] Arthur Schopenhauer, *The World as Will and Representation* (2 vols, New York, 1969), vol. 1, p. 312. It is of interest to note how Pascal anticipated Schopenhauer's analysis: 'The whole of life goes on like this. We seek repose by battling against difficulties, and once they are overcome, repose becomes unbearable because of the boredom it engenders. We have to get away from it, and beg for commotion' (Blaise Pascal, *Pensées* (Oxford, 1999), p. 46 (§168)).

everyone at once found his sweetheart and had no difficulty in keeping her; then people would die of boredom or hang themselves.'[55] Again:

> The striving after existence is what occupies all living things, and keeps them in motion. When existence is assured to them, they do not know what to do with it. Therefore the second thing that sets them in motion is the effort to get rid of the burden of existence, to make it no longer felt, 'to kill time,' in other words, to escape from boredom. Accordingly we see that almost all men, secure from want and cares, are now a burden to themselves, after having finally cast off all other burdens.[56]

Since the 'escape from boredom' is to play a considerable role in this chapter's account of intoxication, it will be worthwhile reflecting on this phenomenon a little further. What *is* boredom, and why is it experienced as something to be escaped? The literature concerning boredom is extensive,[57] reflecting, perhaps, the perception that boredom is the definitive phenomenon of modern civilization ('the disease of our time', indeed).[58] A good understanding of this peculiar mental state is found in Theodor Lipps' definition: 'Boredom is a feeling of unpleasure arising out of conflict between a need for intense mental activity and lack of incitement to it, or inability to be incited.'[59] For the one who is bored, it is the external world that is to blame, since it has failed to supply the excitement sufficient to dispel tedium: 'there is no new thing under the sun', complains the author of Ecclesiastes, while Fernando Pessoa blames 'the contrast between the natural splendour of the inner life, with its natural Indias and its unexplored lands, and the squalor (even when it's not really squalid) of life's daily routine'.[60] Richard Wilbur's diagnosis is more concise still: 'the world is tiresome in itself.'[61] Boredom seems therefore to arise from a clash between a person's expectations about what the world *can* (and *should*) deliver and what it actually *does* deliver: again and again the world comes up empty. Here can be found some degree of unity among the various species

---

[55]   Arthur Schopenhauer, *Parerga and Paralipomena* (2 vols, Oxford, 1974), vol. 2, p. 293.

[56]   Schopenhauer, *World*, vol. 1, p. 313.

[57]   See, for example: Elizabeth S. Goodstein, *Experience Without Qualities: Boredom and Modernity* (Stanford, CA, 2005); Seán Desmond Healy, *Boredom, Self, and Culture* (London, 1984); Patricia Meyer Spacks, *Boredom* (Chicago, IL, 1995); and Lars Svendsen, *A Philosophy of Boredom* (London, 2005).

[58]   *Reader's Digest* (February 1976), quoted in Healy, *Boredom*, p. 36.

[59]   Theodor Lipps, quoted in Otto Fenichel, 'On the Psychology of Boredom', in *The Collected Papers of Otto Fenichel* (2 vols, New York, 1953), vol. 1, p. 292. Fenichel's own definition is also worthy of note: 'the state of mind of boredom is perhaps best characterized as "an unpleasurable experience of a lack of impulse"' (Fenichel, 'Psychology', p. 292).

[60]   Fernando Pessoa, *The Book of Disquiet* (London, 2002), p. 365.

[61]   Richard Wilbur, 'Lying', quoted in Spacks, *Boredom*, p. 10.

of suffering, for there appears in all such cases to be a contradiction between expectation and fulfilment: in the most profoundly painful of sufferings (physical torment, loss of love, and so on) there is a clash between the desire for happiness and the universe's indifference towards that desire; with regard to boredom, there is again a clash between expectation and fulfilment, the expectation that is thwarted in this instance is the expectation that the world should engage our interest or stimulate us in one way or another. This point, as we will later see, will prove to be of considerable significance.

One especially pertinent element of the nature of boredom lies in its relation to the sense of time. (This is of particular significance for our purposes since, as outlined in the preceding chapter, the pessimistic tradition places a not inconsiderable emphasis upon the burden of time as a factor informing human unhappiness.) Kant addresses this theme, noting that 'the more attention we give to time, the more we feel it is empty',[62] and that the act of watching a clock lengthens the experience of time. Things that shorten time are accordingly felt to be enjoyable ('time flies when you're having fun'); hence the need to find and engage in activities that 'pass the time' or (in more aggressive language) *kill* it.[63] Kant is somewhat contemptuous of the usefulness of pleasures and entertainments in the quest to kill time, favouring occupation, projects or work as the best way to dispel its burden ('Young man! (I repeat) get fond of work'[64]), but he recognizes, nonetheless, that the distressing nature of boredom is extraordinarily dangerous, for it often drives us 'to do something harmful to ourselves rather than nothing at all'.[65] This provides a useful context for thinking about the use of certain intoxicating substances. The act of smoking a cigarette, for a start, is frequently undertaken as a way of passing time. Bizet and Baudelaire are among those who have made this observation,[66] while Jules Leforgue's poem 'La Cigarette' links the

---

[62] Immanuel Kant, *Lectures on Ethics* (New York, 1963), p. 162.

[63] Michael Raposa's discussion of the aims of killing time is here worthy of note. Boredom is characterized by Raposa as 'a heightened awareness of the passing of time', the bored person being 'left alone with time'. Such a one, painfully aware of the emptiness of experience, seeks to kill time. Raposa's suggestion is that 'killing time' is 'a rather futile form of self-defense, of self-preservation. One attempts to kill time because time inevitably kills all things' (Michael Raposa, *Boredom and the Religious Imagination* (Charlottesville, VA, 1999), pp. 41–2).

[64] Immanuel Kant, *Anthropology from a Pragmatic Point of View* (Cambridge, 2006), p. 133.

[65] Ibid., pp. 127–8. Note also Kant's description of the distressing condition of boredom: 'The void of sensations we perceive in ourselves arouses a horror (*horror vacui*) and, as it were, the presentiment of a slow death which is regarded as more painful than when fate suddenly cuts the thread of life' (ibid., p. 129).

[66] Baudelaire writes of women who 'display themselves in desperate attitudes of boredom ... smoking cigarettes to kill time' (Charles Baudelaire, quoted in Richard Klein, *Cigarettes Are Sublime* (London, 1995), p. 8), while in Meilhac and Halévy's

act of smoking, not merely with boredom, but with the attendant sense of ennui, of insignificance and a rejection of all that is purportedly transcendent:

> Yes, this world is flat and boring: as for the other, bullshit!
> I myself go resigned to my fate, without hope,
> And to kill time while awaiting death,
> I smoke slender cigarettes thumbing my nose at the gods.
>
> Onward, you living, keep up the fight, poor future skeletons,
> I am plunged into infinite ecstasy by the blue meandering that
> Twists itself toward the sky and puts me to sleep,
> Like dying perfumes from a thousand smoldering pots.[67]

The nihilism exhibited in Leforgue's poem is striking. As Richard Klein perfectly summates, the smoker of the poem has abandoned productive activity, ridicules his more energetic fellows, and resigns himself to insignificance, while in the meantime, 'this mean in-between time between birth into a world of boredom and death with no promise of an afterlife, the poet finds a single activity worth pursuing – killing time'.[68] The cigarette is the weapon of choice in the nihilist's war on time.

The functions of cigarettes (and tobacco products in general) are various, of course. As previously noted, tobacco has a mild anti-anxiety effect, and yet nicotine (only conveyable through the medium of tobacco) is properly classified among that group of substances known as *stimulants*, a group with natural appeal to those for whom the world is not in itself stimulating enough. In stark contrast to the narcotics and depressants discussed earlier (substances, namely, that reduce the activity of the central nervous system), the purpose of a stimulant, as its name suggests, is to stimulate the central nervous system, producing such symptoms as increased heart rate and blood pressure. It is as though the excitement felt to be lacking from an encounter with the world could be generated instead by introducing into one's organism an intoxicating substance. The principal stimulants are cocaine, amphetamines, nicotine and caffeine. The task of dissipating the boredom of everyday life might also be placed in the hands of *hallucinogenic* substances such as mescaline, peyote, psilocybin, LSD and phencyclidine (PCP). The hallucinogens tend to produce a range of subjective effects that might be felt to enliven a world experienced as somewhat dull and even lifeless. These effects include synaesthesia (in which a crossover of sensory experience is felt to occur, the user feeling that he or she can, for example, smell colours), fluidity (in which

---

libretto for Bizet's *Carmen*, Moralés sings that 'to kill time / we smoke, gossip, and watch / the passers-by'.

[67] Jules Leforgue, 'La Cigarette', quoted in Klein, *Cigarettes*, p. 57.

[68] Klein, *Cigarettes*, p. 59.

objects lose their stability and exist instead in a state of flux), spatial distortion, and a general feeling of sensory overload.[69]

One of the most memorable descriptions of the use of stimulants in the fight against life's tedium is found at the very beginning of Arthur Conan Doyle's novel *The Sign of Four*. Sherlock Holmes has injected into his arm a 7-per-cent solution of cocaine, and the disgusted Dr Watson demands a justification from the detective for this dangerous habit ('Why should you, for a mere passing pleasure, risk the loss of those great powers with which you have been endowed?'). The response he receives from Holmes is supremely pertinent:

> 'My mind,' he said, 'rebels at stagnation. Give me problems, give me work, give me the most abstruse cryptogram, or the most intricate analysis, and I am in my own proper atmosphere. I can dispense then with artificial stimulants. But I abhor the dull routine of existence. I crave for mental exaltation.'[70]

It is hard to imagine a more appropriate description of the nature of stimulus hunger and the magnetic appeal of stimulating (and hallucinogenic) substances during those times when the uses of this world indeed appear 'weary, stale, flat and unprofitable'.[71]

None of this is to deny that what people actually seek from the use of intoxicants varies markedly nor that the catalogue of motives is infinitely extendable, but simply that those unsatisfactory elements of the human condition outlined by the pessimistic tradition may provide a useful context for understanding the reasons underlying a large amount of drug use. In short, might not intoxicants function as distinct (perceived) remedies for one or other of those states previously described, for pain and for boredom? The great and abundant variety of psychoactive substances suggests that this may be so. Some drugs may serve to ease troubled, anxious and overstimulated minds. Others may be singularly unfitted to that particular tranquilizing task and may instead *introduce* excitation into a mind uninspired by the common order of things. Even the nightmarish experiences sought by the PCP-user may perhaps be illuminated by such an approach, since the hellish excitement of a trip on angel dust may contrast favourably with a life otherwise pedestrian and bland. Hence, drugs are often used both when the world has become too much for us *and* when it has become too little; both when there is too much going on *and*, conversely, when there is not enough. We can put this point another way by adopting a memorable image offered by Ronald Siegel.[72] Excitation in the brain may be regarded as a fire: sometimes the fire needs to be dampened, while at other times it requires stoking. Narcotics and depressants dampen the fire in the brain; hallucinogens and stimulants stoke it up.

---

[69] See Faupel et al., *Sociology*, p. 95.

[70] Arthur Conan Doyle, *The Sign of Four* (London, 2001), p. 6.

[71] William Shakespeare, *Hamlet* (London, 1996), Act 1, Scene 2, line 133.

[72] Ronald K. Siegel, *Intoxication* (Rochester, VT, 2005), pp. 227–8.

Intoxication as Substitutive Satisfaction

The suggestion thus far explored – namely, that intoxicating substances are utilized to dispel pain and boredom – was also advanced by Huxley in *The Doors of Perception*:

> That humanity at large will ever be able to dispense with Artificial Paradises seems very unlikely. Most men and women lead lives at the worst so painful, at the best so monotonous, poor and limited that the urge to escape, the longing to transcend themselves if only for a few moments, is and has always been one of the principal appetites of the soul. Art and religion, carnivals and saturnalia, dancing and listening to oratory – all these have served, in H. G. Wells' phrase, as Doors in the Wall. And for private, for everyday use there have always been chemical intoxicants.[73]

Here an important connection is drawn between intoxication and two of the other palliative measures – religion and art – isolated by Freud. As in Freud's account, Huxley's desire is to trace these conspicuous features of human life back to a sense of dissatisfaction with some aspect of reality. So pervasive is this dissatisfaction that intoxication is to be regarded as an inevitable feature of human civilization: the 'urge to escape from selfhood and the environment is in almost everyone almost all the time'.[74] Struck by the ubiquity of drug use, some writers – notably Ronald Siegel and Andrew Weil – have claimed that intoxication is 'a basic human appetite',[75] functioning 'like the basic drives of hunger, thirst or sex … *Intoxication is the fourth drive*'.[76] According to Weil, people are 'born with a drive to experience episodes of altered consciousness'.[77] The desire for such a change in consciousness can be seen even in young children, who engage in such activities as whirling themselves into a stupor or auto-choking so as to effect this alteration. As children get older they find other ways (usually chemical methods) to alter their state of mind. Hence a person drinks alcohol, smokes marijuana or swallows ecstasy (or uses any other of the long etcetera of intoxicating substances). In each of these cases, the desire underlying the act is the same: the satisfaction of an inner need to experience different modes of consciousness. Diverging a little from Weil, Siegel concedes that the drive to pursue intoxication is not innate (and differs therefore from the drives associated with survival needs) but is instead acquired. It is thus akin to other acquired (though still perfectly natural) motivations, such as social attachments and the pursuit of love. Unlike other acquired motivations, however, the pursuit of intoxication, Siegel contends, has the strength of a

---

73   Aldous Huxley, *The Doors of Perception and Heaven and Hell* (London, 2004), p. 38.
74   Ibid., p. 39.
75   Andrew Weil, *The Natural Mind* (New York, 2004), p. 14.
76   Siegel, *Intoxication*, p. 10.
77   Weil, *Natural Mind*, p. 19.

primary drive, steering an individual's life, and 'can never be repressed' since it is 'biologically inevitable'.[78]

Nothing in the account of intoxication advanced in this chapter necessitates acceptance of the dramatic claim that drug use constitutes a drive, either innate or acquired. Indeed, the contention that intoxication is a biological inevitability founders on the simple observation that there are individuals (and maybe even entire civilizations)[79] who completely shun such a pursuit. The extraordinary prevalence of intoxicant utilization is, I contend, not to be accounted for by the presence in human beings of some (innate or acquired) drive, but rather by certain distressing features of lived experience that at least appear to the user to be ameliorated by the employment of a psychoactive substance of one kind or another. In other words, a person does not seek intoxication as an end in itself, *maybe not* but instead because the intoxicated state is perceived to mitigate temporarily the unsatisfactory condition of existence felt by the user. If the user's experience of life was less painful or more stimulating, then it is at least plausible that intoxication would hold considerably less of an appeal.

When the determinants of intoxication are presented in this manner we seem to edge close to a standard psychoanalytic explanation, one which stresses that drugs are used as a substitute for a desired satisfaction that has failed to materialize and that they operate as some kind of compensatory gratification. In his early thoughts on the matter, Freud himself was clear about the specific nature of the dissatisfaction underlying intoxication: 'narcotics are meant to serve – directly or indirectly – as a substitute for a lack of sexual satisfaction.'[80] Here Freud's articulation of what ultimately motivates the drug user mirrors his view of the causes of creativity in the artist: unsuccessful in his or her sexual projects, the artist (or drug-user) turns away from reality and finds satisfaction in a secondary, desexualized activity.[81] In a subsequent chapter, the deficiencies of this view as it pertains to art will be exposed, but the most obvious of weaknesses can immediately be detected: it is implausible to suggest that the *sine qua non* of artistic creativity is sexual dissatisfaction, since it would follow that no artist could achieve (or

---

[78]   Siegel, *Intoxication*, p. 208.

[79]   Weil himself describes the Inuit as lacking an intoxicant until white men introduced alcohol to them (Weil, *Natural Mind*, p. 14).

[80]   Sigmund Freud, 'Sexuality in the Aetiology of the Neuroses', S.E. vol. III, p. 276. Freud even justified his own addiction to cigars in these terms. While far away from (and sorely missing) his fiancée, he wrote these words to her: 'Smoking is indispensable if one has nothing to kiss' (Freud, letter to Martha Bernays (22 January 1884), quoted in Peter Gay, *Freud: A Life for Our Time* (New York, 1998), p. 39). In a letter to Fliess, Freud suggests that alcohol, morphine and tobacco addictions enter into life as substitutes for masturbation ('the one major habit, the "primary addiction"') (Freud, letter to Wilhelm Fliess (22 December 1897), in Masson (ed.), *Complete Letters*, p. 287).

[81]   See Sigmund Freud, *Introductory Lectures on Psycho-Analysis* (Part III), S.E. vol. XVI, p. 376.

has ever achieved) sexual fulfilment, and that, if such fulfilment did ever occur for all people then art would simply disappear. Something similar might be said regarding drug-users. A person might feel satisfied in his or her sexual life, and yet still (for some other reason) experience a need for intoxication.

The account of the function of intoxication offered by Freud in *Civilization and Its Discontents* constitutes an improvement upon his earlier, sex-based view. True, the utilization of intoxicating substances is still connected with a sense of dissatisfaction, but (as we have seen) this dissatisfaction encompasses far more than frustration of an exclusively sexual nature. There is nonetheless some danger that an account stressing the role of drugs in compensating for thwarted desires risks eliding the distinction Freud wishes to draw between intoxicating substances and substitutive satisfactions as distinct kinds of palliatives. Some degree of overlap between types of palliative is, of course, to be expected. There is, however, an important difference between intoxicating substances and the substitutive satisfactions offered, for example, by art. Both stem, on Freud's view, from a painful sense of dissatisfaction. In the case of artistic creativity, though, the impulses and desires that have remained unsatisfied undergo *sublimation*, a process whereby an impulse (usually but not exclusively of a sexual nature) is diverted towards a new and socially valued aim. What was originally a base impulse is transformed into something 'finer and higher',[82] and something valuable can in such a manner result from the experience of thwarted desire. Nothing of the kind happens in the case of intoxication. Thwarted impulses are not in this case sublimated, but are just treated chemically; neither pain nor boredom is transformed into something higher, and their distressing effects are instead merely and temporarily ameliorated. The contrast between sublimation and mere amelioration is enough to distinguish intoxicating substances from substitutive satisfactions as different species of palliative. Moreover, since the contrast with artistic creation seems to reflect poorly on intoxication (the latter appears not to produce anything nearly as valuable), we are led inevitably towards the question that arises frequently in discussions of the subject. That question concerns the value judgement one should make regarding drug use.

Questions of Value and Harm

The state of intoxication, we have seen, is commonly – and understandably – valued for its role in the alleviation of some of the most distressing aspects of lived experience. Its effects, of course, may not be entirely beneficial, and it is for this reason that, alone among the palliatives, drug use is frequently seen as something worthy of moral condemnation and legal prohibition. It is to be noted here that this

---

[82]   Freud, *Civilization*, p. 79. See also Jean Laplanche and Jean-Bertrand Pontalis, *The Language of Psychoanalysis* (London, 1973), pp. 431–4 for a concise discussion of sublimation.

judgement does not typically extend to all intoxicating substances. A person, after all, might be heard condemning the use of drugs while quaffing a glass of wine, enjoying an after-dinner cigar, or having their first, much-needed coffee of the day. Having touched on the strange inconsistencies inherent in society's general attitude towards intoxicating substances, we will leave that particular subject on one side and instead take a brief glance at some of the aspects of intoxicating substances that may make them worthy of disapprobation.[83]

Freud's own judgement regarding the injurious aspect of intoxicants has already been noted. He holds them responsible for the waste of a large amount of energy that might have been utilized for the improvement of the human lot. Compared with the act of producing art or of engaging in scientific or intellectual work, both of which stem from an experience of suffering but which seek to bring about some improvement for the human community as a whole ('working with all for the good of all'[84]), the pursuit of intoxication seems a paltry and selfish thing, a cowardly withdrawal from reality worthy only of contempt. Such a view was expressed by Massachusetts judge Joseph Tauro when upholding his state's marijuana law: 'Many succumb to the drug as a handy means of withdrawing from the inevitable stresses and legitimate demands of society. The evasion of problems and escape from reality seem to be among the desired effects of the use of marijuana.'[85] In addition to a failure to contribute anything valuable to the community, the drug user may also be guilty of adding to its sum total of pains. The use of intoxicants not infrequently causes harm to the user, thereby undermining its value as a palliative, while the user in turn inflicts suffering on others through reckless actions, neglect of duties and the criminal activities that appear frequently to accompany drug use and addiction. Since these effects are clearly undesirable, society is justified in morally condemning intoxication and implementing a policy of (selective) prohibition, punishing those who produce, supply and consume (illicit) drugs.

What might be said in response to such claims? One might, first of all, question the extent to which drug use increases crime rates. To shed some light on this matter, it will be helpful to distinguish between different kinds of drug-related crimes. Following Douglas Husak, these crimes may be divided into *systemic*, *economic* and *psychopharmacological* kinds.[86] Systemic crimes arise because of the illegal status of drug use, one consequence of which is that drugs are bought and sold in black markets; since there is no legal process by means of which disagreements

---

[83]   The aspects to be considered in what follows are by no means exhaustive and instead focus predominantly on the negative consequences of the employment of intoxicating substances for palliative purposes. For a more wide-ranging discussion, see Douglas Husak, *Legalize This! The Case for Decriminalizing Drugs* (London, 2002), pp. 64–124.

[84]   Freud, *Civilization*, pp. 77–8.

[85]   G. Joseph Tauro, quoted in Jacob Sullum, *Saying Yes: In Defense of Drug Use* (New York, 2004), pp. 106–7.

[86]   Husak, *Legalize*, pp. 84–9.

regarding black market transactions can be negotiated, such disputes tend to be resolved violently. It is worth remarking here that any activity, however innocuous, will generate systemic crime if it becomes criminalized. Consider, for example, antiquarian book collecting as an example of just such an innocuous activity. If this hobby were to be made illegal, the dealer and the collector would immediately be engaged in a criminal activity simply by virtue of dealing in and collecting antiquarian books, thereby increasing levels of crime. Moreover, transactions would now need to occur in a black market setting, ushering in – for the reasons noted above – a hike in violent conduct. In the case of systemic crimes, therefore, the connection between drugs and crime is merely contingent, arising purely from the illegal status of certain intoxicating substances. Similar observations may be made with regard to economic crime. This category concerns the property crimes (most commonly, burglary) committed by illicit drug-users and addicts in order to fund their habits. These crimes would appear to be more intimately (and less contingently) connected to the nature of drug use itself, since the addict wants drugs badly and will go to great lengths to get them. Again, however, this is a kind of crime that might in fact be generated by the illegality of certain drugs. Those addicted to alcohol and tobacco do not, after all, tend to fund their habits by economic crime. This is not because these licit drugs are any less addictive than illicit ones, but rather because black market prices are inflated. Decriminalization of illicit drugs might serve to bring down their cost, thereby reducing instances of economic crime.[87]

While both systemic and economic crime results largely (or maybe even exclusively) from the fact of prohibition, psychopharmacological crime arises (it is said) from the effects of the drugs themselves: under the influence of drugs, people who would normally behave in a responsible and law-abiding fashion commit criminal and sometimes violent acts. One should be wary of such claims. It is certainly true that a substance capable of turning good citizens into crazed and violent maniacs should be prohibited and its use morally condemned. It would appear, however, that no such substances exist. A great many of the drugs prohibited for recreational use (the narcotics, for example) actually, as we have seen, deliver soporific effects, effectively decreasing the likelihood of aggressive actions. To think, moreover, that a specific piece of behaviour may be entirely caused by the consumption of a particular drug is to fall victim to a belief in what Jacob Sullum colourfully calls 'voodoo pharmacology',[88] and ignores the great extent to which reactions to intoxicants depend upon social context and the characteristics of the individual user. Much more could be said about the connection between drugs and crime, but the foregoing should be sufficient to cast some doubt on the frequently made claim that intoxicating substances are justifiably condemned and prohibited because they exacerbate levels of crime.

[87] For economic arguments of this kind, see William F. Buckley, Kurt Schmoke, Joseph D. McNamara and Robert W. Sweet, 'The War on Drugs Is Lost', in Hugh LaFollette (ed.), *Ethics in Practice* (Oxford, 2002), pp. 300–306.

[88] Sullum, *Saying Yes*, p. 10.

Even if drugs do not bear such a clear relation to crime as commonly thought, the use of intoxicating substances might still have a deleterious effect upon society. As James Q. Wilson, onetime Chairman of the American National Advisory Council for Drug Abuse Prevention, contends, drug use produces 'individuals who regularly victimize their children by neglect, their spouses by improvidence, their employers by lethargy, and their co-workers by carelessness'.[89] Likewise, a report produced by the American Office of National Drug Control Policy declares that drugs erode the user's sense of personal responsibility, diminishing an individual's capacity to operate effectively 'as a student, a parent, a spouse, [and] an employee'.[90] While it is true that the use of intoxicating substances may produce these undesirable results in many people, such effects are not universal, nor may drugs uniquely be responsible for their appearance. The use of alcohol, for example, can lead to an individual being neglectful and improvident, but this is not the case for all those who consume it (even on a regular basis), and this should give one pause before making blanket statements about the consequences of intoxicant utilization. An individual, moreover, may be a poor-performing student, a lethargic employee or an improvident spouse without ever having used intoxicants. These two observations are combined in Michael Huemer's argument for the decriminalization of drugs. Noting that it is not illegal to be lethargic at school or work, nor illegal to be an improvident spouse, it must be unacceptable, he says, for a person to face criminal charges 'for doing something that only has a *chance* of indirectly bringing about a similar result'.[91]

At this stage one might retreat to a less contentious and more demonstrable matter: the harms caused by intoxicants to users themselves. Though often exaggerated, these harms are real enough. A full inventory is unnecessary in this context, but one might in passing mention the damage to lungs and throat caused by tobacco, the cirrhosis produced by heavy alcohol consumption, the brain cell loss resulting from methamphetamines, as well as the psychological and relational problems that may flow from (at least excessive) drug use. Such dangers should constitute enough of a reason to advise individuals against relying on intoxication as their palliative of choice. But it should be emphasized that this would constitute a prudential piece of advice rather than a moral command. Indeed, it is hard to ascertain on what basis a person could be morally condemned for pursuing a state of intoxication, a state in which pleasurable sensations are experienced and unpleasurable sensations are reduced. Evidently, an individual in such a state should not undertake any task in which others are put at risk of harm (he or she should not drive a vehicle while inebriated, for example), nor should a person be negligent in their reasonable duties towards relevant others (spouse, children,

---

[89] James Q. Wilson, 'Against the Legalization of Drugs', in Hugh LaFollette (ed.), *Ethics in Practice* (Oxford, 2002), p. 297.

[90] Quoted in Michael Huemer, 'America's Unjust Drug War', in James Rachels and Stuart Rachels (eds), *The Right Thing To Do* (Boston, MA, 2010), p. 228.

[91] Ibid., p. 226.

work colleagues and so on). But if the harms flowing from an individual's actions affect no person other than that individual, no moral judgement should be made, nor should that individual be punished. Moral judgements – and legal penalties – should extend only to those persons whose actions have harmed others against their will.[92] The pursuit of intoxication does not in itself fall into that category of condemnable actions.[93] There seems to be nothing wrong, therefore, in seeking intoxication, though one should be aware of the potential risks of pursuing pleasure along those lines. The words of Epicurus, written over two thousand years ago, seem in this context as appropriate as ever: 'No pleasure is in itself evil, but the things which produce certain pleasures entail annoyances many times greater than the pleasures themselves.'[94] Epicurus' suggestion, indeed, can be applied neatly to our consideration of intoxicating substances as a specific type of palliative measure. It is perfectly understandable that an individual might turn to intoxicants as a way of either softening the pains of life or else lifting its tedium; such a strategy might, however, be counterproductive, and in certain circumstances and for certain individuals might in fact increase rather than reduce levels of suffering and dissatisfaction.

Before leaving the subject of harms to oneself, it should be remarked that it is rather peculiar that drugs should be singled out as particularly worthy of moral criticism because of the damage they cause to the user. As Husak points out, there are a great many activities – including sunbathing, mountain climbing and many sports – which carry a large degree of risk but are rarely subject to moral criticism and legal prohibition.[95] Few people would think, for example, that a young man devoting his life to playing American football is acting in a morally questionable way, even though he risks inflicting significant harms on himself as a result of his passion.[96] One reason for this odd disparity is (presumably) that society

---

[92]   The classic statement of a position of this kind is, of course, to be found in Mill's *On Liberty*: 'The only part of the conduct of any one, for which he is amenable to society, is that which concerns others' (John Stuart Mill, *On Liberty* (Oxford, 1991), p. 14). Mill makes it clear that a person's own well being is not a sufficient reason for exercising power over that individual. Addressing explicitly the matter of intoxication, Mill says that drunkenness is 'not a fit subject for legislative interference', though special legal restrictions could legitimately be placed upon a person who had previously committed an offence while drunk. Such a person should be liable to penalty if found again drunk, since 'making himself drunk, in a person whom drunkenness excites to do harm to others, is a crime against others' (ibid., p. 108).

[93]   Though see Wilson ('Against', p. 297) for criticism of the view that drug use should be regarded as a 'victimless crime'.

[94]   Epicurus, 'The Principal Doctrines', in J.C.A. Gaskin (ed.), *The Epicurean Philosophers* (London, 1995), p. 6.

[95]   See Husak, *Legalize*, pp. 106–8.

[96]   'According to a recent study, 65 percent of professional football players suffer a major injury while playing – that is, an injury that either requires surgery or forces them to miss at least eight games. Two of every three former professionals indicate that their injuries

places a high value on these other activities (sports, in particular), but can detect little worth in intoxication (especially of the illicit kind). If the argument of this chapter has any weight at all, however, we can begin to see the important value of intoxicating substances: life is extraordinarily difficult and the state of intoxication (of one kind or another) has proven to be of no small benefit in the individual's struggle against misery and unhappiness.[97] Nor should a view touting the positive value of intoxication be regarded as eccentric or even irresponsible. Husak, for example, has argued that the predominant reason for the use of intoxicants lies in their ability to assist a person in altering his or her mood. The effectiveness of this technique can be seen in such quotidian drugs as caffeine and alcohol, without which 'many would be condemned to remain sleepy in the morning, and tense in the evening'.[98] It is the capacity of drugs (both licit and illicit) to function as agents of mood control that accounts for their value, since they allow people to 'exercise more control over their lives and thereby increase their enjoyment'.[99] Moreover, even such a strict moralist as Kant praises drinking in company since it enlivens sociability, 'opens the heart and is an instrumental vehicle of a moral quality, namely frankness'.[100] While few people would deny that there are dangers (both to self and others) in heavy and irresponsible intoxicant use, most would, from their own experience, agree with the observations made by Husak and Kant: intoxication augments one's sense of enjoyment and facilitates a merrier engagement with others, lifting the gloom that settles from time to time over life.

None of the four auxiliary structures examined in this book lends itself more naturally to being characterized in palliative terms than intoxicating substances: the 'recreational' use of chemical agents to mitigate existential pain and lighten mood clearly mirrors the utilization of drugs in palliative medicinal care.[101] As a result of their effectiveness, they have assumed a major role in humanity's battle against dissatisfaction. In closing, we might briefly address Freud's words of rebuke regarding intoxicants: instead of using her energies to assist in the improvement of the human lot, the user withdraws into a world of her own making, choosing to escape from reality rather than to meet its challenges head on. But must we castigate uniquely the user of intoxicants for failing to utilize their energies in the

---

limit their abilities to participate in sports and other recreational activities in retirement' (Husak, *Legalize*, p. 107).

[97] This in itself might constitute an argument for the exercise of greater compassion in drug policy and sentencing.

[98] Husak, *Legalize*, p. 132.

[99] Ibid.

[100] Kant, *Anthropology*, p. 64.

[101] As Husak has shown, the distinction frequently drawn between 'recreational' and 'medicinal' uses of drugs is in fact fraught with difficulties (see Husak, *Legalize*, pp. 33–43). Also of relevance in this context is Siegel's dismissal of the medical/recreational distinction: 'We must recognize that intoxicants are medicines, treatments for the human condition' (Siegel, *Intoxication*, p. xi).

way Freud desires? Why do we not chastise the sports fanatic or the avid reader
of novels for a comparable waste of energy? And is one really obliged to use
one's energies for 'the improvement of the human lot' anyway? After all, a reader
of *Civilization and Its Discontents* might come away with the lesson regarding
cultural endeavour that 'the whole effort is not worth the trouble';[102] in which
case, withdrawing into a world with better conditions of sensibility might seem
a perfectly acceptable course of action. As for that escape from reality itself, our
analysis of the painful elements of the real world should surely make us less critical
of those who, at least for a short while, seek some kind of escapist respite. After
all, the function of certain movies, books and other entertainments is to provide a
means of temporary escape. Why should intoxication be any more reprehensible
than these?[103] It may, on the other hand, be a different (and more culpable) matter
if the withdrawal from reality is less a temporary state and more of a permanent
flight. The next palliative on our list is seen by many to constitute just such a fixed
flight from the real world: *religion*.

---

[102] Freud, *Civilization*, p. 145.

[103] We should not assume that all drug use is an attempt to escape from reality. Huxley,
who has provided us with a description of (certain types of) intoxication as 'a holiday
from the facts', saw that drugs were not always used in an escapist fashion. While *Brave
New World*'s depiction of soma certainly presents the escapist conception, his later novel
Island introduces us to a different substance ('moksha-medicine') the function of which
is to sharpen consciousness and reveal to the user the true nature of reality. See Aldous
Huxley, *Island* (New York, 1962) and M.H.N. Schermer, '*Brave New World* versus *Island*:
Utopian and Dystopian Views of Psychopharmacology', *Medicine, Health Care, and
Philosophy*, 10/2 (2007), pp. 119–28.

Chapter 3
The Second Palliative: Religion

Long enough have the instructors of the people fixed their eyes on heaven; let them at last bring them back to the earth.

Paul Henri Thiry, Baron d'Holbach

A proper understanding of the nature of religious belief, Freud contends, is to be achieved by placing it among the palliative measures utilized by suffering humanity in the battle against life's perennial hardships. In such a context, religion can be seen to emerge from – and to address and soften – distressing aspects of human existence. The precise location of religion in the typology of palliatives is, however, something of a puzzle. Is it to be classified as one among a number of *powerful deflections* allowing people to make light of misery; as a *substitutive satisfaction* providing a displaced gratification for a thwarted impulse; or as something akin to the *intoxicating substances* that, in one way or another, diminish pain and produce pleasurable sensations? A good way to answer that question will be to gain a clear view of the way religion provides a uniquely appealing set of beliefs and expectations, one function of which is to console the faithful for the anxieties, pains and disappointments of earthly existence. One's acceptance of religious ideas brings consolation through its assertions that the universe, far from being a product of chance events and devoid of meaning, is ordered and directed by the intelligent being who originally saw fit to create it; that this being – God – takes a personal interest, not just in the affairs of this world and of our species, but also has a concern for the happiness and well-being of each individual member of that species; that no human life is therefore insignificant since it occupies a position within God's plan and purview; that one can enter into a personal relationship with this being and experience his love as being akin to that of a father for his children; that God has the ability and inclination to intervene in human history, fighting alongside human beings in their struggles, and bringing about events of a miraculous nature; that there is a genuine moral order in the universe, and ultimately, therefore, justice; and that, since God's love for us is perfect and unending, there will be an extension of our life beyond our worldly term, a heavenly existence in which the sufferings of this life are no more and we live in blissful harmony with God, reunited with those we loved during our brief and painful time in the earthly vale of tears.

In its capacity to provide consolations of this magnitude religion stands alone. As Samuel Johnson duly noted, no purely secular system of thought can offer anything comparable to the promise of an afterlife of unending happiness. When friends are lost to death, and our own inescapable annihilation ignites terror, what can non-religious systems offer as solace but resignation? 'Real alleviation of the loss of friends', on the other hand, 'and rational tranquillity in the prospect of our own dissolution, can be received only from the promises of him in whose hands are life and death, and from the assurance of another and better state, in which all tears will be wiped from the eyes, and the whole soul shall be filled with joy.'[1] Nor is it solely in respect of death that religion provides consolations exceeding those of any secular alternative. The total religious vision of the universe – as purposely created, morally ordered and throbbing, indeed, with love – will surely alleviate a person's anxieties more than a bleak naturalistic alternative, in which the processes of the universe are driven by 'blind, pitiless indifference',[2] and the greatest hopes and loves of men and women are 'but the outcome of accidental collocations of atoms',[3] the whole human spectacle 'destined to extinction in the vast death of the solar system'.[4] This melancholy picture marches with our most painful suspicions about our lives, while religion whispers reassuringly to us that those suspicions are wrong, an appearance merely: it is not so that the universe is a mere accident, our lives insignificant and our projects futile; not so that we are ultimately unknown, unloved and doomed only to dusty oblivion. With such anxious concerns banished by religion's gentle balm, one can relax into a condition of tranquillity and repose. This, presumably, is the key to the consoling power of religious belief. As Freud writes, 'it soothes the fear that men feel of the dangers and vicissitudes of life, … it assures them of a happy ending and offers them comfort in unhappiness'.[5]

Before proceeding further, it must be admitted that not *all* systems of religious belief possess the consoling features listed above. Religion, after all, does not possess this kind of uniformity.[6] But this is of little consequence for the discussion to follow, for we will be concerned with the palliative function of a particular kind of religion: namely, the variety of monotheism generally embraced by the Western world's body of believers. Evidently, this is the type of belief that Freud has in mind in *Civilization and Its Discontents*. Eschewing sophisticated philosophical versions of religious belief (referring to these as 'pitiful rearguard actions'[7]), Freud focuses his interest on the religion of 'the common man' – 'the only religion which ought to bear that name'[8] – describing it as 'the system of doctrines and promises

---

[1]   Samuel Johnson, *Consolation in the Face of Death* (London, 2009), p. 116.

[2]   Richard Dawkins, *River Out of Eden* (New York, 1995), p. 133.

[3]   Bertrand Russell, 'A Free Man's Worship', in *Mysticism and Logic* (New York, 2004), p. 37.

[4]   Ibid.

[5]   Sigmund Freud, *New Introductory Lectures on Psycho-Analysis*, in *The Standard Edition of the Complete Psychological Works of Sigmund Freud* (24 vols, London, 1953–74) (hereafter S.E.), vol. XXII, p. 161.

[6]   See Beverley Clack and Brian R. Clack, *The Philosophy of Religion: A Critical Introduction* (Oxford, 2008), pp. 1–7.

[7]   Sigmund Freud, *Civilization and Its Discontents*, S.E. vol. XXI, p. 74.

[8]   Ibid.

which on the one hand explains to him [the believer] the riddles of this world with enviable completeness, and, on the other, assures him that a careful Providence will watch over his life and will compensate him in a future existence for any frustrations he suffers here'.[9] For Freud, this variety of religion is characterized by three functions that it, uniquely, performs. As a system of belief focused upon supernatural beings and afterlife expectations, it provides information about the origin of the universe, it lays down a set of rules of action, and – the source of its greatest influence and appeal – it assures the believer of protection and ultimate happiness. The tranquillizing effect of this system of belief has already been noted, and it is important to reflect on this in a little more detail, for this will allow us to explore the oft-perceived structural similarities between religion and the palliative measure we considered in the previous chapter: drugs.

Religion and Narcosis

Though by no means its exclusive property,[10] the metaphorical characterization of religion as a narcotic is most commonly associated with the Marxist tradition. Here the presence of religious belief in the lives of human beings is traced to some kind of fault in the structure of society: 'the existence of religion is the existence of a defect',[11] Marx writes, the source of this defect locatable in a society's socio-economic basis and the division between oppressor and oppressed, the dominant class and the dominated class. In Western societies, capitalists (and their managerial appointees) constitute the dominant class, luxuriating in wealth, while workers constitute the dominated class, condemned to long hours of tedious work with income and free time insufficient to augment significantly their hard lives. Given the great disparity of wealth and life conditions in capitalist society, it is patently in the interests of the dominating class to retard the capacity of the workers both to see themselves as a dominated class and to recognize the world in which they reside as being fundamentally rotten and in need of revolution. From the perspective of the dominating class, in other words, something needs to be done to prevent the workers from challenging the capitalists' position of unjustifiable privilege. Enter religion. An essentially conservative phenomenon, the acceptance of religion brings with it acceptance of the world as it is (however terrible it may be) and acceptance of the social order (however unequal and unjust it is). Religion achieves this remarkable end by offering consolation to the dominated class in the form of the promise of a better life beyond the grave, a blissful heavenly existence

---

[9]   Ibid.

[10]   Nietzsche, for example, speaks of 'the two great European narcotics, alcohol and Christianity' (Friedrich Nietzsche, *Twilight of the Idols and the Anti-Christ* (Harmondsworth, 1968), p. 61.

[11]   Karl Marx, 'On the Jewish Question', in David McLellan (ed.), *Karl Marx: Selected Writings* (Oxford, 1977), p. 43.

compensating infinitely for all the hardships endured on earth. This consoling notion serves to placate any sense of outrage felt by the workers about their lot and, detaching themselves from a concern with political things of this world, they turn their eyes to heavenly and spiritual matters. With a dominated class thus religiously subdued, the evils of the capitalist system can proceed unchallenged.

Marx, in his most famous words on the subject, described these effects of religion as being narcotic in function:

> *Religious* distress is at the same time the *expression* of real distress and also the *protest* against real distress. Religion is the sigh of the oppressed creature, the heart of a heartless world, just as it is the spirit of spiritless conditions. It is the *opium* of the people.[12]

The charge was to be repeated in even more strident terms by Lenin. More aggressively atheistic even than Marx – describing religion as 'mediaeval mildew' and 'one of the most odious things on earth'[13] – Lenin pointedly altered the phrase 'opium *of* the people' so that it became 'opium *for* the people', thereby suggesting that the religious narcotic was, as it were, *fed* to the workers by their oppressors, rather than, as Marx's words might suggest, something which might have emerged from the dominated class itself (as a protest that might, perhaps, be itself transfigured into revolutionary action).[14] Hence:

> Religion is one of the forms of spiritual oppression which everywhere weighs down heavily upon the masses of the people, over-burdened by their perpetual work for others, by want and isolation. Impotence of the exploited classes in their struggle against the exploiters just as inevitably gives rise to the beliefs in a better life after death as impotence of the savage in his battle with nature gives rise to belief in gods, devils, miracles, and the like. Those who toil and live in want all their lives are taught by religion to be submissive and patient while here on earth, and to take comfort in the hope of a heavenly reward. But those who live by the labour of others are taught by religion to practise charity while on earth, thus offering them a very cheap way of justifying their entire existence as exploiters and selling them at a moderate price tickets to well-being in heaven.

---

[12]   Karl Marx, 'Contribution to the Critique of Hegel's Philosophy of Law', in Karl Marx and Friedrich Engels, *On Religion* (Moscow, 1957), p. 39. It would appear that Marx owed the characterization of religion as an opiate to Bruno Bauer, who had previously spoken of how religion 'in the opium-like stupefaction of its destructive urge, speaks of a future life where all shall be made new' (Bauer, quoted in David McLellan, *The Young Hegelians and Karl Marx* (London, 1969), p. 78).

[13]   V.I. Lenin, quoted in David McLellan, *Marxism and Religion* (London, 1987), p. 4.

[14]   On the differences between Marx and Lenin with regard to the opium metaphor, see Anja Finger, 'The Pains and Pleasures of Opium, Religion, and Modernity: A New View of Robert Owen', in Michael R. Ott (ed.), *The Future of Religion* (Leiden, 2007), pp. 153–6.

Religion is opium for the people. Religion is a sort of spiritual booze, in which the slaves of capital drown their human image, their demand for a life more or less worthy of man.[15]

There is much of significance in this passage. For a start, the connection between the role of religion in both 'savage' and capitalist society is worthy of note. Agreeing with many nineteenth-century theorists that religion arose from the savage's ignorance and sense of helplessness in the face of inscrutable natural powers, Lenin sees the proletarian's faith in comparable terms, namely as an efflux of 'helplessness in the face of the blind forces of capitalism, which every day and every hour inflicts upon the ordinary working people the most horrible suffering and the most savage torment, a thousand times more severe than those inflicted by extra-ordinary events, such as wars, earthquakes, etc.'.[16] For our purposes, however, the crucial element is the contention that religion inculcates a sense of patience and servility, drugging into submission the very ones who should most fervently be fighting for better lives here and now (rather than fixing their sights upon paradise in some illusory hereafter).[17] The 'spiritual booze' provided to the worker performs the same task, therefore, as the literal alcohol recommended by *Proverbs*: the heavy-hearted worker is to drink this booze so as to forget his poverty, his misery and the hopelessness of his exploited life.

One might justifiably take issue with the contention that the religious opiate is one peculiar to capitalist society (or to other societies in which there is a dominant/ dominated class division). This would match the familiar criticism that the Marxist overplays the role of socio-economic factors in the emergence and continued survival of religion, and that it seems implausible that religion will naturally wither away once the defective, exploitative and unsatisfying relationships of capitalist society have been expunged or that the illusions of religion will vanish once one has given up 'a state of affairs which needs illusions'.[18] At the root of such criticisms lies the suspicion that the needs met by religion go deeper than those of a purely economic or political nature. This need not undermine the view

---

[15] V.I. Lenin, 'Socialism and Religion', in *Collected Works*, vol. 10 (Moscow, 1965), pp. 83–4.

[16] V.I. Lenin, 'The Attitude of the Workers' Party to Religion', in *Collected Works*, vol. 15 (Moscow, 1973), pp. 405–6.

[17] Religion may thus be viewed as a kind of plot hatched by the powerful, 'a source', Trotsky held, 'of greater and greater trickery and deliberate deception' (Leon Trotsky, quoted in McLellan, *Marxism*, p. 107). It is to be noted that this suspicious view is not restricted to Marxist thinkers. Jeremy Bentham, for example, maintained that religion was 'an engine, invented by corruptionists, at the command of tyrants, for the manufactory of dupes' (Jeremy Bentham, 'Memorandum Book' of 1822–23, from the University College London collection of Bentham's papers, UC clxxiii.75ᵛ. I am grateful to Michael Quinn of the UCL Bentham Project for providing this reference).

[18] Marx, 'Contribution', p. 39.

that religion functions in a narcotic fashion, nor indeed need it fatally weaken the specifically Marxist version of that view. Kai Nielsen, for example, has powerfully argued that while the sufferings engendered by capitalism (injustice, destitution and so on) might be expected to vanish with the arrival of a fairer society, there is a set of more intractable problems ('existential problems'), such as 'death, failing powers, damaged relations [and] deep human conflicts'[19] which are a perennial part of the human condition and should thus be expected to persist in any kind of society. This expansion of the range of human problems is not intended, however, to throw doubt on the Marxist case as such. Rather, Nielsen wishes to show that there are rival religious and secular responses to both sets of problems: just as such tractable social problems as poverty and exploitation can be addressed in a manner either religious (narcosis) or secular (political and social engagement), so with the existential problems. Evidently, political engagement cannot resolve the intractable problems of human life, but this does not mean that there could be no 'non-religious, broadly secular ethical response to such existential problems'.[20] While Nielsen is a little vague about what form this kind of response might take, one might conjecture that an instilled sense of fortitude in the face of death, a deeper sense of social solidarity and concern for others, and maybe a heightened role for art could take over many of the existential functions traditionally monopolized by religion.[21] In whatever manner these purely secular responses to existential problems developed, they would lack the central element of the religious opiate, namely 'the consoling illusion of a heart in a world that is actually heartless'.[22]

One of the advantages of Nielsen's approach is that it allows us to extend the analysis of religion's narcotic functions from a narrowly circumscribed socio-economic realm to the broader set of existential problems facing all human beings, such problems as were outlined in the first chapter of this book. According to the terms of this (either traditional or revised) Marxist account, the palliative quality of religion is precisely the palliative quality of a narcotic. Its mechanism can be clearly articulated: life brings many pains (both tractable and intractable, economic and existential); rooted in this defect of existence, religious belief (in true palliative fashion) relieves pain without curing the underlying problem; such relief comes in a narcotic form, since the set of beliefs uniquely offered by religion (the idea of a loving God, the promise of a blissful afterlife) serves to benumb the believer, producing a state of beautiful indifference to one's suffering and a sense of being at peace with the world. In the case of economic and tractable problems,

---

[19]   Kai Nielsen, 'Is Religion the Opium of the People?', in D.Z. Phillips (ed.), *Can Religion Be Explained Away?* (Basingstoke, 1996), p. 196.

[20]   Ibid., p. 197.

[21]   Trotsky's policy suggestions as to how religion might be supplanted by 'new forms of life, new amusements' (principally cinema) are, in this context, relevant. See Leon Trotsky, 'Vodka, the Church, and the Cinema', in *Problems of Everyday Life* (New York, 1973), pp. 38–43.

[22]   Nielsen, 'Is Religion?', p. 194.

the effect of religion is generally insidious, since its benumbing and soporific effects serve to diminish the willingness and capacity of a dominated class to improve their real conditions of existence. Its effect is maybe less toxic in its softening of existential problems since these stand less chance of being concretely improved by non-religious means. As we shall later see, however, even here the allure of religion should be resisted. Such resistance is urged by Freud, who was also struck by the intoxicating qualities of religious beliefs, noting that 'the effect of religious consolations may be likened to that of a narcotic'.[23] This observation occurs in Freud's most important book on the nature of religion, *The Future of an Illusion*, a book to which we must now turn.

Religion: Wishes and Illusions

No attempt will be made here to survey the entirety of Freud's multi-faceted thinking on the nature of religion. This is because our focus is to remain resolutely on the palliative function of religious belief, and this theme is pre-eminent in *The Future of an Illusion* (as well as in the lecture on 'The Question of a *Weltanschauung*' in the *New Introductory Lectures on Psycho-Analysis* and, of course, in *Civilization and Its Discontents* itself). This approach has two added advantages also. It will, first of all, allow us to sideline some of the more extravagant elements of Freud's thinking, such as his implausible historical speculations concerning the origins of religion contained within the pages of *Totem and Taboo*.[24] Exposure to those largely unfounded conjectures often leads to a hasty dismissal of the value of the psychoanalytic theory of religion, and confirms the suspicions of many that Freudian theory consists largely of lurid and outlandish flights of fancy.[25] A text such as *The Future of an Illusion* – which might indeed properly be regarded as the least 'Freudian' of Freud's works – exhibits none of that extravagance.[26] It manifests, rather, a strong continuity with other naturalistic accounts of religion, such as David Hume's view that religious belief emerges from humanity's sense of helplessness in the face of nature, the gods originally being personifications of great

---

[23]   Sigmund Freud, *The Future of an Illusion*, S.E. vol. XXI, p. 49.

[24]   See Sigmund Freud, *Totem and Taboo*, S.E. XIII, pp. 140–46, for these speculations.

[25]   Alvin Plantinga says that the historical theory contained in *Totem and Taboo* is merely a 'sensational story' containing 'all the elements – sex, murder, cannibalism, remorse – of a dandy Hollywood spectacular' and 'has little to recommend it and is at best a wild guess' (Alvin Plantinga, *Warranted Christian Belief* (New York, 2000), p. 138). It is to Plantinga's credit, however, that he does engage seriously with other elements of Freud's account of religion, as we will later see.

[26]   Michael Palmer's claim that 'Freud sexualizes religion' is overstated (Michael Palmer, *Freud and Jung on Religion* (London, 1997), p. 17). As we will see, the argument of *The Future of an Illusion* lays no emphasis upon sex whatsoever.

natural forces,[27] and Ludwig Feuerbach's locating of the origin of religion in the contradiction between desire and satisfaction,[28] its essence lying in wishes. It also, of course, has significant connections with the Marxist view earlier expounded. Hence the second advantage of our approach here: Freud's account should not be seen as some perverse aberration in the history of the critical investigation of religion, but as a significant contribution to a tradition that explains religious belief as a product of human beings' engagement with the stresses and anxieties of their lives.[29]

Freud's thinking about religion combines two factors he wants to raise to prominence: the dominance of *wishes* in the mind; and the central role of *parents* in human psychological development. A good place to begin exploring the first of these factors is with Freud's important paper 'Formulations on the Two Principles of Mental Functioning'. Here Freud investigates the development of the relation of neurotics – and of humanity in general – to reality. This he does by considering unconscious mental processes, which he claims to be 'the older, primary processes' of the mind, 'the residues of a phase of development in which they were the only kind of mental process'.[30] The governing purpose obeyed by these primary processes is the *pleasure principle*: the mind seeks to gain pleasure and draws back from any event that might cause unpleasure. In earliest childhood, this pleasure is sought by means of wish and hallucination, and sometimes this appears to be effective: for example, the child is distressed and desires to be comforted, and the mother, sensing the child's distress, provides immediately what is desired; or the child manifests its hunger and the breast appears; in both cases, the child experiences the satisfaction it has hallucinated. The child's belief in the power of wishes is only halted by the non-occurrence of an expected satisfaction, and the disappointment thereby experienced leads to the abandonment of hallucinatory satisfaction. The mind then has to form a conception of the real circumstances of the external world, and a new principle of mental functioning is introduced, one which represents to the mind not just what is agreeable but what is real: Freud dubs this the *reality principle*.

It would be wrong to conclude from this that the reality principle entirely replaces the pleasure principle. Not only does the reality principle seek to ensure a pleasure (a deferred one, rather than an immediate one), but certain aspects of mental activity remain entirely under the rule of the pleasure principle. It is the

---

[27]   See David Hume, *The Natural History of Religion* (London, 1956), pp. 26–32.

[28]   Ludwig Feuerbach, *The Essence of Religion* (Amherst, NY, 2004), p. 30.

[29]   This is a point Freud himself is keen to stress. With regard to his argument in *The Future of an Illusion*, he writes that 'I have said nothing which other and better men have not said before me in a much more complete, forcible and impressive manner ... All I have done – and this is the only thing that is new in my exposition – is to add some psychological foundation to the criticisms of my great predecessors' (Freud, *Future*, p. 35).

[30]   Sigmund Freud, 'Formulations on the Two Principles of Mental Functioning', S.E. vol. XII, p. 219.

activity of the mind during sleep which most explicitly demonstrates this, Freud contends, since dreams show to us how the mind operates when the demands of reality have been withdrawn. Once sleep occurs and the stimuli of the external world no longer act upon it, the mind returns to 'the dominance of the ancient pleasure principle',[31] and gives full license to the demands of its wishes. Hence Freud's familiar judgement that dreams represent the fulfilment of wishes which have remained unsatisfied during waking life. The dreams of children are 'simple and undisguised *wish-fulfilments*',[32] while the dreams of adults, due to the pressure of repression and censorship, are '*disguised fulfilments of repressed wishes*'.[33] Dreams provide evidence of the mind's perennial inclination towards wishful impulses, and these impulses are observable also in waking mental activity – for example, in daydreaming and (with a number of qualifications) in artistic creation. It is, Freud maintains, *science* which has been most successful in making itself independent of the wishful impulses of the pleasure principle. Indeed, it is science's engagement with reality which marks it off so strongly from what he sees to be 'the strangest characteristic' of unconscious mental processes, namely 'their entire disregard of reality-testing; they equate reality of thought with external actuality, and wishes with their fulfilment'.[34]

Freud is not alone in stressing the human animal's immersion in wish-driven thoughts, though few thinkers have wanted to press this point as hard as he does. In her recent text on the philosophy of religion, for example, Linda Zagzebski has noted the dangers of wishful thinking, dangers which philosophy needs to combat.[35] For Freud, however, wishful thinking is not merely a potential danger which one must be on one's guard against: rather, wishful impulses constitute 'the core of our being',[36] a conclusion he reaches by means of the interpretation of dreams. A dream just *is* what the mind produces when the demands of external reality have been put to one side; in other words, once attention to the external world is sidelined, the mind simply delights in its wishes. Any time reality is disregarded in a person's beliefs, therefore, one can be justified in suspecting that what is believed is simply the product of a wishful impulse. For those with a total aversion to psychoanalysis, however, the words of Francis Bacon in the *Novum Organum* of 1620 may show that the emphasis on wishes is not merely a Freudian idiosyncrasy: 'The human understanding is not composed of dry light, but is subject to influence from the will and the emotions, a fact that creates fanciful knowledge; man prefers to believe what he wants to be true.'[37]

---

[31] Ibid., p. 225.

[32] Sigmund Freud, *On Dreams*, S.E. vol. V, p. 644.

[33] Ibid., p. 674.

[34] Freud. 'Formulations', p. 225.

[35] Linda Trinkaus Zagzebski, *Philosophy of Religion: An Historical Introduction* (Oxford, 2007), pp. 22, 228–9.

[36] Sigmund Freud, *The Interpretation of Dreams* (Second Part), S.E. vol. V, p. 603.

[37] Francis Bacon, *The New Organon* (Cambridge, 2000), p. 44 (aphorism XLIX).

Regarding the second factor listed above – namely, the relation of religion to parental figures – we will do no more here than say a brief word. A great deal of Freud's notoriety stems, of course, from his theories concerning the incestuous and aggressive impulses felt by a child towards its mother and father. These impulses crystallize in the form of the 'Oedipus complex', which can most intelligibly be thought of as a child's desire for the exclusive love of one or other of its parents. In the case of a boy, the child wishes the father to depart so as to have a monopoly on the mother's affections. Amidst all the sensationalism surrounding discussions of this issue, it should be recognized that the Oedipus complex, quite simply, revolves around a feeling of *jealousy*: egoistic to the core, children do not want merely a share of parental love, but rather want it all. More will be said about mother–child relations in the later chapter on love. The reading of Freud's interpretation of religion advanced in this chapter will, on the other hand, have no place, nor need, for the concept of the Oedipus complex. This is not to say that reference to parental matters will be absent (far from it), but these matters will be of a less contentious character. The crucial point is a simple biological and psychological fact: the child's lengthy period of dependence upon its parents.[38] With regard to the legacy of childhood, it is this sense of helpless dependence and the protection offered by the parents (rather than any aggressive or erotically charged feeling on the part of the child) that constitute the most compelling components of Freud's account of the origin and appeal of religion as a distinct palliative measure.

Combining the two factors just described, therefore, Freud's suggestion is that religious beliefs are the expression of deeply held wishes and that these beliefs have been built up out of the memories of childhood, principally a memory of feeling loved and protected. In *The Future of an Illusion*, Freud presents this account most clearly, arguing that religious beliefs have the character of *illusions*. He means by this something like the following. As human beings, we find ourselves in a world that is not at all conducive to our happiness. We have to suffer the pain and indignity of illness, frustration, failure and, inevitably, death. How pleasant if things were different, if death did not mark the end of our existence, if there

---

[38]   Freud stresses this point time and again, noting in one place that the 'intra-uterine existence [of the young of the human species] seems to be short in comparison with that of most animals, and it is sent into the world in a less finished state', a consequence of this being that the child remains helpless and dependent for a dramatically extended period after it has been born (Sigmund Freud, *Inhibitions, Symptoms and Anxiety*, S.E. vol. XX, p. 154). See also Anna Freud, *Normality and Pathology in Childhood* (London, 1973), pp. 43–9, and Harry Guntrip, *Personality Structure and Human Interaction* (London, 1968), pp. 381–4, in which we find the following observation: 'We are on solid ground in saying that what makes neurosis possible to begin with is the prolonged biological dependence of the human offspring on the parents. In the lower forms of life, days, weeks or months suffice to make the young independent of those who begot them. The period of dependence lengthens as the forms of life grow more complex, but nowhere is there any real parallel to the case of the human child. Here biological dependence is profound for a very long time, so utterly helpless is the human infant to fend for himself' (Guntrip, *Personality*, pp. 381–2).

were some powerful benevolent figure who cared about our fate! Religion offers us all of this, while at the same time having no evidence in favour of its truth. This leads Freud to claim that religious beliefs are 'illusions, fulfilments of the oldest, strongest and most urgent wishes of mankind'.[39] It is important to understand here precisely what he means by an 'illusion'. In the technical sense in which Freud is employing the term, an illusion is not an error, and it is not even necessarily false. The example Freud provides is that of a middle-class girl who believes that a prince will some day come into her life and marry her. She has no grounds for this belief, and will in all probability be disappointed. There have, nevertheless, been instances in which princes and middle-class girls have wed, so it cannot be said for definite that this state of affairs will not occur. But what is crucial here is simply that the girl's belief is derived, not from reasons nor from evidence, but from *wishes*. A belief can therefore be characterized as an illusion 'when a wish-fulfilment is a prominent factor in its motivation'.[40]

Freud's contention is thus that religion arises from the strength and power of human wishes, principally the wish that one should be protected from harm. A word needs to be said about this. Our very existence, Freud writes, lies in the hands of great and inexorable natural forces – the elements, disasters and diseases – that remind us of our inescapable helplessness. Since nature shows itself able to destroy us with ease, it undermines our narcissistic sense of importance, engendering a state of existential alarm and a demand that this condition of vulnerability should not be so: 'Man's self-regard, seriously menaced, calls for consolation; life and the universe must be robbed of their terrors.'[41] Against this threat, some kind of psychological defence is produced, and Freud locates a first stage of this defence in what he calls the 'humanization of nature'.[42] If these forces of nature are impersonal, then they remain eternally remote and cannot be approached. But if, on the other hand, they have passions, thoughts and a will, then they can – just as human agents can – be adjured, appeased and bribed. Religion thus operates to ameliorate a sense of defenceless vulnerability, since – once nature has been humanized – 'we are no longer helplessly paralysed; we can at least react'.[43] Religious ideas are thus born from a need to make our human helplessness bearable.

Importantly for Freud, human beings have an infantile prototype for this process of transforming awesome powers into gods. The child's representation of its *father* during the earliest, most helpless, years of its life serves as a blueprint for how the superior powers of nature are to be treated. Though a helpless infant, the child nevertheless feels completely safe, protected from all harm by its paternal tower of strength. Powerlessness against the world is not merely an infantile stage to be overcome, however, for we are forever to be at its mercy, and the longing

---

[39] Freud, *Future*, p. 30.

[40] Ibid., p. 31.

[41] Ibid.

[42] Ibid.

[43] Ibid., p. 17.

for protection is thus never entirely outgrown: 'the terrifying impression of helplessness in childhood aroused the need for protection – for protection through love – which was provided by the father; and the recognition that this helplessness lasts throughout life made it necessary to cling to the existence of a father, but this time a more powerful one.'[44] Freud's description of the path to belief in God is worth quoting at length. Noting that God – the creator of the universe – is undisguisedly referred to as 'father', he draws the following conclusion:

> Psycho-analysis infers that he really is the father, with all the magnificence in which he once appeared to the small child ... [T]he same person to whom the child owed his existence, the father (or more correctly, no doubt, the parental agency compounded of the father and mother), also protected and watched over him in his feeble and helpless state, exposed as he was to all the dangers lying in wait in the external world; under his father's protection he felt safe. When a human being has himself grown up, he knows, to be sure, that he is in possession of greater strength, but his insight into the perils of life has also grown greater, and he rightly concludes that fundamentally he still remains just as helpless and unprotected as he was in his childhood, that faced by the world he is still a child. Even now, therefore, he cannot do without the protection which he enjoyed as a child ... He therefore harks back to the mnemic image of the father whom in his childhood he so greatly overvalued. He exalts the image into a deity and makes it into something contemporary and real.[45]

Religious belief is thus representative of a desire to return to childhood, to return to a condition in which we felt completely protected; its contents can be traced to 'the survival into maturity of the wishes and needs of childhood'.[46] The illusory status of this belief is thus revealed: religion is a persisting expression of infantile dependence, and belief in God, at root, arises from an urgent desire to feel loved and protected.

Thus understood, it is not difficult to see how religious belief functions in a palliative manner. The world as experienced by us is troubling and often terrifying: as explored in the opening chapter of this book, we are threatened with pain (indeed, with death) from a variety of sources, we realize the smallness of our lives in the face of the vast magnitude of the cosmos, and we are confronted with the possibility that life is devoid of any significance. The world, in short, does not seem to have our best interests at heart. 'Obscure, unfeeling and unloving

---

[44]   Ibid., p. 30.

[45]   Freud, *New Introductory Lectures*, p. 163.

[46]   Ibid., p. 167. This survival of infantile wishes and needs into maturity is pervasive, and is described well by Guntrip in his discussion of the role of infantile dependence in psychopathology: 'The human child ... does not always grow up to be psychically adult' (Guntrip, *Personality*, p. 381).

powers determine men's fate.'[47] Recognition of this disturbing reality produces in us sadness, terror and anxiety: we feel as though we may be crushed under its weight. Religious belief ameliorates – nay, removes – this terror by denying these details of our experience of existence (by 'distorting the picture of the real world'[48]) and by so doing divesting the world of its terrors. In *Civilization and Its Discontents*, the religious believer is regarded as one who, appalled by the cold truth of reality, tries to 're-create the world, to build up in its stead another world in which its most unbearable features are eliminated and replaced by others that are in conformity with one's wishes'.[49] According to the picture constructed by the believer's wishes, the world is not at all cold and by no means meaningless, all the pains we suffer serve some divine purpose, and death is but a portal to a better life. Experienced now in conformity with one's desires, the world becomes tolerable. Pain is softened and anxiety nullified. The cost, however, is immense, since happiness is attained only by means of a wish-driven retreat from the real world. And unlike the escape from reality offered by intoxication, the religious retreat is of a permanent, rather than merely a temporary, nature.

Delusions and the Claims of Religion

Three important criticisms of the Freudian account of religion need to be addressed before proceeding further. The first of these seeks to cast doubt on the assumption that religion really does constitute a collection of wish-fulfilling notions. Alvin Plantinga articulates this criticism clearly:

> Much of religious belief ... is not something that, on the face of it, fulfills your wildest dreams. Thus Christianity (as well as other theistic religions) includes the belief that human beings have sinned, that they merit divine wrath and even damnation, and that they are broken, wretched, in need of salvation ... Others dislike the lack of human autonomy consequent upon there being a Someone by comparison with whom we are as dust and ashes, and to whom we owe worship and obedience.[50]

'On the face of it', indeed, there is much in religious belief that might run counter to our wishes: there is, admittedly, a God who loves and protects us, but this omniscient God knows our darkest, most shameful thoughts and will hold us accountable for them; there is a God who is perfect and, while this may be a comfort, we appear paltry and amiss in comparison with him; and while there is the promise of an afterlife, this brings with it the prospect of eternal punishment

---

[47] Freud, *New Introductory Lectures*, p. 167.
[48] Freud, *Civilization*, p. 84.
[49] Ibid., p. 81.
[50] Plantinga, *Warranted*, p. 195.

if our actions have met with divine disapproval. A deeper look at these apparently wish-incompatible beliefs illustrates that they do in fact tally with a person's desires. One might be ashamed that God knows one's dark thoughts, but this shame fades when compared with the realization that the omnipotent ruler of the universe takes a keen interest in what we think and do: how important must we therefore be! It is, again, true that we are 'as dust and ashes' when compared with God, and yet we are told, nonetheless, that we have been made in the very image of God (a flattering thought indeed) and occupy a privileged and divinely ordained place in creation.

> When I consider thy heavens, the work of thy fingers,
> the moon and the stars, which thou hast ordained;
> what is man, that thou art mindful of him?
> and the son of man, that thou visitest him?
> For thou hast made him a little lower than the angels,
> and hast crowned him with glory and honour.
> Thou madest him to have dominion over the works of thy hands;
> thou hast put all things under his feet.[51]

As for afterlife punishment, while it is true that this might in theory temper the believer's delight, in practice such post-mortem torments are typically reserved for other people (unbelievers, adherents of other faiths, those who pursue 'deviant' lifestyles), the notion of harsh judgement thus catering to some of the most unsavoury of human wishes, particularly the desire to see others punished and in pain. (Such an observation is central, of course, to Nietzsche's castigation of the religious mentality.) And a crucial wish met by religion stands firm in all of this: the wish that there should be some purpose, some order, in the universe. *God's in his heaven; all's right with the world.*[52]

Freud's account of religion survives, therefore, that first criticism. At this point, however, a second criticism may be levelled: even if Freud has correctly identified wishful thinking as the mechanism that produces religious beliefs, this fact alone has no bearing on the truth of such beliefs. This claim may be made in one of two ways. In its most dramatic form, the claim is that those wishful impulses identified by Freud were in truth implanted in us by God precisely so that we may come to know him. Plantinga advocates this position:

> Perhaps human beings have been created by God with a deep need to believe in
> his presence and goodness and love. Perhaps God designed us that way in order
> that we come to believe in him and be aware of his presence ... Perhaps God has

---

[51]   Psalms 8:3–6.

[52]   See William James, *Pragmatism* (New York, 1907), p. 122.

designed us to know that he is present and loves us by creating us with a strong desire for him, a desire that leads to the belief that in fact he is there.[53]

This suggestion seems somewhat odd. If God has a desire for human beings to 'be aware of his presence' then it seems unreasonable for him to employ for those purposes a mechanism (wishful thinking) which we have found typically to lead us away from truth and into error. God's desire would be better served by providing less ambiguous evidence for his existence. Plantinga might, indeed, be leading us down a very dangerous path if we accept his reasoning. Once the justifiably sceptical attitude towards wish-generated beliefs has been thus loosened, one would be permitted to embrace all sorts of absurdities. Freud's position holds good: one should be suspicious of a belief that is generated from urgent wishes rather than from empirical experience of the world.

The second way of making this claim is less dramatic and more plausible. Freud's claim, as we have seen, is that belief in God is a wish-fuelled projection of an infantile memory of being loved and protected by a powerful paternal figure. But even were this the case, the atheistic conclusion is not bound to follow. Arguing along these lines, Hans Küng has claimed that 'a real God may certainly correspond to the wish for God ... Perhaps this being of our longings and dreams does actually exist'.[54] Küng substantiates this point by drawing an analogy between love relationships and belief in God. Both involve a hefty degree of projection and wish. But from the fact that the lover projects an image onto the beloved, and looks to her to be the fulfilment of all of his wishes, it does not follow that the beloved does not exist. The same may be true of God. Our image of God may indeed be built up from memories of being protected and may indeed cohere with a desire for continued protection, but there might nonetheless in reality be such a loving, protective divine being. This is a straightforward and acceptable criticism, but it doesn't seriously undermine Freud's case. As we have already seen, an illusion is not necessarily false, so the fact that a belief is generated by a wish does not alone destroy its claim to truth. This, as an aside, is why it is wrong to claim that in his critique of religion Freud commits the genetic fallacy: he is not committed to saying that conclusions about the existence or nonexistence of God can be drawn from the influence of psychological factors on the development of religious belief. As we will see, his atheism is rooted elsewhere. Against Küng, however, it must be admitted that a strong presupposition against the truth of religion will arise if it can be shown that religious belief *lacks grounds other than* wishes. And this can indeed be shown.

This issue can be broached initially by noting a third criticism made of Freud, a criticism stridently voiced by Plantinga. Freud, he writes, offers no arguments against the truth of religious belief, and 'simply takes it for granted that there is no God and that theistic belief is false; he then casts about for some kind of explanation of this widespread phenomenon of mistaken belief ... [and] hits on

---

[53]   Plantinga, *Warranted*, pp. 197–8.
[54]   Hans Küng, *Freud and the Problem of God* (New Haven, CT, 1979), pp. 78–9.

wish-fulfilment'.[55] Something is missing in this criticism. It is true that Freud devotes no time to putting forward an argument against the existence of God (in the same way that neither Marx nor Nietzsche spills ink on that matter), but this is not to say that he takes atheism for granted. Freud accepts that earlier thinkers have fatally weakened the rational foundations of belief in God and that there is little to add to that particular atheistic onslaught (as Marx had said, 'the *criticism of religion* is in the main complete'[56]), but he also articulates strong reasons – other than those to do with wish-fulfilment – for denying intellectual legitimacy and warranted status to religious belief. About this more needs to be said.

Freud's atheistic stance stems ultimately from his recognition of the cognitively defective nature of religious beliefs. 'Religious ideas', he writes, 'are teachings and assertions about facts and conditions of external (or internal) reality which tell one something one has not discovered for oneself and lay claim to one's belief.'[57] Now, any assertion that is put forward for acceptance must have supporting grounds, but these are distinctly lacking in the case of religion. Indeed, when asked about the foundations of its beliefs and assertions, religion, Freud says, provides 'three answers, which harmonize remarkably badly with one another. Firstly, these teachings deserve to be believed because they were already believed by our primal ancestors; secondly, we possess proofs which have been handed down to us from the same primaeval times; and thirdly, it is forbidden to raise the question of their authentication at all'.[58]

It must be said that Freud is being unfair here. While it is true that rational criticism of religion is not infrequently met with disapproving censure (something, indeed, which is 'bound to rouse our strongest suspicions',[59] indicating, as it surely does, the insecurity of religious claims), and while it is also true that religious beliefs are largely rooted in ancient tradition, it is incorrect to hold that the sole proofs offered by religious people are 'set down in writings which themselves

---

55   Plantinga, *Warranted*, p. 198.

56   Marx, 'Contribution', p. 38.

57   Freud, *Future*, p. 25.

58   Ibid., p. 26. It is hard not be reminded here of another instance in which Freud talks of three responses being radically out of harmony with one another. He tells the story of a man who was charged by one of his neighbours with having returned a borrowed kettle in a damaged condition: 'The defendant asserted first, that he had given it back undamaged; secondly, that the kettle had a hole in it when he borrowed it; and thirdly, that he had never borrowed a kettle from his neighbour at all. So much the better: if only a single one of these three lines of defence were to be accepted as valid, the man would have to be acquitted' (Sigmund Freud, *The Interpretation of Dreams* (First Part), S.E. vol. IV, p. 120. The defendant's contradictory answers are here an indicator his guilt; the contradictory responses provided by religion when under pressure to provide grounds for its assertions are likewise an indicator that something is seriously wrong with its foundations.

59   Freud, *Future*, p. 26.

bear every mark of untrustworthiness'.[60] Freud is referring in this last point to the appeal to ancient scriptures – and he is right to say that these do not deserve our trust – but believers have offered other kinds of proofs and arguments to support religion, arguments that proceed not by appeal to revelation but to reason and experience. Such are the classical arguments for the existence of God, which proceed by noting some not-to-be-expected feature of the world around us – its very existence, its order and regularity, the sense of moral responsibility felt by each person, so-called 'religious experiences' – and conclude that the best explanation for each of these features is the existence of a God (conceived as the creator of the universe and its order, the author of morality, and the being encountered in religious experiences). These arguments appear to give religion a semblance of rational credibility, though little more than that. There is insufficient space here for a full consideration of these arguments,[61] but two points can briefly be noted. Each argument has faced a barrage of criticisms from philosophical heavyweights (including Hume, Kant, Darwin and Schopenhauer), and one cannot be confident that anything substantial is really left after those critiques have been made. Moreover, even if something *is* established by these putative proofs, they cannot go far beyond the suggestion that there might possibly be a creator of the universe (and some of its conspicuous features). The most cherished beliefs of the religious – that this creator has the characteristics of a father, that he loves us, and that he holds out to us the promise of a blissful afterlife – could never be established on the basis of these arguments alone.[62] Support for those more comforting beliefs can come only from those ancient scriptures, which, as Freud reminds us, are not sufficiently trustworthy to earn our acceptance. Secondly, one needs to be reminded of the very basic point that no religious person comes to accept their beliefs on the basis of any of these arguments, which may properly rather be viewed as later rationalizations of an earlier, independently held belief.

Further problems await the attempt to provide religion a rational foundation. The project of the believer engaged in natural theology is to direct attention to features of the empirical world that are seen to demand a theistic explanation. That might seem a promising strategy for the believer. However, once a person chooses to look seriously at the nature of the world, that observer will unavoidably come face to face with the undeniable existence of suffering, the various manifestations of which were surveyed in the opening chapter of this book and do not require

[60] Ibid., p. 27.

[61] I have addressed these arguments elsewhere: see Clack and Clack, *Philosophy*, pp. 13–53.

[62] Hume's position regarding the design argument seems most appropriate here. A person following the hypothesis of design, he writes, 'is able, perhaps, to assert or conjecture that the universe sometime arose from something like design; but beyond that position he cannot ascertain one single circumstance, and is left afterwards to fix every point of his theology by the utmost license of fancy and hypothesis' (David Hume, *Dialogues Concerning Natural Religion* (New York, 1948), p. 40).

repeating here. It is sufficient merely to stress that observation of life as we find it must include these facts of suffering, and thus arises the most intractable theological problem of all: the problem of evil. Easily stated, the problem revolves around the apparent contradiction between the existence of a loving, omnipotent God and the existence of suffering. Philosophers friendly to religious belief have worked strenuously to show that the contradiction spoken of here is more apparent than real, and that the co-existence of suffering and a loving, omnipotent God is perfectly possible.[63] Those efforts may or may not be successful, but the important thing to echo is Hume's rejoinder to all such attempts to render God and evil compatible:

> Is the world, considered in general and as it appears to us in this life, different from what a man or such a limited being would, *beforehand*, expect from a very powerful, wise, and benevolent Deity? It must be strange prejudice to assert the contrary. And from thence I conclude that, however consistent the world may be, allowing certain suppositions and conjectures with the idea of a Deity, it can never afford us an inference concerning his existence. The consistency is not absolutely denied, only the inference. Conjectures … may perhaps be sufficient to prove a consistency, but can never be foundations for any inference.[64]

The point should not be lost. No person observing the world dispassionately and without theological assumptions would draw the conclusion that it was authored by a being possessing the characteristics of omnipotence and omnibenevolence. The facts of the world as we know them do not permit such an inference. Our lived experience thus stands in marked contrast to the comforting doctrines of religion. Noting this very contrast, Freud writes of religion that its 'consolations deserve no trust. Experience teaches us that the world is no nursery'.[65]

The source of religious belief cannot lie in a calm, unbiased examination of the world, therefore. Believers accept the specific doctrines of religion, rather, on the basis of what others have told them is the case, without being in a position to investigate and verify those doctrines themselves. This is what Freud finds most disreputable about religion. These beliefs, which concern such important matters of existence and which have the task of reconciling people to suffering, are the least well authenticated of all claims to knowledge: 'We should not be able to bring ourselves to accept anything of so little concern to us as the fact that whales bear young instead of laying eggs, if it were not capable of better proof than this.'[66] In questions of religion, it would therefore appear, people have a tendency to lay

---

[63]	For representative examples, see: John Hick, *Evil and the God of Love* (London, 1966); Alvin Plantinga, *God, Freedom and Evil* (Grand Rapids, MI, 1977), pp. 7–64; Richard Swinburne, *The Existence of God* (Oxford, 1979), pp. 200–224.

[64]	Hume, *Dialogues*, p. 73.

[65]	Freud, *New Introductory Lectures*, p. 168.

[66]	Freud, *Future*, p. 27.

aside their intellectual scruples, and are 'guilty of every possible sort of dishonesty and intellectual misdemeanour'.[67] And it is here that the full force of the theory of religion as wish-fulfilment is felt. It is not merely the fact that religion so closely matches our wishes that is damaging. What is truly damaging is that *in the absence of any compelling evidence that there is a loving God and a blissful afterlife awaiting us*, people believe these things that so thoroughly conform to their wishes. Religious belief is a case of all wish and no evidence. Küng, as we earlier saw, noted that the wish for God was not incompatible with the real existence of God, but admits that 'religious belief would be in a bad way if there were no genuine grounds for it or if no grounds remained after a psychoanalytic treatment of the subject'.[68] The bad news is that religion really *is* in a bad way, since it does appear to have no basis other than wishes; wishes so strong that they override all evidence contradicting their content. Hence Freud's judgement on religion, which brings together data concerning wishes, insufficient theological evidence, and the origin of religion in the distant past of humanity:

> We know approximately at what periods and by what kind of men religious doctrines were created. If in addition we discover the motives which led to this, our attitude to the problem of religion will undergo a marked displacement. We shall tell ourselves that it would be very nice if there were a God who created the world and was a benevolent Providence, and if there were a moral order in the universe and an after-life; but it is a very striking fact that all this is exactly as we are bound to wish it to be. And it would be more remarkable still if our wretched, ignorant and downtrodden ancestors had succeeded in solving all these difficult riddles of the universe.[69]

The threads of Freud's critique can be brought together thus. The consoling beliefs offered by religion are not supported by evidence; on the contrary, the presence and extent of suffering should lead one to conclude that there is no benevolent God. One can accept these beliefs, therefore, only on the basis of authority, but since such beliefs cannot even in principle be tested, their acceptance constitutes a kind of 'intellectual misdemeanour'. Religion, moreover, bears all the marks of its antique origination, and can be regarded therefore as a product of superannuated mental operations. These features taken together cast doubt on the verisimilitude of religious belief, and when one adds to this the central Freudian insight that wishes are supremely operative in the construction of religion, the prosecuting case becomes very strong indeed.

---

[67] Ibid., p. 32.
[68] Küng, *Freud*, p. 78.
[69] Freud, *Future*, p. 33.

Love, Drugs, Art, Religion

Much is made of the fact that classifying something as an illusion does not disallow its truth.[70] In the case of religion, however, suspicion-generating factors other than wish fulfilment alone are present. The presence of these proves sufficient for Freud to elide, in this particular instance, the distinction between an *illusion* (a belief generated by a wish) and a *delusion* (a false belief resistant to influence by actual fact). Freud writes that delusions are ideas 'which are inaccessible to logical criticism and which contradict reality';[71] they are fantasies or imaginings that have 'gained the upper hand – that is, have obtained belief and have acquired an influence on action'.[72] Freud is certainly struck by the affinities between delusions and religious beliefs: both disregard the contrary indications of reality, both are resistant to rational criticism, and both influence behaviour. In *The Future of an Illusion*, he suggests that some religious beliefs 'are so improbable, so incompatible with everything we have laboriously discovered about the reality of the world, that we may compare them – if we pay proper regard to the psychological differences – to delusions'.[73] By the time Freud came, three years later, to write *Civilization and Its Discontents*, the idea that religion had a delusional quality had taken a firmer hold on him, and it is in its character as a delusion that religion is seen to function in a palliative manner. Its technique, he says, consists in 'distorting the picture of the real world in a delusional manner',[74] creating an alternative world more in conformity with one's wishes, and living as though that wishful fantasy were in fact reality; in this manner, protection against suffering is sought by means of 'a delusional remoulding of reality'.[75] 'The religions of mankind', he concludes, 'must be classed among the mass-delusions of this kind.'[76]

In classifying religion as a delusion driven by a desire to escape from the stresses of real life, Freud is asking us to regard it as a form of collective mental disorder. This is, of course, a familiar and persistent element of the Freudian approach: he famously characterized religion as 'the universal obsessional neurosis of humanity',[77] while as early as 1907 he was seeking to chart the affinities he had detected between the ritual actions of religious people and the quasi-ceremonial performances of those suffering from obsessive disorders.[78] In *The Future of an Illusion*, he offers, almost as an aside, a very specific diagnosis of the religious illness, which he says 'comprises a system of wishful illusions

[70] See James J. DiCenso, *The Other Freud: Religion, Culture and Psychoanalysis* (London, 1999), p. 32.
[71] Sigmund Freud, 'Constructions in Analysis', S.E. vol. XXIII, p. 269.
[72] Sigmund Freud, *Delusions and Dreams in Jensen's 'Gradiva'*, S.E. vol. IX, p. 45.
[73] Freud, *Future*, p. 31.
[74] Freud, *Civilization*, p. 84.
[75] Ibid., p. 81.
[76] Ibid.
[77] Freud, *Future*, p. 43.
[78] See Sigmund Freud, 'Obsessive Actions and Religious Practices', S.E. vol. IX, pp. 115–27.

together with a disavowal of reality, such as we find in an isolated form nowhere else but in amentia, in a state of blissful hallucinatory confusion'.[79] The reference here is to the condition known as 'Meynert's amentia'. It consists in a 'reaction to a loss which reality affirms, but which the ego has to deny, since it finds it unsupportable';[80] the individual, horrified thus by the real world, turns away from it, and into the place vacated by reality there presses forward a wishful fantasy which is affirmed as a better reality, and which is 'often completely well-ordered like a perfect day-dream'.[81] It is with this comparison that we find an appropriate depiction of religion and its consolations, which may be summarized thus: religious belief constitutes a rebellion against reality, a disavowal of all the elements threatening a person's narcissistic self-regard (principally: their insignificance, and the absolute finality of death); in the place of a cold and indifferent universe it establishes a hallucinatory alternative which, in its delusional quality, is immune both to rational criticism and the demands of reality-testing; its appeal lies simultaneously in its well-ordered structure (witness the internal consistency of theological systems which seem, nonetheless, to lack points of contact with actual reality) and (crucially) in its conformity to human wishes; amidst all the terrors of existence, therefore, religion consoles and palliates by means of the blissful state of confusion its hallucinations generate in the faithful.

Leaving Heaven to the Angels and the Sparrows

Freud's antipathy towards religion is unambiguous. 'The whole thing', he writes, 'is so patently infantile, so foreign to reality, that to anyone with a friendly attitude to humanity it is painful to think that the great majority of mortals will never be able to rise above this view of life.'[82] Close to the heart of this antipathy lies the sense that religion involves a contemptible abrogation of responsibilities both intellectual and social. These responsibilities should be addressed one at a time.

As we have seen, Freud's case against religion is that it signifies a triumph of wishes over reality, an equation of desire with its fulfilment. It violates its intellectual duty by altogether disregarding the responsible practice of reality-testing, and by setting up and accepting, in place of a dispassionate depiction of things as they are, a fantastic representation of things as we would like them to be. It might be tempting to think of these intellectual misdemeanours as being the preserve of unsophisticated religious believers only, but this would be wrong, since we have ample evidence of theologians and Christian philosophers articulating positions that can have no basis in lived reality. For example, the Oxford philosopher Tim

---

[79]   Freud, *Future*, p. 43.

[80]   Sigmund Freud, 'A Metapsychological Supplement to the Theory of Dreams', S.E. vol. XIV, p. 233.

[81]   Ibid., p. 230.

[82]   Freud, *Civilization*, p. 74.

Mawson has written that our afterlife existence will be 'an embodied one, where we eat, drink, and sing' and where there will be intellectual, moral, emotional, spiritual and physical fulfilment.[83] It barely requires remarking that Mawson's contentions are not rooted in any observational evidence and seem to be generated instead entirely by wishes concerning post-mortem existence. Nor is this peculiar to Mawson, or to other rogue thinkers who engage in this kind of speculation. It is, rather, an endemic function of religious belief itself, which, divorced from the demands and restrictions of real-world observations, permits the proliferation of groundless and otherworldly fantasies.

A great many philosophers – into whose tradition we may place Freud – have warned against the flights of fancy ensuing from this loosening of empirical anchorage. Hume, at the end of the *Enquiry Concerning Human Understanding*, cautioned that reasoning without appeal to experience could 'produce anything', giving the pertinent example that in such a case the wish of a man could be believed to control the planets in their orbits;[84] Kant's critical project demonstrated that pure reason was incompetent to know things lying outside experience; while Wittgenstein's informally stated desire to 'cut out the transcendental twaddle'[85] received a famously austere articulation in the *Tractatus Logico-Philosophicus*: 'Whereof one cannot speak, thereof one must be silent.'[86] The basic insight of this tradition is expressed clearly by Cheryl Misak in her fine study of verificationism (itself a maligned and yet powerful combatant in the fight against religious fantasies): 'a belief with no connection to experience is spurious.'[87] Theologians and philosophers of religion – as well as the massed ranks of ordinary believers – have been extraordinarily resistant to such warnings. Indeed, those warnings have, in the main, simply been ignored in favour of a continuation of fanciful theological speculation, thus – at least for Freud – violating one's intellectual responsibilities.

Intellectual responsibility is simply, therefore, taking care to accept only those things that it is reasonable to believe, not accepting beliefs that lack empirical anchorage, and not succumbing to the seductive allure of wishes. One must, therefore, hold fast to the reality principle and to reality-testing, however uncomfortable the results of such testing may be. Freud casts religion as the enemy of the intellect, not simply because its claims extend well beyond what any person could confidently assert, but also in virtue of its detrimental effects on a person's critical apparatus: 'When a man has once brought himself to accept uncritically all the absurdities that religious doctrines put before him and even to overlook the

---

[83] T.J. Mawson, *Belief in God: An Introduction to the Philosophy of Religion* (Oxford, 2005), p. 86.

[84] David Hume, *Enquiries Concerning Human Understanding and Concerning the Principles of Morals* (Oxford, 1975), p. 164.

[85] Letter to Paul Engelmann (16 January 1918), in Paul Engelmann, *Letters from Ludwig Wittgenstein with a Memoir* (Oxford, 1967), p. 11.

[86] Ludwig Wittgenstein, *Tractatus Logico-Philosophicus* (London, 1922), 7 (p. 189).

[87] C.J. Misak, *Verificationism: Its History and Prospects* (London, 1995), p. ix.

contradictions between them, we need not be greatly surprised at the weakness of his intellect.'[88] In other words, the outlandish ideas of religion – the existence of a loving God, an afterlife of disembodied bliss, efficacious prayers, miraculous occurrences, and so on – can only be accepted by means of a suspension of critical thinking skills, and it is to be expected that this weakening of criticism will bleed into other areas of a person's mental life.[89] Voltaire had famously detected a link between believing absurdities and committing atrocities, and Freud is likewise of the view that any weakening of intellectual responsibility poses a grave threat to the future of humanity. 'Our best hope for the future', he writes, 'is that intellect – the scientific spirit, reason – may in process of time establish a dictatorship in the mental life of man.'[90]

Here one can see how for Freud intellectual and social responsibilities intersect. In both cases there is a responsibility to keep our eyes focused on the material world around us, to come to know it and, where necessary, to change it. Nietzsche had this in mind when he urged his readers to 'stay loyal to the earth' and to keep their virtue targeted on body and life: 'Do not let it fly away from the things of earth and beat with its wings against the eternal walls!'[91] The objection to religion is that it exhibits disloyalty to the earth, keeping its eyes on a fantastic world of the imagination to the detriment of the real world. In his assault on the otherworldly outlook of religion, in part undertaken so that people can revert their attention to the conditions of real life, Freud can, once more, find an ally in the Marxist tradition. 'Criticism', Marx declared, 'has torn up the imaginary flowers from the chain not so that man shall wear the unadorned, bleak chain but so that he will shake off the chain and pluck the living flower.'[92]

Friedrich Engels' essay on the early history of Christianity is especially helpful here, since it serves to highlight two possible ways in which groups of people can respond to their own sufferings. Engels contrasted the character of the early Christian church with that of the socialist movement in his own time. Both of these movements consisted of oppressed people and of a response to that oppression, and Christianity is to be distinguished from socialism primarily by the location of its hopes for liberation:

---

[88]   Freud, *Future*, p. 48.

[89]   It is not difficult to draw connections between Freud's concerns in this regard and W.K. Clifford's castigation of the irresponsibility of religious believing. 'Every time we let ourselves believe for unworthy reasons,' Clifford writes, 'we weaken our powers of self-control, of doubting, of judicially and fairly weighing evidence' (W.K. Clifford, *The Ethics of Belief and Other Essays* (London, 1947), p. 76). One catastrophic consequence of giving one's assent to some dubious and ill-founded proposition of religion is that it unleashes a habitual credulousness. (In other words, if you can bring yourself to believe *that*, then you'll probably be able to bring yourself to believe just about *anything*.)

[90]   Freud, *New Introductory Lectures*, p. 171.

[91]   Friedrich Nietzsche, *Thus Spoke Zarathustra* (Harmondsworth, 1961), p. 102.

[92]   Marx, 'Contribution', p. 39.

> Both Christianity and the workers' socialism preach forthcoming salvation from
> bondage and misery; Christianity places this salvation in a life beyond, after
> death, in heaven; socialism places it in this world, in a transformation of society.[93]

This theme is by now familiar to us. The suffering of life can produce both a
religious and a this-worldly response. The religious response is escapist, soothing
the blows of life with the idea of divine love. Yet however effective it may be as
an analgesic, its fantastical quality cannot be denied (it 'stands furthest away from
material life and seems to be most alien to it'[94]). Less removed from material life
is the other response, which rebels against extant conditions and takes the fight
to them, transforming society so that suffering is lessened in a real rather than in
an illusory manner. In this struggle, religion stands as the dragon to be defeated,
since its illusory consolations reduce the sense of urgency for social change. Here
the thoughts of Feuerbach are apposite. Having diagnosed religion as 'the dream
of the human mind',[95] and exposing theology as anthropology (claims about the
divine nature being disguised claims about human nature), Feuerbach saw religion
as an impediment to progress, stripping human beings of their self-confidence
and ability to alter their lives for the better. The critic's task must therefore be a
transformative one:

> The purpose of my lectures as of my books is to transform theologians into
> anthropologists, lovers of God into lovers of man, candidates for the next world
> into students of this world, religious and political flunkeys of heavenly and
> earthly monarchs and lords into free, self-reliant citizens of the earth.[96]

The undeniably soothing quality of religion is thus tempered by the recognition
that its absence would, in the long run, facilitate a real improvement in the
conditions of life.

Freud stands in (qualified) agreement with these Marxist and Feuerbachian
contentions. Though bereft of the humanistic optimism of these earlier writers,
and under no illusion that the aggressive tendencies of human beings ('this
indestructible feature of human nature'[97]) might be eliminated by a restructuring
of society, he nonetheless indicates that an improvement of the human lot could
ensue from a thoroughgoing rejection of religious belief. These thoughts occur in
a passage in which Freud wonders whether people would be able to do without
'the consolation of the religious illusion', whether they could without it 'bear the

but liberation theologies

---

[93]   Friedrich Engels, 'On the History of Early Christianity', in Karl Marx and Friedrich
Engels, *On Religion* (Moscow, 1957), p. 275.

[94]   Friedrich Engels, 'Ludwig Feuerbach and the End of Classical German Philosophy',
in Karl Marx and Friedrich Engels, *On Religion* (Moscow, 1957), p. 229.

[95]   Ludwig Feuerbach, *The Essence of Christianity* (New York, 2008), p. xii.

[96]   Ludwig Feuerbach, *Lectures on the Essence of Religion* (New York, 1967), p. 23.

[97]   Freud, *Civilization*, p. 114.

troubles of life and the cruelties of reality'.[98] One can be in no doubt, he writes, that the surrender of religious belief will entail human beings accepting harsh alternative views: a recognition of 'the full extent of their helplessness and their insignificance in the machinery of the universe' and an awareness that they are 'no longer the object of tender care on the part of a beneficent Providence'.[99] True to his view concerning the infantile nature of faith, Freud likens this perceptual change to a child leaving the warmth and comfort of the parental home and going out into hostile life. While it may be nicer to stay under the protective care of one's parents, every capable person ultimately needs to strike out on their own. No one can remain forever a child. The same is true of religion. And maybe, Freud suggests, we are not entirely without aid, since humanity's scientific knowledge can greatly assist us in our struggles with this world and its newly recognized cold heart. It is true that the terrible inevitabilities of life cannot be softened without religious aid, but with that truth we shall simply have to live:

> [A]s for the great necessities of Fate, against which there is no help, they will learn to endure them with resignation. Of what use to them is the mirage of wide acres in the moon, whose harvest no one has ever yet seen? As honest smallholders on this earth they will know how to cultivate their plot in such a way that it supports them. By withdrawing their expectations from the other world and concentrating all their liberated energies into their life on earth, they will probably succeed in achieving a state of things in which life will become tolerable for everyone and civilization no longer oppressive to anyone. Then, with one of our fellow-unbelievers, they will be able to say without regret:
>
> Den Himmel überlassen wir
> Den Engeln und den Spatzen.[100]

Here the connection between Freud and Feuerbach can clearly be seen. A withdrawal of attention from an illusory set of compensatory beliefs can free one's energies to engage in really useful work: namely, altering the conditions of the world so that we – and, crucially, future generations – can experience conditions of life somewhat better than those under which we and our forebears have laboured.

With this strangely upbeat assessment, our initial assessment of the palliative qualities of religion is complete. As we have seen, religion has an enviable and incomparable strength in its amelioration of life's various sufferings: none of the other auxiliary constructions can compete with its ability to dismiss perennial human anxieties concerning transience, death and insignificance. Ultimately, however, it claims too much for itself. Rather than admitting that it functions simply as another form of narcotic, it stakes a claim to truth: the ideas it advances

---

[98]   Freud, *Future*, p. 49.

[99]   Ibid., p. 49.

[100]   Ibid., p. 50. The quotation is from Heinrich Heine's poem 'Deutschland': 'We leave Heaven to the angels and the sparrows.'

are not merely comforting but are held to correspond to the way things really are. This claim is unsustainable once subjected to criticism, and religion is revealed to be 'a product of our wishes too unmistakable to lay claim to reality'.[101] It is important, further, to note that religious ideas cannot survive being exposed as having a quality that is merely palliative. Religion, in other words, is a palliative *and nothing more*. Of course, drugs can be regarded as merely palliative in quality (palliatives and nothing more) and their use still survive that characterization, but this is because the person who (for example) imbibes alcohol might full well recognize and accept that she does this to offset the strains and tensions of her life. But the important thing about religion for the believer is not merely that it lessens suffering: it does this only when held to be the truth. Once the question of the truth of religion is answered in the negative, it is highly unlikely that believers could persist in this way of life. Other palliatives will instead be sought. It should once more be reiterated, however, that our conclusions apply only to a particular set of religious beliefs, those revolving around the consoling nucleus of a loving God, an afterlife of bliss, and a cosmic moral order. A different type of religion might be better able to survive the criticisms outlined in this chapter. We will return to that possibility at the very end of this book.

---

[101] Sigmund Freud, 'On Transience', S.E. vol. XIV, p. 305.

Chapter 4
The Third Palliative: Art

Beauty and art, no doubt, pervade all the business of life like a kindly genius, and form the bright adornment of all our surroundings, both mental and material, soothing the sadness of our condition and the embarrassments of real life, killing time in entertaining fashion, and where there is nothing good to be achieved, occupying the place of what is vicious, better, at any rate, than vice.

G.W.F. Hegel

While one may be prepared to admit that the nature of both religion and drugs is predominantly palliative, to consider *art* in a comparable manner seems fraught with difficulties and laden with implausibility. Can it really intelligibly be contended that the products of artistic creation – widely regarded as counting among the highest achievements of the human spirit – function simply as substitutive satisfactions, offering a merely illusory happiness in place of that real happiness which must forever elude us? Can one seriously advance the view that enjoyment of Bach and Wagner, of Shakespeare and Proust, and of Vermeer and Picasso, has any connection – let alone a profound one – with either the reality-fleeing use of intoxicants or the embracing of an infantile, compensatory faith? It would seem, in other words, that to conceive of art in terms of its palliative function involves an unpalatable denigration of its value and significance in human life. For while both drugs and religion may (not entirely unreasonably) be regarded as merely escapist strategies, the role of art in human life seems far more elevated, more worthy; and while one might intelligibly think that drugs and religion are an impediment to human flourishing (and are, as a consequence, unnecessary) art, on the other hand, seems indispensable. It is precisely this worthiness and indispensability that would appear to call for something other than a palliative interpretation. In this chapter, however, it will be contended that to conceive of art as one of humanity's auxiliary constructions is not inappropriate. In order to make this case, though, it will be necessary to move beyond Freud's own interpretation of art, which is now generally held to be inadequate and reductive. Notwithstanding its limitations, however, Freud's account of the origins of art – and the enjoyment it provides – constitutes a provocative view of the palliating role of art in human life, so with this we will begin.

Art: The Freudian Perspective

Let us first revisit *Civilization and Its Discontents*. Freud there classifies art as one of the substitutive satisfactions serving to diminish misery. Such satisfactions are 'illusions in contrast with reality, but they are none the less psychically effective, thanks to the role which phantasy has assumed in mental life'.[1] The effectiveness of art (either its creation or its enjoyment) lies in the sublimation of instincts so that such instinctual aims 'cannot come up against frustration from the external world'.[2] If one seeks satisfaction and pleasure from intellectual work – from, say, listening to a piece of music or reading a novel – rather than from trying to alter a typically intransigent external reality, a great many disappointments may thereby be avoided: 'When that is so, fate can do little against one.'[3] Art might, therefore, be regarded as having a vital role in a person's quest to ameliorate the pains of life, and this is a judgement which would be echoed by many individuals of an artistic disposition: 'People who are receptive to the influence of art cannot set too high a value on it as a source of pleasure and consolation in life.'[4] Although art holds out this promise, Freud thinks its ability truly to console is severely limited, and this for two reasons. First, the joys offered by artistic creation have no general application, presupposing the possession of 'special dispositions and gifts which are far from being common to any practical degree'.[5] This is probably accurate, but, one might argue, those of us who cannot create art may nonetheless gain enormous consolation from the artistic achievements of more creative types. I may gain considerable delight from listening to Strauss' 'Four Last Songs', even though I am no musician myself. Freud, of course, would agree, noting that the artist makes accessible the enjoyment of art to those who themselves lack artistic creativity, but his second point aims to undermine our hopeful expectations: 'the mild narcosis induced in us by art can do no more than bring about a transient withdrawal from the pressure of vital needs, and it is not strong enough to make us forget real misery.'[6] To use an image of Schopenhauer's, taken from a rather different context, in the face of the misery and horrors of life, the consolations offered by art are 'as effective as a syringe at a great fire'.[7] Aesthetic pleasure just isn't pleasurable enough; its consolations mild and fleeting.

Freud's ambivalent attitude towards art is in these thoughts apparent. Artistic pleasure is 'finer and higher' than (presumably) religious and intoxicating

1   Sigmund Freud, *Civilization and Its Discontents*, in *The Standard Edition of the Complete Psychological Works of Sigmund Freud* (24 vols, London, 1953–74) (hereafter S.E.), vol. XXI, p. 75.

2   Ibid., p. 79.

3   Ibid.

4   Ibid., p. 81.

5   Ibid., p. 80.

6   Ibid., p. 81.

7   Arthur Schopenhauer, *On the Basis of Morality* (Oxford, 1995), pp. 75–6.

palliatives, but its consoling power fades in comparison. This ambivalence mirrors a deeper tension in Freud's more general thoughts concerning art and its production. His attitude towards artistic creation is at times respectful, reverential even. For example:

> [C]reative writers are valuable allies and their evidence is to be praised highly, for they are apt to know a whole host of things between heaven and earth of which our philosophy has not yet let us dream. In their knowledge of the mind they are far in advance of us everyday people, for they draw upon sources which we have not yet opened up for science.[8]

Alongside this admiring attitude, however, sits Freud's more famous (and far less glowing) account of the nature of artistic production. According to this latter account, the artist is less a pioneer of the scientific study of the mind, and more akin to a *neurotic*. What Freud says about this is important for our purposes, for his account can be applied *mutatis mutandis* to the enjoyment of art and not exclusively to its creation.[9] We should thus turn our attention to the details of the Freudian theory of artistic production.

Freud thinks of art as providing a substitutive gratification, and the artist as one who, disappointed by reality, creates in its place a phantasy world in which his or her wishes can find their fulfilment. The theoretical foundation for this contention lies in a conjecture of Freud's which we have in a previous chapter already had reason to consider: the interplay of the pleasure principle and the reality principle. With the emergence of the reality principle, 'one species of thought-activity was split off; it was kept free from reality-testing and remained subordinated to the pleasure principle alone':[10] this activity is the world of phantasying and day-dreaming, out of which, Freud claims, art is ultimately derived. Hence, in 'Formulations on the Two Principles of Mental Functioning' he describes the artist thus:

> An artist is originally a man who turns away from reality because he cannot come to terms with the renunciation of instinctual satisfaction which it at first

---

[8] Sigmund Freud, *Delusions and Dreams in Jensen's 'Gradiva'*, S.E. vol. IX, p. 8.

[9] Freud forges the connection between the creation and the enjoyment of art when he writes that the works of an artist 'were calculated to arouse sympathetic interest in other people and were able to evoke and to satisfy the same unconscious wishful impulses in them too' (Sigmund Freud, *An Autobiographical Study*, S.E. vol. XX, p. 65). There is scope here to draw connections between Freud's account of art and that advanced by Tolstoy, since in both cases a work of art *transmits* the feelings of the artist to the audience: 'Art is a human activity consisting in this, that one man consciously by means of certain external signs, hands on to others feelings he has lived through, and that others are infected by these feelings and also experience them' (Leo Tolstoy, *What Is Art?* (New York, 1962), p. 123).

[10] Sigmund Freud, 'Formulations on the Two Principles of Mental Functioning', S.E. vol. XII, p. 222.

demands, and who allows his erotic and ambitious wishes full play in the life of phantasy.[11]

This disparaging claim is formulated in an even more dramatic fashion in the *Introductory Lectures on Psycho-Analysis*, where Freud contends that the artist differs from the average person, not in being necessarily more insightful, but rather in being more neurotic:

> An artist is once more in rudiments an introvert, not far removed from neurosis. He is oppressed by excessively powerful instinctual needs. He desires to win honour, power, wealth, fame and the love of women; but he lacks the means for achieving these satisfactions. Consequently, like any other unsatisfied man, he turns away from reality and transfers all his interest, and his libido too, to the wishful constructions of his life of phantasy, whence the path might lead to neurosis.[12]

The theory of artistic production allied to this slighting description is most fully worked out in Freud's famous paper on 'Creative Writers and Day-Dreaming', and to understand fully his view that art constitutes a neurotic variety of wish-fulfilling illusion a brief explication of this paper is required.

It is a mark of the ambivalence felt by Freud towards art both that he thinks that psychoanalysis cannot throw light on the origin of the work of art ('Before the problem of the creative artist analysis must, alas, lay down its arms'[13]), and that he nonetheless attempts to do precisely that. Contrary to his protestations, in other words, Freud does not lay down his analytic arms. The key to understanding the work of an artist, he contends, lies in the behaviour of a child at play. 'Might we not say that every child at play behaves like a creative writer, in that he creates a world of his own, or, rather, re-arranges the things of his world in a new way which pleases him?'[14] Though a child is able perfectly well to distinguish play from reality, he takes play-activity very seriously indeed. The creative writer does precisely the same. 'He creates a world of phantasy which he takes very seriously – that is, which he invests with large amounts of emotion – while separating it sharply from reality.'[15] If one objects here that what the artist does is surely very different from that which the child does with its toys, then Freud discerns a closer connection between the work of the artist and what develops and extends from the world of play, namely the enjoyment provided by daydreaming, by the creation and entertainment of phantasies. The work of an author, for example,

---

[11]   Ibid., p. 224.

[12]   Sigmund Freud, *Introductory Lectures on Psycho-Analysis* (Part III), S.E. vol. XVI, p. 376.

[13]   Sigmund Freud, 'Dostoevsky and Parricide', S.E. vol. XXI, p. 177.

[14]   Sigmund Freud, 'Creative Writers and Day-Dreaming', S.E. vol. IX, pp. 143–4.

[15]   Ibid., p. 144.

derives from the writer's daydreams, in which desires and wishes unsatisfied by reality can, in the pages of a story, finally be fulfilled. But this means, of course, that the artist is a frustrated type, disappointed by reality and taking refuge in the illusory life of phantasy:

> We may lay it down that a happy person never phantasies, only an unsatisfied one. The motive forces of phantasies are unsatisfied wishes, and every single phantasy is the fulfillment of a wish, a correction of unsatisfying reality. These motivating wishes vary according to the sex, character and circumstances of the person who is having the phantasy; but they fall naturally into two main groups. They are either ambitious wishes, which serve to elevate the subject's personality; or they are erotic ones.[16]

This returns us, naturally, to the disparaging claim noted earlier. The artist is one who wanted to achieve power and love in the real world; finding these goals thwarted, he seeks fulfilment in the wish-fulfilling life of phantasy.

These contentions may also be employed to account for the valued place occupied by art in the lives of people in general, artists and non-artists alike, and thus the nature of art-as-palliative might perhaps be explicated in analogous terms. The person who takes delight in art, and who finds consolation in it, has turned away from reality because he or she finds it too difficult, too painful. Art offers us something more pleasant than reality – more beautiful, better ordered – and at the same time returns us to the delightful life of infantile play. But a return to an infantile mode constitutes a kind of *regression*, and one of the key contentions of psychoanalytic theory is that human beings regress to more childlike stages when they find their instinctual satisfactions thwarted. The allure of a return to childhood is strong – how delightful those years were, how free from adult cares! – but there is surely something terribly immature about such a fleeing from the adult present. As Anthony Storr says, regarding the psychoanalytic teaching, 'regression to infantile modes of satisfaction and communication is to be deplored: at best, it is a respite from the burden of being an adult; at worst, a permanent failure to grow up'.[17] Art, moreover, is subject to the same criticism one might level against religious belief: in its opposition to reality, and in its presentation of a world more in conformity with our wishes, it constitutes an *illusion*. It is, of course, a less harmful illusion than the fantastical creations of religion, simply because it does not confuse the realm of wishes with the realm of reality. As Freud writes:

---

[16] Ibid., pp. 146–7.
[17] Anthony Storr, *Music and the Mind* (London, 1997), p. 92.

> Art is almost always harmless and beneficent; it does not seek to be anything but an illusion. Except for a few people who are spoken of as being 'possessed' by art, it makes no attempt at invading the realm of reality.[18]

Harmless and beneficent as it is, however, art is an illusion nonetheless, set up in opposition to the harshness of the real world. Delight in it is infantile, a sign that one lacks the courage to face up to life as it really is. The consolations art offers, then, are mild, infantile and illusory. Human beings would do better to turn away from its allure, and to concentrate instead upon engaging with the world as it actually stands.

This conception of art, however distinctive and recognizably Freudian it may be, is not without its precursors. The Marxist view, for example, lays its stress on the unsatisfactory nature of life in capitalist society and on how the function of art is to ease that pain, by entertaining, relaxing, *distracting*. Art, therefore, can be seen – just as religion can be seen – as merely an epiphenomenon of a cruel and heartless socio-economic order, an indicator, as it were, that something is wrong. Ernst Fischer quotes Piet Mondrian's view that 'Art will disappear as life gains more equilibrium'.[19] On such a view reality would increasingly displace the work of art once the social order became more rational and equitable. As things stand, however, art serves simply to placate and anaesthetize, to make people placid and content, when they should rather be rebellious.[20] This is a judgement that one finds voiced also by Nietzsche in *Human, All Too Human*:

---

[18]   Sigmund Freud, *New Introductory Lectures on Psycho-Analysis*, S.E. vol. XXII, p. 160. Compare in this respect Christopher Butler's comment on the difference between fiction and theology: 'Fictions are of course more rational than theology in that they don't try to populate the *real* universe with types of entity that don't exist' (Christopher Butler, *Pleasure and the Arts* (Oxford, 2004), p. 62).

[19]   Ernst Fischer, *The Necessity of Art* (Harmondsworth, 1986), p. 7.

[20]   Such a contention gains in plausibility when one reflects upon the contents of the most pervasive entertainment-medium of our time: television. It is heartbreaking to see that while television could be a source of edification and enlightenment, hundreds of television channels flood our homes with mind-numbing entertainment-industry gossip, 'reality TV' (note the insidious irony of that term), glorified karaoke contests, chat-shows and game-shows. A US-based production company, responsible for the game-show 'Deal or No Deal', is named *Entertain the Brutes*, and – clever allusions to *Heart of Darkness* notwithstanding – this might well be revelatory of the extant function of television. For it is hard to escape the conclusion that such mindless outpourings serve the purpose of anaesthetizing viewers, deadening their intellects and sensibilities, and making them pliant assenters to the structure of a rotten world which really should be overthrown and transformed. Theodor Adorno's conception of 'the culture industry' is, of course, pertinent here. Adorno contends that popular culture serves to secure the capitalist system, as the consumption of unsophisticated and sentimental movies, music and television programmes creates a passively satisfied populace stripped of any desire to overthrow the existing socio-economic order. More difficult, intellectually-challenging art-forms provide people with

Insofar as they want to alleviate the life of men, poets turn their eyes away from the toilsome present or they procure for the present new colours through a light which they direct upon it from the past ... There are, to be sure, several things to be said against their means of alleviating life: they soothe and heal only provisionally, only for a moment; they even hinder men from working for a real improvement in their conditions by suspending and discharging in a palliative way the very passion which impels the discontented to action.[21]

Hence, Freud's position occupies a place in a tradition castigating art for masking the real pains of existence rather than healing those pains. It distracts and diverts merely, and without its palliating effects people might actually engage with the real world and alter it for the better, thereby reducing (even eradicating) the need for art altogether. What Freud adds to this tradition, of course, are those distinctive thoughts concerning the illusory and childish nature of the creation and enjoyment of art.

Provocative as the Freudian view is, it has generally been found wanting. Both Anthony Storr and Lionel Trilling have powerfully expressed the flaws in Freud's account. 'It simply will not do,' Storr writes, 'to assume that the artist is a man who can only achieve satisfaction of his instinctual drives in phantasy', since this would put the work of great artists such as Tolstoy or Beethoven upon 'the same level as a masturbatory phantasy'.[22] The contention that artists create because their erotic and personal ambitions have been thwarted has the odd consequence that 'if total sexual fulfillment were possible by means of a complete adaptation to reality, the arts ... would become otiose'.[23] It would also suggest that the artist – pre-eminently – is one who cannot find satisfaction in their personal life, cannot establish and maintain a successful romantic relationship. This is simply implausible, and the connection drawn between the artist and the neurotic relies on a misunderstanding of the relation of each to their world of phantasy. As Trilling notes, 'the poet is in command of his fantasy, while it is exactly the mark of the neurotic that he is possessed by his fantasy'.[24] Moreover, art does not remain simply at the level of phantasy; rather, it explores the realm of phantasy in order to lead us to a deeper understanding of reality. 'Freud's assumption of the almost exclusively hedonistic nature and purpose of art bar him from the perception of this.'[25] It is important to emphasize this point. Freud seems to think that the purpose of art is simply to ease the harshness of life, and it does this by constructing an alternative (more agreeable) version of the world. Thus Freud

---

the tools to question and critique the status quo, but the culture industry has no desire to produce such an effect, and instead churns out merely stupefying nonsense, the aim of which is simply narcosis.

[21] Friedrich Nietzsche, *Human, All Too Human* (Cambridge, 1986), p. 81.

[22] Anthony Storr, *The Dynamics of Creation* (London, 1972), p. 3.

[23] Storr, *Music*, p. 92.

[24] Lionel Trilling, *The Liberal Imagination* (New York, 1950), p. 45.

[25] Ibid.

attributes to art a narcotic function. But even the most cursory glance at the nature of art shows that it does not always – or even usually – function in this manner. Think of *Macbeth*, or of *Rigoletto*, or of Francis Bacon's paintings. To what extent can these plausibly be thought of as 'more agreeable' versions of reality? Or as wish-fulfilling, comforting illusions? Something else is plainly taking place there.

The insight lying at the heart of Freud's consideration of art in *Civilization and Its Discontents* should not, however, be lightly dismissed. This core insight relates to the role art has in ameliorating (in some fashion) the pains of existence, and it will be the contention of this chapter that to conceive of the function of art in these terms is quite correct. However, two weak elements of the original Freudian position will need to be banished. It was wrong, first of all, for Freud to think of art in narcotic terms, and we will need here to modify this position so that art can be viewed as a *non-narcotic palliative*, so that it can be seen to ease our troubles and pains without merely *anaesthetizing* them. Art will thus be seen to help us *deal* with reality, not *deny* it. A second weakness concerns Freud's failure to distinguish between good and bad art. His account of the narcotic, wish-fulfilling appeal of art simply does not apply to *all* art, though it may apply to *some*. It is undeniably true that there are certain species of art which serve the function of merely presenting a sugar-coated alternative version of reality. This is the realm of *the sentimental*; and the Freudian view of art might explain the appeal of this completely. Yet merely sentimental art might be felt to contrast sharply with what good art does. This requires a little more investigation.

The pleasure derived from sentimental art can be straightforwardly explained. As Christopher Butler says, this pleasure 'depends upon a fantasized simplification and idealization in which we are released from the fatigue of too much reality-testing'.[26] Sentimental art – and sentimentality as a character trait in a person – is generally regarded as undesirable ('There is always something wrong with it'[27]), and is castigated for its excess of inappropriately directed and unearned emotion. Oscar Wilde's famous definition of a sentimentalist as 'one who desires to have the luxury of an emotion without paying for it'[28] encapsulates this criticism, as does Roger Scruton's comparable view that sentimentality is 'the desire for the glory of some heroic or transfiguring passion, without the cost of feeling it'.[29] The feelings of a sentimentalist are thus 'in some important way unearned, being had on the cheap, come by too easily, and … are directed at unworthy objects'.[30] The criticism voiced by Freud and Butler, on the other hand, moves on a different tack, and is motivated by a moral censure of the falsification of reality found in art that is sentimental in

---

[26] Butler, *Pleasure*, pp. 65–7.

[27] Anthony Savile, 'Sentimentality', in Alex Neil and Aaron Ridley (eds), *Arguing About Art* (London, 2008), p. 337.

[28] Oscar Wilde, *De Profundis and Other Writings* (Harmondsworth, 1986), p. 196.

[29] Roger Scruton, 'The Aesthetic Endeavour Today', *Philosophy*, 71/277 (1996), p. 343.

[30] Michael Tanner, 'Sentimentality', *Proceedings of the Aristotelian Society*, 77 (1976–77), p. 128.

character. In sentimental art we find 'a selective editing of the world'[31] in which all that is ugly or disagreeable is erased, and an idealized, simplified version of things put forward instead, one which can inspire and console. Butler provides, as an example of this, Monet's paintings of Argenteuil 'which put in the boats and leave out the factories',[32] though any number of examples spring readily to mind (think of saccharine paintings of children and pets). The operatic portrayal of consumption is also a frequently cited case in point: 'The soprano lead will manage a discreet little cough but producers never give us blood and phlegm.'[33]

One especially incisive account of the process involved in the production of sanitized sentimental art is given by I.A. Richards in his classic book on *Practical Criticism*. Richards wishes to pursue the line (indicated above) that sentimental art is *selective* in nature, 'confining itself to one aspect only of the many that the situation can present, or by substituting for it a factitious, illusory situation that may, in extreme cases, have hardly anything in common with it'.[34] This much is familiar, of course, and is entirely of a piece with the Freudian view outlined earlier, whereby art filters out unpleasant aspects of things as they actually stand, leaving us with a wish-derived alternative: the sentimentalist is driven by a desire, not for truth, but for 'reassurance in a world that is found unsettling',[35] this aim being served by presenting objects in a false light, thereby making 'what is in truth rather alien and off-putting quite docile to his wishes and tastes'.[36] Richards extends beyond this, however, by linking sentimentality with *inhibitions*, and showing how an excessively sentimental depiction of some thing, phenomenon or situation (childhood or schooldays, for example) is a result of a desire not to look too closely at the painful reality of that which is being depicted. His words are worth quoting at length:

> Most, if not all, sentimental fixations and distortions of feeling are the result of inhibitions ... If a man can only think of his childhood as a lost heaven it is probably because he is afraid to think of its other aspects ... The mind is curiously quantitative in some of its operations; undue curtailment in one direction seems to imply excess in an opposite direction ... As a rule the source of such inhibitions is some painfulness attaching to the aspect of life that we refuse to contemplate. The sentimental response steps in to replace this aspect by some other aspect more pleasant to contemplate or by some factitious object which flatters the contemplator ... For the curse of sentimentality ... is not that

---

[31] Butler, *Pleasure*, p. 69.

[32] Ibid., p. 70.

[33] R.A. Sharpe, 'Solid Joys or Fading Pleasures', in Eva Schaper (ed.), *Pleasure, Preference and Value* (Cambridge, 1983), p. 88.

[34] I.A. Richards, *Practical Criticism* (New York, 1929), p. 246.

[35] Savile, 'Sentimentality', p. 339.

[36] Ibid.

its victims have too much feeling at their disposal, but that they have too little, that they see life in too specialised a fashion and respond to it too narrowly.[37]

In this passage the moral failings of sentimentality become clear. Sentimental art originates from the inability to look at existence as it really is, and constitutes therefore a kind of cowardice, as the mind of the sentimentalist flees from (or simply fails to acknowledge) the frequently harsh and painful character of reality. Note that the sentimentalist is not being scolded for his or her excess of emotion. It is, after all, perfectly appropriate to weep over the nature of existence ('the whole of it calls for tears', as Seneca reminded us). No, the problem with the emotional life of the sentimentalist (as with the emotions produced by sentimental art) is that the feelings expressed are not deeply felt, but are, rather, shallow and clichéd. As Roger Scruton writes, 'the vice of sentimentality … causes us not merely to speak and write in clichés, but to *feel* in clichés too, lest we should be troubled by the truth of our condition'.[38]

It is not difficult to see where the connections lie between sentimentalism in art and the phenomenon of kitsch, for the world of kitsch, as Scruton tells us, 'is a world of winsome make-believe, of sugary promises, of instant reward',[39] which has as its goal the falsification of reality. Milan Kundera, whose words have become the *locus classicus* on the subject, stresses how kitsch constitutes a 'beautifying lie'.[40] As with Richards' account of the origin of the sentimental in the denial of some unpleasant reality, Kundera claims that kitsch emerges from a (very specific) denial. Kitsch, he famously declares, 'is the absolute denial of shit'.[41] Importantly for our purposes here, Kundera links the origin of kitsch with religious belief, and in so doing makes clear what the denial of shit's existence means. The Western religious attitude, he maintains, encapsulates a *categorical agreement with being*. This is most clearly seen in the first book of Genesis, of course, in which God's verdict on the world after each day of creation is that it is 'good'. This categorical agreement comes into conflict with those features of the world that seem to be the opposite of 'good', a prime and visceral example of which is defecation:

> The fact that until recently the word 'shit' appeared in print as s--- has nothing to do with moral considerations. You can't claim that shit is immoral, after all! The objection to shit is a metaphysical one. The daily defecation session is daily proof of the unacceptability of Creation. Either/or: either shit is acceptable (in which case don't lock yourself in the bathroom!) or we are created in an unacceptable manner.[42]

---

[37] Richards, *Practical Criticism*, pp. 252–4.
[38] Scruton, 'The Aesthetic Endeavour Today', p. 339.
[39] Ibid., p. 344.
[40] Milan Kundera, *The Art of the Novel* (New York, 1988), p. 135.
[41] Milan Kundera, *The Unbearable Lightness of Being* (New York, 1999), p. 248.
[42] Ibid.

Kitsch serves the purpose of shielding us from the most unacceptable aspects of reality, thereby preserving our desire to live in agreement with being, but this can only be done by creating (in one's mind) a world 'in which shit is denied and everyone acts as though it did not exist'.[43] Hence, and this is important for the Freudian view of art-as-palliative, 'kitsch excludes everything from its purview which is essentially unacceptable in human existence'.[44] Here one can see that the 'shit' Kundera speaks of is not just literal shit (though that is bad enough), but figurative shit, namely everything that is unacceptable and damaging to our perception of the beauty of things. Of principal note here is, naturally, our mortality, something denied both by kitsch and by traditional religious faith: 'kitsch is a folding screen set up to curtain off death.'[45]

Freud's thoughts about the palliative nature of art cohere well with the accounts of kitsch and the sentimental offered by Kundera and Richards. With these kinds of creative work we find precisely the kind of thing Freud is talking of: something wish-driven, fantastical and ultimately illusory, a pleasing rearrangement of the world in a selective and falsifying way.[46] The failure of the Freudian view of art is simply that when he speaks of art he is talking merely of sentimental art, or as though art and kitsch were equivalents. So his view of the narcotic, palliating effect of art is correct, provided that he restricts his account to kitsch (or to other varieties of sentimental and merely escapist art). As Wittgenstein wrote in a different context, 'Yes, [this description] is appropriate, but only for this narrowly circumscribed region, not for the whole of what you were claiming to describe'.[47] Evidently, art's territory extends far beyond the realm of kitsch, and great art likewise does so much more than create shit-denying alternative realities. What possible relevance can Freud's thoughts regarding cultural palliatives have with regard to the work of Shakespeare, Goya and Mozart? To answer this, we may now seek to elaborate three ways in which the enjoyment of art may ameliorate the pain of existence without functioning merely as a narcotic or anaesthetic.

---

[43]   Ibid.

[44]   Ibid.

[45]   Ibid., p. 253.

[46]   It would be remiss not to mention that sentimental art has its defenders, some of whom have argued that selectivity does not by itself equate to falsification, nor is it the sole preserve of the sentimental: 'This process of abstracting from the rest of what life actually presents (and even idealising it) to secure concentration and expressive force is characteristic of art' (David Pugmire, 'Sentimentality and Truthfulness', in Alex Neill and Aaron Ridley (eds), *Arguing About Art* (London, 2008), p. 354. Given that all art involves selectivity, it may be unfounded to castigate the sentimental for possession of that property alone.

[47]   Ludwig Wittgenstein, *Philosophical Investigations* (Oxford, 1953), §3.

Art and Pleasure

That people gain pleasure from art is no profound observation. The enjoyment of music, of theatrical performance, of literature, and of the other many forms of artistic production, has such a valuable and firmly embedded place in human life that one is tempted to say that it should be reckoned among the features of a natural history of human beings.[48] But why should art provide such pleasure to people in the first place? Is this not a strange phenomenon? As Wittgenstein advises, 'Don't take it as a matter of course, but as a remarkable fact, that pictures and fictitious narratives give us pleasure, occupy our minds.'[49] And – of particular relevance for a view of art-as-palliative – how might the pleasures arising from art serve to ameliorate our pains, console us in our human misery?

Let us start with that second question. One way to address this might be to consider the central role of pleasure-seeking impulses in the human person. Freud, of course, is himself a significant advocate of the primacy of hedonistic drives in the psyche, as were the architects of utilitarianism, Jeremy Bentham and John Stuart Mill. We have already had reason to address Freud's notion of the 'pleasure principle', and a consideration of the comparable ideas of Bentham and Mill will take us some way to understanding how the experiencing of pleasurable sensations can simultaneously be felt as a diminution of painful ones.

The theory of life upon which both Bentham and Mill built their moral theory was straightforwardly stated, namely that 'pleasure, and freedom from pain, are the only things desirable as ends; and that all desirable things ... are desirable either for the pleasure inherent in themselves, or as a means to the promotion of pleasure and the prevention of pain'.[50] The claim is not, however, simply that pleasure is the most desirable of things. Beyond that value judgement there is a descriptive claim about the wellsprings of all human actions; namely, that all actions are oriented towards the attainment of pleasure. The famous first lines of Bentham's *Principles of Morals and Legislation* bring out this contention clearly:

> Nature has placed mankind under the governance of two sovereign masters, *pain* and *pleasure*. It is for them alone to point out what we ought to do, as well as to determine what we shall do. On the one hand the standard of right and wrong, on the other the chain of causes and effects, are fastened to their throne. They govern us in all we do, in all we say, in all we think: every effort we can make to throw off our subjection, will serve but to demonstrate and confirm it. In words

---

[48]   See here Wittgenstein: 'What we are supplying are really remarks on the natural history of human beings; we are not contributing curiosities, however, but observations which no one has doubted, but which have escaped remark only because they are always before our eyes' (Wittgenstein, *Philosophical Investigations*, §415).

[49]   Ibid., §524.

[50]   John Stuart Mill, *Utilitarianism* (London, 1864), p. 10.

a man may pretend to abjure their empire: but in reality he will remain subject to it all the while.[51]

Upon this basis, Bentham proceeds to elaborate how the value of any particular pleasure or pain may be estimated by appeal to a number of dimensions or 'circumstances'. Considered by itself, he claims, a pleasure or pain will be greater or less according to (i) its *intensity*, (ii) its *duration*, (iii) its *certainty* or *uncertainty* (in other words, the certainty (or uncertainty) that a pain or a pleasure will result from a particular course of action) and (iv) its *propinquity* or *remoteness* (namely, how near or distant in the future the expected pain or pleasure will follow that course of action). Two supplementary circumstances of a pleasure or pain are then taken into account: (v) its *fecundity* (the chance the sensation has of being followed by sensations of the same kind), and (vi) its *purity* (the chance it has of *not* being followed by sensations of the opposite kind; for example, the chance of pleasurable sensations not being followed by painful ones).[52] These six circumstances allow us to see the goal of all individual actions: it is to achieve (for oneself) pleasures which are intense and of long duration, which are relatively certain to flow from that course of action, which will follow shortly from the performance of the action, and which will bring in its wake similar desirable pleasures; put negatively, the goal is to avoid intense, long-lasting pains. A seventh and final circumstance comes into play only when a group of people is affected by the action, and is termed by Bentham the *extent* of the pleasure or pain. This is where the moral content of utilitarianism comes into play, since a moral act would be one seeking to maximize the pleasurable sensations (and minimize the painful sensations) of others. This moral aspect need not concern us greatly here, since our concern is with Bentham's account of the individual person's pleasure-seeking, pain-avoiding behaviour.

On this account, therefore, the individual's hardwired goal is to secure for him- or herself as much pleasure, and as little pain, as possible. It is not hard to see that this can be achieved by cumulatively adding pleasures so that, on balance, one's life may be more pleasurable than painful. If sensations are regarded as discrete units of experience, then the more pleasurable units one can amass, the more the painful units of one's life may be outweighed and counterbalanced. In other words, pains and pleasures offset one another, and the pain one experiences can be made more manageable if a greater percentage of one's sensations are of the pleasurable sort. There may be a strange artificiality in speaking of pain and pleasure in these vaguely quantifiable terms, and yet there is, nonetheless, some intuitive plausibility

---

[51]   Jeremy Bentham, *An Introduction to the Principles of Morals and Legislation* (Amherst, NY, 1988), p. 1.

[52]   The Benthamite way of framing the issue may be useful for explicating the problematic nature of drug use, as considered in a previous chapter. The pleasures of intoxication are typically *impure*, as those pleasures are not unusually followed by painful sensations.

to the notion. It surely makes sense to think that the enjoyment of an experience might be heightened by the addition of further pleasurable factors. For example, the delight caused by listening to a favourite piece of music might be further enhanced by the addition of other units of pleasure: a glass of good whiskey; a comfortable chair in which to relax while listening; a nicely lit room; the close presence of one's beloved; and so on. In this manner, a pleasurable experience can become – by supplementation – *more* pleasurable than it would otherwise have been. By extension, the strategy of adding pleasures could serve to diminish the amount of pain as a percentage of one's overall experiences. Here, then, is one way of achieving happiness in life and counteracting pain: add as many pleasures to one's life as possible, for in such a manner pain may be overshadowed. And a life which is judged to be painful can be understood in like terms, namely as one in which pleasurable units of sensation are outweighed – in drastic cases overwhelmed and eclipsed – by painful units.

One may suspect that what is being presented here is an unrealistic ideal of the happy life as one of constant and intense pleasurable excitation, but Mill properly dispelled that impression when he reflected on criticisms of utilitarian and Epicurean philosophers:

> The happiness which they meant was not a life of rapture; but moments of such, in an existence made up of few and transitory pains, many and various pleasures, with a decided predominance of the active over the passive, and having as the foundation of the whole, not to expect more from life than it is capable of bestowing.[53]

Reflecting on whether such a moderate conception of happiness could be of sufficient appeal to human beings, Mill noted that 'great numbers have been satisfied with much less', and offered a memorable recipe for a satisfied life:

> The main constituents of a satisfied life appear to be two, either of which by itself is often found sufficient for the purpose: tranquillity, and excitement. With much tranquillity, many find that they can be content with very little pleasure: with much excitement, many can reconcile themselves to a considerable quantity of pain.[54]

Mill's words may be used as a rejoinder to the bleak Freudian diagnosis of the impossibility of happiness, and they present to us, once again, the notion that the addition and accumulation of pleasurable experiences may serve to undercut the ever-threatening painful elements of a human existence.

Before applying to the question of art the thoughts voiced above, an important criticism must be noted. It is a criticism already familiar to us, and stems from Schopenhauer. On the Benthamite view under consideration, sensations, of either

---

[53]   Mill, *Utilitarianism*, p. 18.
[54]   Ibid., p. 19.

the painful or the pleasurable type, are positively felt, one kind of sensation (for example, eating a gourmet meal or engaging in sexual activity) yielding pleasure, another kind (being tortured, feeling unbearably hungry, and so on) yielding pain. Successful management of sensations would result in a favourable balance of pleasure over pain, units of pleasure outweighing units of pain. From Schopenhauer's perspective, however, such a view is radically confused, since pleasures and pains do not both enjoy the privilege of positive status: a pleasurable sensation has no positive reality at all, but is simply the (temporary) abatement of what has genuine positive reality, namely a painful sensation. That 'which is good, in other words, all happiness and satisfaction, is negative, that is, the mere elimination of a desire and the ending of a pain', he writes, noting as a consequence of this that 'as a rule, we find pleasures far below, but pains far beyond, our expectation'.[55] This objection need not derail our project. Whether pleasurable sensations are positive or merely negative, they may nonetheless be supremely valuable in the economy of a human life. It seems hard to deny that there is at least *some kind* of pleasure to be had from food, sex, music (and so on), and whether such pleasurable experiences have a foundational positive reality or merely a negative one must surely seem irrelevant to the person seeking delight, consolation or comfort by means of them. Remove one pleasurable experience from a person's life (without replacing it with another pleasurable experience of equal or greater value) and that person's life will (presumably) be counted, on balance, less pleasurable, and more painful, than it hitherto was. As for the second aspect of his diagnosis (namely that pleasures are less pleasurable and pains more painful than expected), all we can say here is that such a diagnosis may well be true. Such is part and parcel of a pessimistic view of things. All the more reason, then, for aiming to keep those painful experiences to a minimum.

One further objection may be noted. It may seem that Benthamite considerations are less than helpful when exploring the significance of art. Bentham would appear to be that philosopher *par excellence* who seems to find little place for the value of art within his system. His avowed opinion regarding the poetic arts – no better, famously, than push-pin[56] – suggests impatience only (in a letter to Lord

---

[55] Arthur Schopenhauer, *Parerga and Paralipomena* (2 vols, Oxford, 1974), vol. 2, p. 292.

[56] Bentham's judgement regarding the relative merits of poetry and push-pin deserves to be quoted in full, since it manifests not merely an egalitarian view of the value of different pleasures, but also a harsh criticism of the poetic arts: 'Prejudice apart, the game of push-pin is of equal value with the arts and sciences of music and poetry. If the game of push-pin furnish more pleasure, it is more valuable than either. Everybody can play at push-pin: poetry and music are relished only by a few. The game of push-pin is always innocent: it were well could the same be always asserted of poetry. Indeed, between poetry and truth there is a natural opposition: false morals, fictitious nature. The poet always stands in need of something false. When he pretends to lay his foundations in truth, the ornaments of his superstructure are fictions; his business consists in stimulating our passions, and exciting our prejudices. Truth,

Holland he comments that poetry is where some of the lines do not go as far as the margins[57]). More important than Bentham's own preferences and personal idiosyncrasies, however, are the varieties and dimensions of pleasure he outlines, a typology not smoothly applicable to aesthetic experience. Of the list of 14 simple pleasures Bentham provides in *The Principles of Morals and Legislation*, only three – the pleasures of sense, the pleasures of imagination and the pleasures dependent on association – would seem to be at work in the enjoyment of art.[58] The pleasures of sense, as one would expect, encompass first of all those agreeable sensations presented to us by our perceptual organs – taste, smell, touch, sight and hearing – but are extended to cover more specific pleasures, such as intoxication, sex, good health and the gratification of curiosity. Pleasures of imagination are derived from the contemplation of an experience but put together and extended in a different order. One is here speaking of fantasy. Lastly, pleasures of association are pleasures afforded by a particular object or incident, not due to the object or incident in itself, but because of some association that is itself pleasurable. One might, for example, gain pleasure from listening to a particular piece of music, not because one regards it as being of value in itself, but because it brings to mind happy memories of youthful experiences.

As Bentham does not grant a place to aesthetic pleasure in his typology of simple pleasures, he must think of it either as one of the pleasures of sense, or as a complex pleasure. He might subsume musical enjoyment within the category of 'the simple pleasures of the ear', while the delight occasioned by looking at a painting might be placed within the category of 'the simple pleasures of the eye'. Listening to music and looking at visual art can thus be regarded as simple sensory pleasures. Alternatively, aesthetic pleasure could be seen as a complex pleasure. True to form, Bentham does not include an analysis of an experience occasioning aesthetic delight, but his dissection of 'the pleasures of a country scene'[59] can

---

exactitude of every kind, is fatal to poetry' (Jeremy Bentham, 'The Rationale of Reward', in *The Works of Jeremy Bentham* (11 vols, Edinburgh, 1843), vol. 2, pp. 253–4). Here Bentham reveals himself to be the heir of Plato's intolerance of art, viewed as being three steps removed from reality (see Plato, *The Republic* (Harmondsworth, 1955), pp. 359–69).

[57]   '*Prose* is where all the lines but the last go on to the margin—poetry is where some of them fall short of it' (letter to Lord Holland (31 October 1808), in *The Works of Jeremy Bentham* (11 vols, Edinburgh, 1843), vol. 10 (*Memoirs and Correspondence*), p. 442).

[58]   The full list of simple pleasures is this: 1. The pleasures of sense; 2. The pleasures of wealth; 3. The pleasures of skill; 4. The pleasures of amity; 5. The pleasures of a good name; 6. The pleasures of power; 7. The pleasures of piety; 8. The pleasures of benevolence; 9. The pleasures of malevolence; 10. The pleasures of memory; 11. The pleasures of imagination; 12. The pleasures of expectation; 13. The pleasures dependent on association; 14. The pleasures of relief (see Bentham, *Introduction*, p. 33). By a 'simple pleasure' Bentham means a pleasure which cannot be resolved into other simpler ones; he thus contrasts simple pleasures with complex ones, the latter being those which can be further dissected.

[59]   Bentham, *Introduction*, p. 42.

Figure 4.1   John Constable, *The Cornfield*, 143 × 122 cm, oil on canvas, 1826,
             National Gallery, London (Getty Images / The Bridgeman Art
             Library)

be employed as a blueprint for how to proceed. Consider, for example, John
Constable's painting *The Cornfield* (Figure 4.1). Constable gives us a view of an
elm-bordered country lane, leading into a glowing cornfield beyond which we catch
sight of a river, a church tower and green meadows. In the foreground a shepherd
boy is drinking from a stream, leaving his dog to watch the sheep. A donkey and
her foal stand peacefully nearby. All of this takes place under clouds both grey and
white, which part at times to give sight of a bright blue sky. A Benthamite analysis

of the pleasure engendered by a viewing of this painting would, first of all, direct our attention to the pleasures of the senses excited by the scene. The pleasures of the sight are here clearly the relevant ones, and, indeed, our eyes find delight in Constable's painting, with its agreeable colours and figures (it is surely noteworthy here that Constable himself described this particular painting as 'eye salve'[60]). Beyond the sensory pleasure given to our sight by Constable's brushwork we also experience what Bentham would call 'pleasures of the imagination produced by association'. Each viewer would here have to speak for him- or herself (and there is, of course, always the possibility that some viewers would experience no such pleasures at all), but possible associative and imaginative pleasures might include the following: the idea of the gentleness, innocence and loyalty of certain animals; the idea of the carefree days of youth; certain imaginative auditory sensations (birdsong, the murmur of a stream, distant church bells); imagination of other sensory experiences (the warmth of the sun on one's skin, the refreshing coolness of a drink of water on a hot day); the idea of a simpler life, uncorrupted by the demands, business and shallowness of the modern world; and maybe even the pleasing idea of a divine providence, occasioned by the sight of the church and a felt appreciation of the harmony and beauty of nature.

By means of such a dissection of aesthetic experience, one may come to see how the viewing of a painting (or some other experience) may bring about pleasurable sensations. Even with such a possibility of analysis open to us, it might be felt that a Benthamite analysis of art would still struggle to provide a feasible account of the power of art. Given an overarching concern with the intensity and duration of pleasurable experiences, and a marked emphasis on the sensual, Bentham's verdict on the pleasures of aesthetic experience would undoubtedly concur with that provided by Freud: such pleasures are too mild to make one forget real misery. More potent solace must be sought elsewhere.

It is, of course, well known that one of Mill's central revisions of utilitarianism was the rejection of Bentham's monolithic conception of pleasure, and in so doing he arguably bequeathed to us a hedonic theory more conducive to an assessment of the value of aesthetic experience in the economy of human life. Bentham had resolutely denied that there were any differences in *kinds* of pleasure, holding instead that pleasures could only be ranked in terms of intensity, duration, purity and so on. Mill rejects this, and introduces a distinction between *higher* (mental) and *lower* (physical) pleasures, the former preferable to and ultimately more desirable than the latter. That value-based distinction is rooted in a view of what fundamentally divides humans from nonhuman animals: bodily pleasures are enjoyed by both humans and nonhumans, but those higher (intellectual) pleasures – opera, philosophy, poetry and so on – are definitive of the human, and should accordingly be pursued. Importantly, however, it is also supported by the

---

[60]   John Constable, quoted in Graham Reynolds, *Constable's England* (New York, 1983), p. 76.

preferences of sophisticated human agents, who, given a choice, will always opt for the higher of two pleasures:

> Now it is an unquestionable fact that those who are equally acquainted with, and equally capable of appreciating and enjoying, both, do give a most marked preference to the manner of existence which employs their higher faculties. Few human creatures would consent to be changed into any of the lower animals, for a promise of the fullest allowance of a beast's pleasures; no intelligent human would consent to be a fool, no instructed person would be an ignoramus, no person of feeling and conscience would be selfish and base, even though they should be persuaded that the fool, the dunce, or the rascal is better satisfied with his lot than they are with theirs.[61]

For our purposes these thoughts have a twofold importance. First, the refined nature of Mill's reformulation of hedonism softens the apparently philistine quality of a pleasure-seeking guide to life. And secondly – and more significantly – Mill provides us with a framework capable of undermining the Benthamite/Freudian suspicion that the pleasures of art are just too mild to be of use in our struggles against the inevitable pain and potential misery of life. For Mill, aesthetic pleasure is not merely one mild pleasure eclipsed by the more convulsing pleasures of the body. Rather, it is what people ultimately yearn for; it is what brings with it the greatest satisfaction and the very highest of pleasures.

That may sound encouraging, but how exactly does art provide us with a yield of pleasure? The Benthamite analysis considered earlier provides one answer to that question, but there are competing alternatives. One of the most impressive of these can be found in Christopher Butler's *Pleasure and the Arts*. Butler offers a markedly cognitive account of the pleasures provided by art, for he emphasizes how aesthetic pleasure results from the process of *understanding*. It is 'the urge to find meaning', 'a drive to understanding', which lies behind aesthetic enjoyment, and this drive is, Butler says, 'a built-in feature of brain function'.[62] When we are brought face to face with a work of visual art, of literature, or a piece of music, we experience a sense of puzzlement (*'What is going on here?'*), and then, by calling up memories and associations, we construct 'a narrative scene or universe within an imagined world',[63] an achievement which we find inherently pleasurable. Something of the kind can be seen quite clearly in the enjoyment we get from understanding a joke. Take the following example, gleefully told by Freud in *Jokes and Their Relation to the Unconscious*:

> Two not particularly scrupulous business men had succeeded, by dint of a series of highly risky enterprises, in amassing a large fortune, and they were now

---

[61]   Mill, *Utilitarianism*, p. 12.
[62]   Butler, *Pleasure*, p. 15.
[63]   Ibid.

making efforts to push their way into good society. One method, which struck them as a likely one, was to have their portraits painted by the most celebrated and highly-paid artist in the city, whose pictures had an immense reputation. The precious canvases were shown for the first time at a large evening party, and the two hosts themselves led the most influential connoisseur and art critic up to the wall upon which the portraits were hanging side by side, to extract his admiring judgement on them. He studied the works for a long time, and then, shaking his head, as though there was something he had missed, pointed to the gap between the pictures and asked quietly: 'But where's the Saviour?'[64]

Finding delight in this joke here depends in part upon understanding the allusion made by the art critic to Christ's crucifixion and how that allusion takes the place of a biting criticism: 'You are a couple of rogues, like the two thieves between whom the Saviour was crucified.'[65] Accompanying the pleasure of this act of understanding is delight both in the ingenuity of the allusion and in the spectacle of self-aggrandizing, pretentious and unscrupulous individuals being brought down to size: 'What do I care about your pictures? You are a couple of rascals – I know that!'[66]

The critic's piece of ego-deflation amuses us, partly, because it brings about a situation of justice. We are delighted by the order brought into the world by such an interjection. For Butler, one of the pleasure-bringing elements of aesthetic experience is precisely the perception of coherence and order to be found within a work of art. Though we like the process of problem solving and meaning finding, we are ultimately left unsatisfied and frustrated by art of a disordered and fragmentary nature. This may be why David Lynch's movie *Mulholland Drive* makes for such exasperating viewing. Bringing these thoughts together, Butler writes:

> If we need these kinds of formal order to be satisfied by our experience, then great works of art are our supreme examples of the ordering and making intelligible of miscellaneous materials. The finding of a hidden order (through an appreciation of the point of the apparently disordered techniques of the artist) is one of the greatest pleasures of puzzle-solving interpretation.[67]

What Butler calls 'our desire for conceptual order' is likewise brought into prominence in Anthony Storr's theory of music. As human beings we are compelled to make sense of the world around us and cannot avoid trying to find coherence and order within it. Auditory sensations are generally chaotic and therefore disturbing (just *stop* for a moment and listen to the world outside the window: the sounds are unpredictable, disordered and grating). The joy of music is that it imposes order on the world of sound, structuring our auditory experience

---

[64] Sigmund Freud, *Jokes and Their Relation to the Unconscious*, S.E. vol. VIII, p. 74.

[65] Sigmund Freud, *Five Lectures on Psycho-Analysis*, S.E. vol. XI, p. 31.

[66] Freud, *Jokes*, p. 75.

[67] Butler, *Pleasure*, p. 156.

so as to make sense of it. When we listen to music, we 'enter a special, secluded world in which order prevails and from which the incongruous is excluded'.[68] The fact that music provokes *movement* in us, inspiring in our bodies the rhythmic orderliness of dance, is likewise pleasurable; it replaces the often disjointed nature of our movements with a mellifluous silkiness making us feel in harmony with our own physical being.[69]

There are two polar ways of thinking about the relationship between art and pleasure. On the Platonic end of the spectrum, art is always disappointing, constituting merely a copy of some object in the material world.[70] In Roland Barthes' version of this view, art can never quite give us what we want, for 'our desire is typically directed to real *objects in the world*, like real lovers, good food, and enjoyable possessions';[71] since art never gives us real things, we are left with our appetites whetted but no satisfaction. The result is simply deflation. On the spectrum's other end, however, we see theorists such as Butler and Storr lauding the pleasures of art. Far from disappointing, art – so much more than the hurly-burly of reality – gives us order and beauty, and the pleasures it provides are, significantly, *reliable* ones. In other words, while the pleasures of our material world are often not forthcoming or can let us down, this does not happen when we listen to a recording of a favourite piece of music. Hence, our experiences of art 'tend to be more reassuringly satisfactory than those of risotto, blondes, or men with moustaches'.[72] This reliability may be just one more reason why aesthetic pleasures may be a source of consolation in a world which not infrequently upsets and disappoints us.

Art and the Denial of Desire

If one's wish is to show how art can serve to ameliorate, soften or palliate the sufferings of our human condition, then there is an important and influential view that can operate as a rival to the hedonistic conception just considered. It is a view powerfully articulated by Schopenhauer in the third book of *The World as*

---

[68]   Anthony Storr, *Music*, p. 105.

[69]   For some, the delight produced by listening to music may even be the one thing redeeming existence from its arguably 'erroneous' character, as discussed in the first chapter of this book. Nietzsche makes this point most powerfully: 'Without music life would be a mistake' (Friedrich Nietzsche, *Twilight of the Idols and the Anti-Christ* (Harmondsworth, 1968), p. 26).

[70]   It should be noted that there is more ambivalence in Plato's account of art than this might suggest (see Wayne D. Bowman, *Philosophical Perspectives on Music* (New York, 1998), pp. 19–68).

[71]   Butler, *Pleasure*, p. 194.

[72]   Ibid., p. 108.

Will and Representation.[73] We are already familiar with the multifaceted character
of Schopenhauer's pessimistic diagnosis of existence (this much was addressed
in our opening chapter), but one significant detail should here be mentioned and
reiterated: the ubiquity of *willing*. It is not reason which drives human beings,
but rather an endless striving after objects of desire. A necessary consequence
of this ever-present willing, Schopenhauer thinks, is suffering. This is because
desire arises from a feeling that we *lack something*. That feeling is itself painful.
Moreover, the end result of the process of willing is inevitably one species or
other of suffering. A person either fails to secure an object of desire or, conversely,
succeeds. In the first case, of course, suffering ensues; but suffering also flows
from the successful attainment of the desired thing; since the satisfaction is not
as great as one had anticipated, boredom sets in (itself an unpleasant feeling), and
another object of desire takes the place of the former one. The cycle of willing thus
starts all over again. If the operations of the will are in such a manner productive
of suffering, the conclusion must be straightforward. Suffering will be lessened
(maybe even eliminated) by the denial of desire. It is art's great gift to humanity
that it does precisely this. It eliminates desire and quiets the will. The palliative
qualities of art, on this view, must be considerable.

Schopenhauer's account turns on a distinction he draws between the intellectual
operations employed in aesthetic contemplation and those at work in all others
areas of knowledge. As a rule, Schopenhauer tells us, knowledge serves the will,
and is subordinate to it, the pursuit and attainment of knowledge being undertaken
so as to satisfy one or other of the pressing demands of the all-encompassing, all-
demanding will; it is, in other words, instrumental in character.[74] In the case of nonhuman animals, this subservience can never be eliminated, but in humans there is
one exception to that rule, and this exception is to be found in the appreciation of
art. The clearest way to state this is to say that, while all other operations of the
intellect are driven by a desire to sate some personal interest, the engagement with
art is *disinterested*.

An emphasis on the disinterested nature of aesthetic contemplation is not
peculiar to Schopenhauer, of course. It is, indeed, a prominent feature of Kant's
Critique of Judgement that judgements of beauty are evaluations made 'by
means of a delight or aversion *apart from any interest*';[75] these consist in 'pure
disinterested delight'[76] and are at the mercy of no sensual impulse, manifesting,

---

[73]   A great deal will need to be omitted from our discussion of Schopenhauer's view of
art, since we need to focus on the question of how artistic contemplation eliminates suffering.
The Platonic dimension of his aesthetic theory – namely, how art reveals to us timeless
realities (Platonic 'ideas') – will thus be passed over here, its importance notwithstanding.

[74]   See Arthur Schopenhauer, *The World as Will and Representation* (2 vols, New
York, 1969), vol. 1, p. 177.

[75]   Immanuel Kant, *Critique of Judgement* (Oxford, 1952), p. 50.

[76]   Ibid., pp. 43–4.

rather, an 'active engagement of the cognitive powers *without ulterior aim*'.[77] The distinction Kant wishes to draw – between pleasures of *sensation* (the satisfaction of physical urges) and the aesthetic pleasures of *reflection* – is further radicalized by Schopenhauer, since for him all non-aesthetic intellectual operations are slaves to desire, but the idea of disinterestedness nonetheless lies at the heart of both thinkers' theories of art. Hegel likewise embraces this idea, expressing clearly how desire does not enter into aesthetic contemplation:

> In this appetitive relation to the outer world [i.e. desire], the man stands as a sensuous particular over against the things as likewise particulars; he does not open his mind to them with general ideas as a thinking being, but has relations dictated by particular impulses and interests to the objects as themselves particulars, and preserves himself in them, inasmuch as he uses them, consumes them, and puts in act his self-satisfaction by sacrificing them to it. In this negative relation desire requires for itself not merely the superficial appearance of external things, but themselves in their concrete sensuous existence. Mere pictures of the wood that it wants to use, or of the animals that it wants to eat, would be of no service to desire. Just as little is it possible for the desire to subsist in its freedom. For its impulse urges it just precisely to destroy this independence and freedom of external things, and to show that they are only there to be destroyed and consumed ... This relation of desire is not that in which man stands to the work of art. He allows it to subsist as an object, free and independent, and enters into relation with it apart from desire, as with an object which only appeals to the theoretic side of the mind. For this reason the work of art, although it has sensuous existence, yet, in this point of view, does not require concrete sensuous existence and natural life; indeed, it even *ought* not to remain on such a level, seeing that it has to satisfy only the interests of the mind, and is bound to exclude from itself all desire.[78]

Schopenhauer's emphasis on disinterestedness falls into a well-trodden path in aesthetic theory, therefore, though he extends these thoughts further so as to grant to art a unique role in the mitigation of pain.

A first thing briefly to note is a distinction Schopenhauer draws between art and what he calls the *charming* or *attractive*.[79] He sees this latter as the opposite of *the sublime*, the feeling of which is provoked by the sight of some incomparable power threatening the individual with annihilation. The examples Schopenhauer provides are of 'nature in turbulent and tempestuous motion' (barren deserts, darkness visible through thunder clouds, vast and inhospitable landscapes).[80] This feeling of the sublime arises when something unfavourable to the will (something

---

[77] Ibid., p. 64, emphasis added.

[78] G.W.F. Hegel, *Introductory Lectures on Aesthetics* (London, 1993), p. 41.

[79] See Schopenhauer, *World*, vol. 1, p. 207.

[80] Ibid., pp. 204–5.

which, if experienced in reality, would annihilate the viewer) becomes an object of contemplation. In such cases, the desire is inoperative (since no viewer could wish really to experience that harsh and destructive reality), so we are left in a state of pure contemplation. The merely charming, on the other hand, stirs the will by presenting objects which directly appeal to it (paintings of prepared and served-up food, and many representations of nude figures), exciting desirous or lustful feelings, thereby transforming the beholder into a 'needy and dependent subject of willing'.[81] Art which is in this sense charming must clearly be divorced from the category of true art if art is to fulfil its promise of eliminating desire.

When we reflect upon the experience of engaging with art, we find relinquished the ordinary way of considering things (objects seen as means to ends, objects of desire). Our entire consciousness, rather, is now devoted to perception, and is filled with a calm contemplation of what is presented to us. As a result, we '*lose* ourselves entirely in this object', forgetting both our will and our individuality, 'so that it is as though the object alone existed without anyone to perceive it'.[82] In losing himself in such a fashion, the individual has become a 'will-less, painless, timeless *subject of knowledge*'.[83] The vehicles for this experience are, predominantly, architecture and the natural beauty of the inorganic and vegetable kingdoms (and their representation in art).[84] In landscape painting, paintings of still life, in ruins and church interiors, will-less knowing is experienced, and one can relax 'in the bliss and peace of mind of pure knowledge free from all willing'.[85] We may ask how such tranquillity can ensue. Schopenhauer provides us with a very moving answer. Willing enmeshes our lives and a throng of desires enslaves us, always demanding and yet never finding satisfaction. What we need for peace would seem to be some kind of respite:

> When … an external cause or inward disposition suddenly raises us out of the endless stream of willing, and snatches knowledge from the thralldom of the will, the attention is now no longer directed to the motives of willing, but comprehends things free from their relation to the will. Thus it considers things without interest, without subjectivity, purely objectively; it is entirely given up to them in so far as they are merely representations, and not motives. Then all at once the peace, always sought but always escaping us on that first path of willing, comes to us of its own accord, and all is well with us. It is the painless

[81]   Ibid., p. 207.

[82]   Ibid., p. 178.

[83]   Ibid., p. 179.

[84]   It is to be noted here that Schopenhauer did not think that *all* artistic forms served the function of securing blissful peace of mind. This, he thinks, happens only when inorganic and vegetable life is the focus of aesthetic contemplation. When, on the other hand, animals and human beings are the object, aesthetic enjoyment will consist in the apprehension of timeless Platonic realities (see Schopenhauer, *World*, vol. 1, pp. 212–13).

[85]   Ibid., p. 212.

state, prized by Epicurus as the highest good and as the state of the gods; for that moment we are delivered from the miserable pressure of the will. We celebrate the Sabbath of the penal servitude of willing; the wheel of Ixion stands still.[86]

This deliverance is brought about by the pleasing sensation we can feel when looking at a still life or landscape painting. The calm tranquillity of such paintings contrasts with our own restless state of mind, perennially disturbed by desiring and by striving, and we find ourselves in 'another world, so to speak, where everything that moves our will, and thus violently agitates us, no longer exists'.[87]

This much accounts for the will-less, painless state caused by aesthetic contemplation. But what of that other dramatic claim, namely that the subject becomes *timeless* through such an engagement with art? We can begin to answer that question by noting one feature of painting highlighted by Schopenhauer: its apparent ability to bring time to a halt. There are two ways of considering things, according to Schopenhauer: firstly, there is the 'rational method', employed in both science and in practical life; and there is, alternatively, 'the method of genius', valid in art alone. His way of describing these two methods opens up the possibility of timeless aesthetic knowing:

> The first is like the mighty storm, rushing along without beginning or aim …; the second is like the silent sunbeam, cutting through the path of the storm, and quite unmoved by it.[88]

In line with the terms of this second methodology, art at its best manages to freeze the whirligig of temporal processes:

> For it plucks the object of its contemplation from the stream of the world's course, and holds it isolated before it … It therefore pauses at this particular thing; it stops the wheel of time.[89]

Everything we experience in our world lives in time and is at the mercy of its vicissitudes. The dinner party one enjoys, the smelled rose, the face of one's beloved, the shifting beauty of a sunset – all of these are essentially evanescent, their transience definitive of a life lived within an inescapable spatiotemporal setting. The work of art, however, selects a particular object or scene and makes it stand still so that it can be contemplated outside of the order of time. And when one engages with that work of art (and loses oneself within it), it is as though time has itself stopped and we achieve that most wonderful of things: a view of life *sub specie aeternitatis*. If the burden of time really is (as contended in the opening

---

[86] Ibid., p. 196.

[87] Ibid., p. 197.

[88] Ibid., p. 185.

[89] Ibid.

chapter) a source of human suffering, then the timeless perspective offered to us by art will be of great assistance in our quest for consolation.[90]

Schopenhauer's emphasis upon art's ability to quell excitations (to be, as he puts it, a *quieter* of the will)[91] would seem to be particularly apposite for a Freudian view of the palliative nature of the aesthetic. For, to recall Freud's view, the mental apparatus seeks to keep all stimulations to a minimum. If art were to do this it would truly be working in the best interests of suffering humanity. Freud himself, however, seems to be suspicious of the view – a view from which the Schopenhauerian perspective seems to stem – that aesthetic engagement is disinterested. In one of his characteristic gibes at philosophy, Freud, in his book on jokes, tells us that the philosophers 'define an aesthetic idea by the condition that in it we are not trying to get anything from things or do anything with them, that we are not needing things in order to satisfy one of our major vital needs, but that we are content with contemplating them'.[92] Freud finds this view inapplicable with regard to jokes (since evidently we are trying to get something from joking activity, that thing being *pleasure*), but he also extends that conclusion to aesthetic phenomena more generally:

> I doubt if we are in a position to undertake *anything* without having an intention in view. If we do not require our mental apparatus at the moment for supplying one of our indispensable satisfactions, we allow it itself to work in the direction of pleasure and we seek to derive pleasure from its own activity. I suspect that this is in general the condition that governs all aesthetic ideation, but I understand too little of aesthetics to try to enlarge on this statement.[93]

Freud's (real or sardonic) modesty notwithstanding, there may be something of importance in the view that there is nothing really disinterested in the aesthetic attitude, and that it is operating to produce pleasure in one form or another. That, of course, would return us to the Benthamite model of art considered in a previous section of this chapter. One might, nonetheless, be sufficiently impressed by art's capacity to quiet our strivings and to produce a timeless (or at least quasi-timeless) perspective on things to reject Freud's criticism as being a cavil merely.

A different objection might hold greater force, and this relates to the contention that excitation and desire are always in themselves unpleasant sensations and that what we yearn for is an end to such stimulation, art offering us one such route to that end. This objection may express scepticism towards the notion that human beings always seek to put a period to excitation. We have already encountered a

note

---

[90] One must be careful not to overstate Schopenhauer's view of art's usefulness in this respect, however, since it offers us merely a temporary respite from the pains of existence: art, he declares, 'is not the way out of life, but only an occasional consolation in it' (ibid., p. 267).

[91] See ibid., p. 233.

[92] Freud, *Jokes*, p. 95.

[93] Ibid., pp. 95–6.

criticism of this kind during our discussion of intoxicants in a previous chapter, and it has an equal power when we think about art. For surely art does not just subdue and quiet but can at times bring about quite ferocious stimulations, and these are often actively sought out. Think about our never-ending appetite for horror movies and edge-of-the-seat thrillers.[94] A prominent feature, moreover, of Anthony Storr's theory of music is that it causes arousal just as much (and maybe more) than it tranquilizes: 'Lullabies may send children to sleep; but we listen to Chopin's *Berceuse* or the *Wiegenlieder* of Brahms and Schubert with rapt attention.'[95] And therefore a similar conclusion to that drawn with regard to drugs would be appropriate here also: sometimes we suffer from 'stimulus overload' and need quieting; at other times we experience 'stimulus hunger' and require arousal. The lesson is thus a familiar one: generalizations are to be avoided wherever possible, and the variability of art – and the variability of the human needs it addresses – must always be borne in mind. It is in this respect, at least, that art and drugs are motley bedfellows.

Mithridatism

Thus far, our enquiry has yielded two possible ways in which art may be said to mitigate suffering: it might cause pleasure in us, thus offsetting pain; or the disinterestedness inherent in aesthetic engagement might produce an (albeit temporary) end to willing and a corresponding diminution of pain. To those two may be added, as has just been observed, the role of art in lifting the burden of boredom. There is still a further way in which art may exhibit a palliative function. Given that any human life will inevitably encounter obstacles, frustrations, losses and pains, art may provide a unique set of resources for dealing with these. This would help to explain the perennial appeal of tragedy and other art forms either distressing or disturbing or in some manner lacking a 'happy ending'. For this is a significant problem facing any hedonic theory of art. If the purpose of art really is to produce pleasant sensations, its palliative dimension lying precisely in this function, then how can we hope to understand the appeal of *Hamlet*, the novels of Thomas Hardy or the paintings of artists such as Lucien Freud or Hieronymous Bosch? On a Benthamite understanding, should not all art be delightfully soothing? How could we ever on

---

[94] If a person were to object that horror movies did not qualify as art, then they would only need to be reminded that at least certain instances of that genre must be seen to have substantial artistic merit (Stanley Kubrick's *The Shining*, for instance). But our business here is not to evaluate the merit of an entire genre, but simply to draw attention to the possible weaknesses of a view stressing that the value of art lies in its diminution of excitation. Addressing this very issue, Butler writes: 'We are supposed to find tension unpleasurable and its reduction pleasurable. But we like the arousal within these horrifying and suspense narratives' (Butler, *Pleasure*, p. 56).

[95] Storr, *Music*, p. 25.

such a view make sense of the appeal of the tragic? Such a concern patently extends beyond an objection to Benthamism alone. We are trying here to conceive of art as a way of softening, mitigating or even eliminating suffering, but how can pain-alleviation possibly be aided by adding to our sum total of pain the woes of King Oedipus or Tess Durbeyfield? Would it not be better to immerse oneself in the kind of sentimental art earlier castigated? It is, after all, easy to see why *that* would make a viewer happy. Schopenhauer's theory of art, of course, provides a more conducive home for the tragic, conceived by him as a depiction of 'the terrible side of life'.[96] Tragedy takes as its theme humanity's misery, highlighting the fall of the just and the triumph of the wicked. It thus, Schopenhauer holds, hints at the true nature of the world, and leads the spectator to a rejection of that world, to resignation and the peace resulting from a denial of the will-to-live.

The view we need briefly to expound here moves on a somewhat different tack. If one is *prepared* for an ordeal or a loss, then one is (at least arguably) in a better position to deal with it and suffer less. Engagement on an artistic level with 'the terrible side of life' might furnish one with a greater understanding of life's torments and afflictions, with resilience in the face of it, and maybe even with an internalized conceptual and existential framework enabling one to rise above one's troubles or to make something noble out of them. If A.D. Nuttal is right in holding that the appeal of tragedy is that it shows 'the worst we can imagine ennobled by form',[97] then by engaging with it we can, as it were, prepare for the worst that can happen. In such a fashion, the attainment of what we might call 'tragic literacy' could bring enormous benefits in the struggle against suffering. It is at least possible that a great many of the problems (either inevitable or potential) awaiting all of us may be managed better and (again to use Nuttal's word) ennobled if we can bring to them the tools garnered from art and tragedy, and we might thereby shoulder better the sufferings engendered by ageing (*King Lear*, Richard Strauss' *Der Rosenkavalier*), damage to name and reputation (J.M. Coetzee's *Disgrace*), love (lots to choose from here, though *Remembrance of Things Past* is the classic example), illness and dying (Tolstoy's *Death of Ivan Ilych*), and the long etcetera of human torments. We might thus attribute to art (and specifically art of the tragic kind) a mithridatic function. Just as Mithridates of Pontus cultivated immunity to poisons by regularly ingesting them in sub-lethal doses, so tragedy might be used as 'the homeopathic administration of pain to inure ourselves to the greater pain which life will force upon us'.[98] From a safe distance, as it were, we watch, learn and prepare for what is to come. Nuttal suggests in this context that tragedy may serve a comparable function to that of frightening dreams, which allow us, perhaps, to 'practice for crises':

---

96   Schopenhauer, *World*, vol. 1, p. 252.
97   A.D. Nuttall, *Why Does Tragedy Give Pleasure?* (Oxford, 1996), p. 99.
98   Trilling, *The Liberal Imagination*, p. 56.

The human capacity to think provisionally, to do thought-experiments, to form hypotheses, to imagine what may happen before it happens – is fundamental to our nature and to our spectacular biological success (so far). I think the cleverest thing Sir Karl Popper ever said was his remark that our hypotheses 'die in our stead'. The human race has found a way, if not to abolish, then to defer and diminish the Darwinian treadmill of death. We send our hypotheses ahead, an expendable army, and watch them fall. It is easy to see how the human imagination might begin to exhibit a need, in art, for a death-game, a game in which the muscles of psychic response, fear and pity, are exercised and made ready, through a facing of the worst, which is not yet the real worst.[99]

The palliative benefits of art are, on this view, not to be enjoyed immediately but at some point in the future, when their effectiveness will be required.

In *Beyond the Pleasure Principle*, Freud himself hints at such a function during his discussion of repetition-compulsion. Children's games, he notes, exhibit a repetitive quality. A child will insist that a story or game that has given pleasure must be repeated in an identical way, and this, of course, contrasts with the reaction of adults, for whom '[n]ovelty is always the condition of enjoyment'.[100] But it is not enjoyable experiences alone that a child desires to repeat: unpleasurable experiences are repeated too. 'If the doctor looks down a child's throat or carries out some small operation on him, we may be quite sure that these frightening experiences will be the subject of the next game.'[101] Reflection on what he dubs the 'daemonic' character of these repetitions leads Freud ultimately to posit the existence of a 'death drive' in human beings, but for our purposes here a less dramatic element of his conclusion may simply be noted. Children, remember, do not recoil from repeating unpleasurable experiences, and this seems to have something to do with a desire to 'make themselves master of the situation'.[102] This, for Freud, may provide a clue to the appeal of the tragic arts, in which spectators are not spared the most painful experiences. What may be happening here is a comparable desire to master some dreadful possible situation, to work it over in the mind, and to make us less unprepared for its actual arrival.

This chapter has sketched a number of ways in which the difficulties of the human condition may be eased and palliated by art. No conclusion needs to be drawn concerning which of these perspectives holds most truth. It is probably the case that all may work together to produce a composite picture of the value of art with regard to suffering: engagement with artworks of one kind or another may bring pleasure, thereby counterbalancing pain; it may put a temporary halt to the apparently incessant striving which only seems to bring dissatisfaction; when we lack stimulation, contrariwise, it may step in to fill that void, enlivening periods

---

[99] Nuttall, *Tragedy*, pp. 76–7.
[100] Sigmund Freud, *Beyond the Pleasure Principle*, S.E. vol. XVIII, p. 35.
[101] Ibid., p. 17.
[102] Ibid.

of boredom; and it may habituate us to the undesirable elements of a potentially painful future. At any rate, art would seem to be an invaluable palliative for most sensitive human beings. Without its presence, existence would be distinctly more painful. A similar judgement might be made regarding the final palliative calling for our attention: *love*.

Chapter 5
The Fourth Palliative: Love

Remember all along that there is no embrace in this world that won't finally unclasp.

Joseph Brodsky

If one conceives of palliative measures as auxiliary structures lending support to our troubled and vulnerable lives, then it will be easy to see why love should occupy a central position in this set of techniques. For the promise of love is precisely that of something which can in some way soften the impact of the worst of our experiences and – as Dickens puts it – 'calm the wild waters' of the soul.[1] This is, indeed, a common enough sentiment: how many movies, poems, songs and novels are dedicated to this theme? For many, its effects may even exceed what we expect of a mere palliative, love holding out the hope of real healing and a permanent cure for human woe. From the book of Genesis to the speech of Aristophanes in Plato's *Symposium*, the human condition has been viewed as something incomplete or broken, a condition that love can restore to wholeness. Pursuing this line, the psychoanalyst Erich Fromm has argued that love is best regarded as 'the answer to the problem of human existence',[2] the thing which uniquely overcomes the pain of our separateness, meeting the 'deepest need of man … to leave the prison of his aloneness'.[3] More modestly (and maybe even cynically), the excitement and turbulence of love might simply be seen as another of those deflections which serve to distract a person – sometimes temporarily, sometimes more durably – from the pains and tedium of existence.[4] But in whatever fashion and to whatever magnitude the alleviating power of love is presented, it is widely regarded as the most indispensable of the auxiliary structures we are in this book examining. A person might, after all, make little or no use of intoxicants, have no time at all for religion, and maybe even be impervious to the allure of

---

[1]   Charles Dickens, *Hard Times* (Harmondsworth, 1969), p. 115. Dickens is here describing the love felt by Stephen Blackpool for Rachael.

[2]   Erich Fromm, *The Art of Loving* (New York, 2006), p. 7.

[3]   Ibid., p. 9.

[4]   Note in this context Hardy's presentation, in *Two on a Tower*, of Lady Constantine's amatory interest in Swithin St Cleeve, who 'had, in fact, arisen as an attractive little interpolation between herself and despair' (Thomas Hardy, *Two on a Tower* (London, 1999), p. 46).

art, but a life without *love*, on the other hand, might very well prove untenable: 'Destroy love and friendship; what remains in the world worth accepting?'[5]

The word 'love' encompasses a wide range of phenomena and relations. C.S. Lewis famously documented its four varieties as being *storge* (familial love), *philia* (the love between friends), *agape* (charitable love, the reciprocal love of God and humanity, the love of one's fellow human beings) and *eros* (romantic love).[6] Of these four types, it is romantic love that is to command our attention in this chapter. I am not going to devote a great deal of space here to defining romantic love – in agreement with Alan Soble, 'I assume that the reader knows what I am talking about'[7] – but will nonetheless mention a number of characteristics that are typically present in instances of romantic relationships. We thus might say that romantic love is a set of feelings and pieces of behaviour occurring in a relationship between two people in which is manifested an intense and reciprocated concern for each other's happiness and well-being; it usually has a sexual dimension (something which serves to distinguish romantic love from both friendship and familial love); it is typically of an exclusive nature; it involves the creation of shared projects and goals; and it may (frequently but by no means always) lead to marriage and procreation. To repeat, this depiction is not intended to be at all definitive, and it raises many problematic questions. Are there not non-exclusive (that is, 'open') romantic relationships? Is love not infrequently unreciprocated? Must it be intentionally long-term? Given, however, that I have only wished to outline typical (rather than necessary) features of romantic love, these questions may be put on one side.[8] Our concern here is with the role romantic love plays in the fight against personal suffering, and we may once more begin our investigation by turning our attention to *Civilization and Its Discontents*.

Love's Palliative Appeal: Freud's View

The palliative measures of intoxicants, religion and art all function, Freud thinks, by means of a turning away from the external world and its painful conditions of sensibility. Love stands apart from these other techniques in that 'it takes a firm hold of its objects and obtains happiness from an emotional relation to them'.[9] Moreover, instead of merely – morphine-like – aiming at a diminution or

---

5   David Hume, 'Of Polygamy and Divorces', in *Essays: Moral, Political, and Literary* (Indianapolis, IN, 1985), p. 185.

6   See C.S. Lewis, *The Four Loves* (London, 1960).

7   Alan Soble, *The Structure of Love* (New Haven, CT, 1990), p. 3.

8   See Raja Halwani, *Philosophy of Love, Sex, and Marriage* (New York, 2010), pp. 7–28 for a thorough discussion of the problems relating to these (and to other) features of romantic love.

9   Sigmund Freud, *Civilization and Its Discontents* (J.R.) (London, 1930), p. 37.

avoidance of pain ('that goal of weary resignation'[10]), love 'holds fast to the deep-rooted, passionate striving for a positive fulfilment of happiness'.[11] Freud's words on the matter of seeking satisfaction through loving and being loved will here be quoted at length. They serve as the initial orientation for this chapter's discussion:

> This attitude is familiar enough to all of us; one of the forms in which love manifests itself, sexual love, gives us our most intense experience of an overwhelming pleasurable sensation and so furnishes a prototype for our strivings after happiness. What is more natural than that we should persist in seeking happiness along the path by which we first encountered it? The weak side of this way of living is clearly evident; and were it not for this, no human being would ever have thought of abandoning this path to happiness in favour of any other. We are never so defenceless against suffering as when we love, never so forlornly unhappy as when we have lost our love-object or its love.[12]

Three distinct claims are made by Freud in this passage: sexual love provides the 'most intense' of pleasures; it is the earliest experienced of our pleasures; and the vulnerable condition one enters when in a romantic relationship makes love a high-risk strategy, thereby attenuating its palliative promise. We'll examine these claims one at a time.

The first claim is straightforward enough and is consistent with the experience of (at least) a great many people. What is highlighted is simply the intensity of sexual love and sexual sensations. Within this category we should include both the intense emotional pleasure of being in love and the specific set of pleasurable sensations produced by (a certain kind of) physical contact with another person's body and by the attainment of orgasm. These have provided us with the very model and standard by which other pleasurable experiences are judged. It is on this basis, presumably, that Freud can judge artistic pleasure to be a mild experience (it's mild *compared with sex*), while the appeal of intoxication is that its pleasure can be extraordinarily intense (the rush accompanying intravenous heroin use, for instance, not uncommonly depicted as being similar in intensity to the release of orgasm). Indeed, in everyday discourse people typically describe pleasurable experiences in these terms: a wonderful (non-sexual) experience is sometimes called 'orgasmic', while certain foodstuffs (chocolate cake, for instance) are not uncommonly referred to as being 'better than sex'. If, therefore, a person desires a life in which pleasurable experiences outweigh (or at least significantly counterbalance) painful ones – what we might for shorthand call a 'happy' life – or if he or she simply wishes for a pleasurable dimension in life, then it is reasonable to think that romantic love and its attendant experiences, as the very acme of pleasure, should be recommended and sought.

---

[10] Ibid.
[11] Ibid.
[12] Ibid., pp. 37–8.

With the second claim we move into more contentious territory. Sexual love presents itself to us as a natural route to felicity because it was our first encountered form of happiness. This idea is spelled out in detail in the *Three Essays on the Theory of Sexuality*, in which Freud develops the idea that sexuality (and sexual pleasure) is present in an individual from infancy and is not, as commonly thought, something ushered in with puberty. The child's sexual life has a marked autoerotic quality, sexual pleasure being experienced by stimulation of one or other of the erotogenic zones of its body (principally: mouth, anus, penis/clitoris), but amidst this is to be found the first stirrings of erotic interest in an external object, namely the mother (and, more specifically, her breast). This original erotic relation is to leave a defining mark on a person's subsequent quest for love. Freud writes:

> At a time at which the first beginnings of sexual satisfaction are still linked with the taking of nourishment, the sexual instinct has a sexual object outside the infant's own body in the shape of his mother's breast. It is only later that the instinct loses that object, just at the time, perhaps, when the child is able to form a total idea of the person to whom the organ that is giving him satisfaction belongs. As a rule the sexual instinct then becomes auto-erotic, and not until the period of latency has been passed through is the original relation restored. There are thus good reasons why a child sucking at his mother's breast has become the prototype of every relation of love. The finding of an object is in fact a refinding of it.[13]

Two things need to be drawn out of this pregnant passage. It is, first of all, vital to note the importance to Freud of the uniquely satisfying experience of feeding at the breast. I say 'uniquely satisfying' because it is in this event alone that the two driving forces of life – conceived by Freud in his earliest theory of instincts as 'hunger' (an instinct for self-preservation) and 'love' (the sexual instinct)[14] – come together: in the moment of breastfeeding, therefore, the infant satisfies its nutritional needs and simultaneously achieves non-nutritional, and (therefore for Freud) sexual pleasure as a result of the rhythmical stimulation of the mucous membrane of the mouth. The importance of this paradisiacal past for Freud's account of love cannot be overstated. Love, as we will see, promises us a return to this kind of all-encompassing happiness.

The other thing we need to note is perhaps the most striking, and constitutes the most distinctive thing about the Freudian contribution to the understanding of

---

[13]   Sigmund Freud, *Three Essays on the Theory of Sexuality*, in *The Standard Edition of the Complete Psychological Works of Sigmund Freud* (24 vols, London, 1953–74) (hereafter S.E.), vol. VII, p. 222.

[14]   Sigmund Freud, 'The Psycho-Analytic View of a Psychogenic Disturbance of Vision', S.E. vol. XI, pp. 214–15; see also Sigmund Freud, 'Instincts and Their Vicissitudes', S.E. vol. XIV, pp. 123–5.

romantic love.[15] The claim is that the child's relationship to its primary caregiver (principally its mother) constitutes the 'prototype' of all later love objects and all later quests for love: the finding of an object (in other words, the experience of falling in love with another person) is a refinding of it (a response to some individual who resuscitates in us memories of that caregiver and of long gone pleasures at the breast). As with so many other of his conjectures (for example, concerning religion or morality), Freud is intent upon emphasizing the determining role of child–parent relations in a person's subsequent quest for love, and he employs an *ok* extraordinarily visceral image to ram this point home. Noting that all instances of love are 'derived from the infantile fixation of tender feelings on the mother',[16] he draws our attention to the differences between normal and more neurotic types of love. In the former, there is some (more or less) discernible connection between the mother and the new love-object (we will shortly consider the forms that connection may take); in the latter, on the other hand, maternal characteristics are completely *stamped* on the love-object, so that the latter becomes a mother-surrogate. And here Freud draws a comparison with the manner in which the skull of a newly born child is shaped: 'after a protracted labour it always takes the form of a cast of the narrow part of the mother's pelvis.'[17]

As with his view that attention to sexual perversions throws light on so-called 'normal' sexuality, so the explicitly mother-determined choice of object found in neurotic love is seen to illuminate how the romantic choices of all of us are rooted in childhood experiences. Some details of the case history of the patient known as the 'Wolf Man' can also be utilized for this end, showing (again, in exaggerated, neurotic form) how a pattern for loving is laid down in childhood. The conditions in which the Wolf Man falls in love are traceable back to an experience he had when he was just one and a half years old. At that young age, he observed his parents in sexual intercourse. The father was positioned behind the mother, with the mother on her knees before him. At the age of two and a half, the Wolf Man saw a nursemaid scrubbing the floor in a similar position; with her buttocks projecting and her back raised, she 'became his mother to him; he was seized with sexual excitement owing to the activation of this picture'.[18] In adulthood he continues this pattern, his amatory interests provoked by witnessing women in kneeling positions. Freud tells us that, in one such case (one among many) the Wolf Man

[15] Martin Bergmann writes that 'Freud made significant discoveries never made before about love because he looked for love in a place only a few observers before him had thought of looking: in the years of infancy' (Martin Bergmann, *The Anatomy of Loving* (New York, 1987), p. 158).

[16] Sigmund Freud, 'A Special Type of Choice of Object Made by Men (Contributions to the Psychology of Love I)', S.E. vol. XI, pp. 168–9.

[17] Ibid., p. 169.

[18] Sigmund Freud, *From the History of an Infantile Neurosis*, S.E. vol. XVII, pp. 92–3.

'fell in love with the girl instantly and with irresistible violence, although he had not yet been able to get even a glimpse of her face'.[19]

While the idea of the formative potency of early experiences is not, of course, uniquely Freudian – centuries previously, John Aubrey had written that 'Who loses his maidenhead with a bare-legged wench will never run after silk stockings'[20] – the distinctive element of the psychoanalytic perspective is the emphasis upon parental imprints. This is then typically brought into connection with the satisfaction of instinctual needs, as when Freud declares that a child's 'first erotic object is the mother's breast that nourishes it; love has its origin in attachment to the satisfied need for nourishment'.[21] Just as the child's love for its mother is here regarded as resting upon the gratification of needs both sexual and self-preservative, so later romantic relations may also be conceived as gaining their strength and appeal from a comparable satisfaction. Hence, regarding the formation of the family, Freud suggests that this institution arose because of the desire to keep near at hand those objects necessary for genital satisfaction.[22] Here we find a view of love as a fundamentally self-regarding phenomenon, the allure of love being that of the establishing of a relationship in which our keenly felt needs for self-preservation and sexual satisfaction are met. With this conception, one is not too far from Georg Christoph Lichtenberg's pronouncement that it is impossible truly to care for or feel for others: 'One loves neither father, nor mother, nor wife, nor child, one loves the pleasant sensations they produce in us.'[23] Less dramatically stated, love can be regarded as a learned response to people who provide us with satisfying rewards. These people function as 'secondary positive reinforcers', that is as people who fulfil primary needs, such as nourishment, sex and the avoidance of pain.[24] It is important to emphasize the secondary nature of

---

[19]   Ibid., p. 93.

[20]   Quoted by Frank Cioffi in 'Explanation and Biography: A Conversation', in *Freud and the Question of Pseudoscience* (Chicago, IL, 1998), p. 265. In this piece Cioffi trenchantly criticizes the Freudian 'infatuation' with tracing adult behaviour back to early childhood.

[21]   Sigmund Freud, *An Outline of Psycho-Analysis*, S.E. vol. XXIII, p. 188.

[22]   See Freud, *Civilization* (J.R.), pp. 65–7. The point is made in the most graphic terms in *Group Psychology and the Analysis of the Ego*: 'In one class of cases being in love is nothing more than object-cathexis on the part of the sexual instincts with a view to directly sexual satisfaction, a cathexis which expires, moreover, when this aim has been reached; this is what is called common, sensual love. But, as we know, the libidinal situation rarely remains so simple. It was possible to calculate with certainty upon the revival of the need which had just expired; and this must no doubt have been the first motive for directing a lasting cathexis upon the sexual object and for "loving" it in the passionless intervals as well' (Sigmund Freud, *Group Psychology and the Analysis of the Ego*, S.E. vol. XVIII, p. 111.

[23]   This remark is approvingly quoted in Friedrich Nietzsche, *Human, All Too Human* (Cambridge, 1986), p. 71.

[24]   See the discussion of this in Irving Singer, *The Nature of Love: The Modern World* (Chicago, IL, 1987), pp. 347–8.

love in this view: our needs – both self-preservative and sexual – are primary, and the object is loved on the basis of its ability to meet those primary needs.

In his groundbreaking book *Attachment*, John Bowlby refers to the aforementioned view of secondary drive as the 'cupboard love theory of object relations'.[25] Bowlby takes issue with this theory, rejecting Freud's idea that the child's love for the mother is a derivative development constructed upon the mother's gratification of the infant's instinctual needs. Attachment to the mother, he argues, is instead primary and independent of the mother's role as gratifier, the child entering the world with an instinct to participate in social interaction. Bowlby's explanation flows from his biological perspective, and he concludes that, both in human beings and in other species, the original function of attachment behaviour was protection against predators. Such protection is especially vital when an individual is young, sick or pregnant. Attachment behaviour has, therefore, a significant evolutionary purpose, for the survival of vulnerable individuals of a species is greatly assisted by an innate predisposition to hold close to parents and others. Bowlby's conclusions were supported by evidence from other researchers who demonstrated that, in primates other than human beings, the need for attachment and comfort was primary and instinctive rather than derived from a more basic desire for the gratification of nutritional needs. Harry Harlow, for example, famously showed that given a choice between a soft terrycloth mother surrogate yielding no nourishment and a wire surrogate yielding milk, young rhesus monkeys almost universally attached themselves to the former. On this basis, Harlow contended that there was a primary desire for 'contact comfort' that was not derived from the instinctual needs emphasized by Freud.[26] Considerations of this nature, moreover, led Bowlby to contend that intimate attachments to others 'are the hub around which a person's life revolves, not only when he is an infant or a toddler or a schoolchild but throughout his adolescence and his years of maturity as well, and on into old age'.[27] Viewed from this perspective, romantic love can be seen as an example of hardwired attachment behaviour, a primary need distinct from the instincts for nutrition and sexual satisfaction.[28]

For our immediate purposes, the virtue of Bowlby's account is that it allows us to downplay the classical psychoanalytic view of love as a secondary phenomenon while still emphasizing the importance of childhood and infancy for our understanding of the way in which a person's choice of love object might be formed. And Freud still has things of considerable importance to tell us regarding these matters. Hitherto, the lesson we have taken is that a child's relationship to its

---

[25] John Bowlby, *Attachment* (Harmondsworth, 1971), p. 222.

[26] See Harry F. Harlow, *Learning to Love* (New York, 1974), p. 28. See also Bowlby, *Attachment*, pp. 262–4.

[27] John Bowlby, *Loss* (London, 1991), p. 442.

[28] See Robert S. Weiss, 'Attachment in Adult Life', in Colin Murray Parkes and Joan Stevenson-Hyde (eds), *The Place of Attachment in Human Behavior* (New York, 1982), pp. 171–84, and Anthony Storr, *Solitude* (London, 1997), pp. 8–15.

primary caregiver forms the prototype for later love objects (and it should here be stressed that this idea can be presented either in terms of the strict Freudian view concerning love as satisfaction of primary needs or in terms of the attachment view that regards love as non-derivative). In a footnote added to the *Three Essays* ten years after its original publication, however, the picture becomes somewhat less straightforward: 'Psycho-analysis informs us that there are two methods of finding an object',[29] Freud now writes, referring to an idea put forward in his important paper 'On Narcissism'. This deserves our attention.

A central contention in this paper is that before the libidinal drive is directed towards an external object, the infant takes its own body as a sexual object (that is to say, the earliest erotic life of the infant is *auto*-erotic). Hence, the stages of development in the child's love-relationships are twofold: it first of all takes itself as its object of desire, and only subsequently directs its libido outwards, towards its caregiver. As he says, 'We say that a human being has originally two sexual objects – himself and the woman who nurses him.'[30] This two-stage development manifests itself in later erotic relations. Given that the years of infancy are going to provide the prototype of loving, we will find in their later lives people loving according to what Freud calls an attachment (or anaclitic)[31] model. This is what everyone thinks they know about Freud already: a person falls in love with someone who resembles in some fashion their mother or their father. However, the phenomenon of primary narcissism blurs this picture somewhat. It is possible that narcissism can leave its mark, and provide a person with another love object prototype: him- or herself.

This provides the basis for Freud's famous classification of the ways of loving:

> A person may love:—
>> (1) According to the narcissistic type:
>>> (a) what he himself is (i.e. himself),
>>> (b) what he himself was,
>>> (c) what he himself would like to be,
>>> (d) someone who was once a part of himself.
>> (2) According to the anaclitic (attachment) type:
>>> (a) the woman who feeds him,
>>> (b) the man who protects him,
> and the succession of substitutes who take their place.[32]

To amplify this just a little, narcissistic object choices range from what we might call 'easily identifiable' narcissism (in which, true to the mythical derivation of the

---

29   Freud, *Three Essays*, p. 222, n. 1.

30   Sigmund Freud, 'On Narcissism: An Introduction', S.E. vol. XIV, p. 88.

31   The term 'anaclitic type' is the translator's rendering of Freud's *Anlehnungstypus* (literally: 'leaning-on type').

32   Ibid., p. 90.

term, a person is in love with himself and 'treats his own body in the same way in which the body of a sexual object is ordinarily treated'[33]) to cases in which the narcissistic attitude is more indirect. In these latter three cases, we find the love felt for children (one was formerly a child oneself), the love felt for an object representing an idealized version of oneself, and – highly controversially – the only way that narcissistic women can achieve complete object-love (namely by way of an object that was once a part of them: 'In the child which they bear, a part of their own body confronts them like an extraneous object, to which, starting out from their narcissism, they can then give complete object-love'[34]). In comparison with this, the attachment subdivisions are straightforward. Since 'the persons who are concerned with a child's feeding, care, and protection become his earliest sexual objects',[35] one who loves according to the anaclitic model will direct their love towards a person who is reminiscent of their mother, their father or some surrogate parental figure. The nature of this 'refinding of the object' will, of course, be various. Maybe what is refound is the mother's smile, or the colour of her eyes; maybe it is the sense of comfort she provided; and similar things may be said concerning the father: strength, power or authority, in addition to some merely physical feature.

It is little more than a commonplace to state that Freud's account of infantile sexuality is notorious and controversial. Much of the outraged response to it – even among philosophers – is, however, shrill and a little hysterical.[36] On the other hand, Irving Singer's sober judgement concerning Freud's speculations should be registered. Freud, he says, is too hasty in concluding that, purely because an instance of mouth stimulation (thumb-sucking, for example) has no nutritional value, its pleasure must be of a sexual nature. Rather, the most that Freud is justified in inferring from his overview of human development is that 'a great deal of adult sexuality includes traces, sequelae, sometimes duplications of affective occurrences that belong to the individual's earlier life'.[37] Since our discussion of Freud's view of the palliative nature of romantic love is not dependent upon defending the existence of infantile sexuality, I am happy simply to accept that more modest conclusion concerning 'traces, sequelae and duplications'. These traces might, to some extent at least, account for the consoling power of romantic love, which resuscitates the feelings of security, comfort and protection we felt during our most vulnerable years. There need thus be nothing overtly sexual in the original relation to the mother or father, and we are left simply to note that, in matters of love as in so many other things, the child's lengthy period of dependence on its parents leaves its mark. In

---

[33]   Ibid., p. 73.

[34]   Ibid., pp. 89–90.

[35]   Ibid., p. 87.

[36]   Roger Scruton, for example, in an interview with BBC Radio 4 complained that Freud's contention that 'the child comes, as it were, as a fully sexualised being into this world' was akin to 'the thoughts of a paedophile' ('Freudian Slip?', broadcast 3 May 2001).

[37]   Singer, *Modern World*, p. 108.

part, therefore, our search for love can be regarded – analogously, perhaps, with the allure of religious belief – as a nostalgic yearning for our past, an attempt 'to restore the happiness that has been lost'.[38]

After this extended discussion of Freud's second claim, reflection on his third claim need only be brief. This is because he simply reminds us here of what we must already know, namely that the palliative promise of love is compromised by the vulnerable position we occupy once we have attached ourselves, and the fate of our happiness, to another person. Robert Nozick has, I think correctly, suggested that what is common to all instances of love is that '[y]our own well-being is tied up with that of someone (or something) you love',[39] and with this idea in mind we can see all too clearly the dangers of romantic love. If the person I love ceases to love me, or if – and here, terribly, we might properly say *when* – that person sickens and dies, I will succumb to the most dreadful emotional pain, a pain I would have avoided had I refrained from investing my happiness in another person. In addition, the expansion of my concern to include, not merely what happens directly to me, but also the troubles befalling the loved person, has the potential to produce a greater amount of suffering in my life. We will later have cause to return to these matters, but one can already see why, as Freud notes in his treatment of romantic love, 'wise men of all ages have … warned us emphatically against this way of life'.[40] Reflection on the dangers of making oneself dependent upon another might even lead us to a sympathetic entertainment of Napoleon's claim that, in love, the only victory is *escape*.[41]

Merging (and Its Discontents)

Let us return to Freud's memorable remark that the finding of an object is in fact a refinding of it. While the tracing of love's determining factors to the years of infancy is certainly an innovation, the idea that love is (or, at least, might be experienced as) an ecstatic reunification with someone or something previously lost is nothing new. The classic statement of such a view is found in the speech of Aristophanes in Plato's *Symposium*. According to the terms of this mythical account, human beings were originally of a circular nature with eight limbs, two faces and two sets of genitals. Threatened by the strength and vigour of these original humans, Zeus decided to cut each individual in two, producing in such a manner the familiar and current human form. But to be so divided proved a terrible

---

[38]   Freud, *Three Essays*, p. 222.

[39]   Robert Nozick, 'Love's Bond', in Robert M. Stewart (ed.), *Philosophical Perspectives on Sex and Love* (Oxford, 1995), p. 231.

[40]   Freud, *Civilization* (J.R.), p. 69.

[41]   See Napoleon Bonaparte, *Aphorisms and Thoughts* (Richmond, Surrey, 2008), p. 59 ('En amour, la seule victoire, c'est la fuite'). 'Shun this hell', says Propertius likewise (quoted in Irving Singer, *The Nature of Love: Plato to Luther* (Cambridge, MA, 2009), p. 136).

fate for the humans, each of whom 'yearned for the half from which it had been severed',[42] the two parts of the original embracing each other desperately as if they could thereby grow together and become whole once more. This yearning that constitutes love – this 'desire and pursuit of the whole'[43] – was felt not just by the first-generation divided humans of Aristophanes' myth, but is the experience of all later-generation humans too: 'Each of us then is the mere broken tally of a man, the result of a bisection which has reduced us to a condition like that of flat fish, and each of us is perpetually in search of his corresponding tally.'[44] Many popular ideas concerning sexual love (reciprocity, exclusivity, the idea that there is for each of us 'one true mate'[45]) are contained in this myth, but of especial importance to us is the notion that what a lover wants above all is to *merge* with the beloved. This merging of individuals is deemed to lessen the suffering characteristic of a solitary, incomplete state. It is, indeed, a view of this kind that animates Fromm's account of the healing power of love: the full answer to the unbearable problem of a separate, disunited existence lies in 'the achievement of interpersonal union, of fusion with another person, in *love*'.[46]

In Aristophanes' speech, the idea of merging comes to the fore when Hephaestus (the god of blacksmiths and metalworking) asks a pair of lovers what they hope to gain from one another:

'Is the object of your desire to be always together as much as possible, and never to be separated from one another day or night? If that is what you want, I am ready to melt and weld you together, so that, instead of two, you shall be one flesh; as long as you live you shall live a common life, and when you die, you shall suffer a common death, and be still one, not two, even in the next world. Would such a fate as this content you, and satisfy your longings?' We know what their answer would be; no one would refuse the offer; it would be plain that this is what everybody wants, and everybody would regard it as the precise expression of the desire which he had long felt but had been unable to formulate, that he should melt into this beloved, and that henceforth they should be one being instead of two.[47]

In the history of ideas concerning love, this concept of merging has been a dominant notion.[48] Samuel Taylor Coleridge, for example, even defined love in these terms,

---

[42]   Plato, *The Symposium* (Harmondsworth, 1951), p. 61.

[43]   Ibid., p. 64.

[44]   Ibid., p. 62.

[45]   For a discussion of these ideas in relation to the Aristophanic myth, see Soble, *Structure*, pp. 78–90.

[46]   Fromm, *Art*, p. 17.

[47]   Plato, *Symposium*, pp. 63–4.

[48]   See Irving Singer's trilogy on *The Nature of Love* for a full and detailed historical survey of the roots, nature and difficulties of this idea.

holding that love is 'a desire of the whole being to be united to some thing, or some being, felt necessary to its completeness, by the most perfect means that nature permits, and reason dictates'.[49] A total merging of two previously separate individuals is required for this unity to occur: 'Each strives to be the other.'[50] A sentiment of this kind will inevitably remind a reader of the most famous literary expression of love as merging, namely Cathy's dramatic declaration of her love for Heathcliff in Emily Brontë's *Wuthering Heights*: 'I *am* Heathcliff – he's always, always in my mind – not as a pleasure, any more than I am always a pleasure to myself – but as my own being.'[51]

That the characterization of love as a merging of two selves is not merely a mythical or poetic flourish can be seen if we examine the theories of love advanced by two important and sober philosophers of recent years: Robert Solomon and Robert Nozick. Solomon contends that 'the dominant conceptual ingredient in romantic love' is an 'urge for *shared identity*, a kind of *ontological dependency*'.[52] Once the absurd mythology of the Aristophanic conception is stripped away, there can be seen 'a real psychological mechanism'[53] at work in the merging of two individuals. Such merging is possible because individual selves 'are not in fact so individual after all',[54] our fluid identities being formed by way of an extensive network of interactions with others. Since an individual person is thus capable of forming and reforming his or her own character and identity in an intersubjective fashion, the merging required for love – we 'do literally "merge ourselves" in love, for this, and nothing less, is what love is'[55] – is secured by the plausibility of two individuals re-defining their selves in terms of each other. Love is, therefore, 'the mutual creation of self-identity',[56] a process of development in which two people,

---

[49]   Samuel Taylor Coleridge, quoted in Irving Singer, *The Nature of Love: Courtly and Romantic* (Cambridge, MA, 2009), p. 288.

[50]   Coleridge, quoted in Singer, *Courtly*, p. 290.

[51]   Emily Brontë, *Wuthering Heights* (Harmondsworth, 1965), p. 122. It is interesting to note that Simone de Beauvoir sees Cathy's declaration, not as an expression of the merging felt by all genuine lovers, but as, rather, specific to *female* experience, 'the cry of every woman in love': 'the centre of her world is no longer the place where she is, but that occupied by her lover; all roads lead to his home, and from it' (Simone de Beauvoir, *The Second Sex* (Harmondsworth, 1972), p. 663). In this context it is also worth noting the radical contentions of another feminist philosopher, Ti-Grace Atkinson, who sees in heterosexual love the attempt of the powerless to merge with the powerful (for a discussion of Atkinson's view, see Singer, *Modern World*, pp. 419–21; see also Alan Soble, 'Union, Autonomy and Concern', in Roger E. Lamb (ed.), *Love Analyzed* (Boulder, CO, 1997), p. 73).

[52]   Robert C. Solomon, 'The Virtue of (Erotic) Love', in Robert C. Solomon and Kathleen M. Higgins (eds), *The Philosophy of (Erotic) Love* (Lawrence, KS, 1991), p. 511.

[53]   Robert C. Solomon, *About Love: Reinventing Romance for Our Times* (Indianapolis, IN, 2006), p. 63.

[54]   Ibid., p. 197.

[55]   Ibid., p. 64.

[56]   Ibid., p. 203.

growing together, construct a shared self. Rather than being a feeling, love is best regarded as 'an opening up of ourselves, not to the world, but to a single other person, struggling to redefine ourselves in his or her terms'.[57]

While Solomon, as we will later note, stresses how the ever-present tensions between two individuals do not permit a complete merging to occur, Nozick is more sanguine. The love of two people results, he says, 'in the formation of a joint and wondrous enlarged identity for both',[58] a new entity that can be called a 'we'. This 'we' is the product of a new web of shared relationships and concerns that serve to make the lovers less separate. Features of this web include: a pooling of autonomy (crucial life-decisions now being made jointly); a new social identity in which the two people are viewed as a couple rather than as isolable individuals; and, crucially, a uniting of one's own well-being with that of the beloved. This last feature is worth emphasizing. Love, as was earlier noted, places a person at considerable risk, since the 'bad things that happen to your loved one happen to you'.[59] That danger is, however, counterbalanced (and even outweighed) by the benefits flowing from this pooling of well-being. For a start, good things happen to your loved one, too, and you can gain some satisfaction from those. Moreover, your loved one helps you cope with the vicissitudes and misfortunes of life, thus softening the suffering of life: as Nozick notes, 'love places a floor under your well-being; it provides insurance in the face of fate's blows'.[60] This may seem a somewhat prosaic thought when compared with the lofty declarations of romantic poets, but it is not inappropriate, particularly when one is exploring, as we are here, the palliative quality of love, and we will have reason to return to the idea of love as insurance later. A further feature of the bond of love that contributes to a person's well-being is the ecstatic experience of sexual intercourse: 'two persons flowing together and intensely merging, mirror and aid the formation of the *we*.'[61] Once the 'we' has been established, there is a desire for it to continue and persist. Marriage (seen as a 'knitting ... together more fully'[62]) and the incarnation of the 'we' in the form of a home both contribute to this continuation and concretization, as does parenthood: 'As egg and sperm come together, two biographies have become one.'[63]

Both Solomon and Nozick lay stress on the softening of boundaries between two individuals occurring within a loving relationship, this softening being what facilitates the process of merging. The imagery is simple enough to understand. Our everyday interpersonal dealings are conducted according to a structure of formality, with roles, masks, circumspection and protection of personal space all serving as barriers between oneself and others. In the physical, intellectual and

---

57   Ibid., p. 82.
58   Nozick, 'Love's Bond', p. 233.
59   Ibid., p. 232.
60   Ibid.
61   Ibid., p. 233.
62   Ibid., p. 239.
63   Ibid.

emotional intimacy of romantic love, these boundaries are crossed and erased. Freud himself addresses this perceived softening of boundaries when he discusses the psychical origins of an 'oceanic feeling' purported to be experienced by many people (and regarded by Romain Rolland as the very fountainhead of religious sentiments). In Freud's depiction of this feeling of limitlessness, the ego (usually 'an independent unitary thing, sharply outlined against everything else'[64]) senses a loss of its lines of demarcation, a feeling of oneness with the external world resulting. This Freud links with romantic love:

> At its height the state of being in love threatens to obliterate the boundaries between ego and object. Against all the evidence of his senses the man who in love declares that he and his beloved are one, and is prepared to behave as if it were a fact.[65]

As with his other thoughts concerning love, Freud seeks to explain this oceanic feeling by reference to early childhood experiences, this time to the infant's experience of total unity with its mother. During its earliest days, Freud contends, the child does not distinguish its ego from the external world, and this differentiation only occurs in response to certain promptings, such as its inability to make appear at will desired sources of satisfaction (the breast, for example). With this realization, the ego 'detaches from itself the external world',[66] and the division between self and other arises. Our present sense of self is thus 'only a shrunken vestige of a far more extensive feeling – a feeling which embraced the universe and expressed an inseparable connection of the ego with the external world'.[67] If a trace of this more expansive ego-feeling were to remain in (at least some) people, then the resuscitation of that feeling caused by the ecstatic experience of romantic love could account for the sense of fusion purportedly felt by some lovers, and we would, once more, recognize in love the characteristic return to a harmony and a happiness that had previously been lost.

With this explanation, Freud seeks both to account for the oceanic feeling and to indicate the impossibility of any true instantiation of merging. The discrete and entirely physical quality of each person's being will not permit of any such fusion. A stress on the unbridgeable separateness of people links Freud's account with those of other notable critics of the possibility of romantic merging, principally Jean-Paul Sartre and Marcel Proust. For Sartre, both love and sex consist of a futile attempt to overcome, via a desired process of merging, the conflict between two subjectivities. This idea is prominent in the chapter of *Being and Nothingness* concerning 'the look', where Sartre explores the situation he calls 'being-seen-by-

---

[64]　Freud, *Civilization* (J.R.), p. 10.

[65]　Ibid., pp. 10–11.

[66]　Ibid., p. 13.

[67]　Ibid.

the gaze

another'.[68] I experience myself as a subjectivity, but when I am seen by another person I become for him or her an object. Ashamed by our reduction to the status of a mere object in another's visual field, we seek for a strategy that will place us once more at the centre of the world. Love appears to offer just such a solution to this humiliating problem, since when another person loves us we are regarded by them as so much more than just another object in the world: in love, we become for that other person exceptional, 'the unsurpassable', 'the very condition of the upsurge of a world'.[69] Before being loved, our existence is felt to be gratuitous (an 'unjustifiable protuberance'[70]); once loved, we are justified and saved from objectification. The uselessness of this enterprise, according to Sartre, results from its mutuality: what each person desires is to be loved, rather than to love, and thus in this 'system of indefinite reference',[71] the lovers can never give each other what is required. The 'fusion of consciousnesses'[72] desired in love cannot therefore occur. Another layer of Sartre's critique stresses, more simply, the unavoidable struggles perpetually woven into romantic relationships, notably the tension between wanting to be free and independent while also bound to another.[73] In amatory relations, no less than in all our dealings with others, the 'essence of the relations between consciousnesses is … conflict'.[74]

Selfishness ✓

In Proust we find a comparable picture of the impossibility of attaining that which love promises. In *Remembrance of Things Past*, love is depicted – just as Fromm depicts it – as an attempt to overcome our separateness as individuals and to penetrate into 'the secret' of another.[75] Proust's narrator, Marcel, first recognizes this painful separateness one evening when his mother, entertaining guests, fails to deliver to him his cherished good night kiss. Marcel's subsequent quest for love takes the form of an attempt to re-create the original unity he sensed with his mother, but to no avail. Two things stand intractably in the way of love's attempts at merging with another. First, Proust contends that what is loved is not the individual him- or herself, but rather a personal assemblage of images and fantasies projected on to the blank canvas of another human being, who is actually

---

[68] Jean-Paul Sartre, *Being and Nothingness* (New York, 1956), p. 257.

[69] Ibid., p. 369.

[70] Ibid., p. 371.

[71] Ibid., p. 376.

[72] Ibid.

[73] Solomon likewise stresses – though without Sartre's sense of despair – this 'dialectical tension between union and individuality', referring to it as 'the paradox of love' (Solomon, *About Love*, p. 198; see also Irving Singer, *Philosophy of Love: A Partial Summing-Up* (Cambridge, MA, 2009), pp. 89–93). A 'paradox of love' is voiced also by Fromm, who sees it, one might say, in almost theological terms, with all the mystery that inevitably entails: 'In love the paradox occurs that two beings become one and yet remain two' (Fromm, *Art*, p. 19).

[74] Sartre, *Being*, p. 429.

[75] See Fromm, *Art*, pp. 27–9.

to the lover an 'almost unknown object', 'scarcely more than a silhouette'.[76] As a result, one is never truly even in contact with the loved person, let alone engaged in a process of merging or fusion. We will return to this thought when we examine the phenomena of transference and idealization later in this chapter. One might take issue with this first claim and the theory of (the impossibility of) interpersonal relations upon which it rests, but Proust's second challenge to the idea of romantic merging is independent of the first and is in itself compelling. He recognizes that, when in love, a person has a very strong desire to fuse their life with that of the beloved, but this desire can never be fulfilled, since there are always parts of the other's life and mind that remain dark and forever elusive to the lover. This emerges powerfully in Marcel's description of his inability to penetrate into the soul of Albertine Simonet. In her he senses 'regions more inaccessible to me than the sky, in which Albertine's memories, unknown to me, lived and moved'.[77] It is this thought of the other's past experiences that proves most heartrending: Albertine 'existed on so many planes and embodied so many days that had passed' that there accordingly 'yawned like a gulf the inexhaustible expanse of the evenings when I had not known [her]'.[78] Of course, you may hold a beloved person in your arms, and even spend every moment of your life with that adored being, but you will remain forever separate, the loved object being 'no more than the sealed envelope of a person who inwardly [reaches] to infinity'.[79]

A common pattern is discernible in the claims of both Sartre and Proust: love is properly to be regarded as the longing for a merged union with another person; this union would bring about a resolution to one or other of the wrenching difficulties of our condition (separateness, perhaps, or the threat of objectification); the conditions under which merging would occur are, however, unrealizable; as a result, love is a futile endeavour. The despairing conclusion follows, of course, only if one accepts that love *is* properly to be regarded in terms of merging or fusion, and there is really no good reason to accept that at all. Despite its perennial appeal, the idea of merging can be shown to be both confused and a misrepresentation of the actual dynamics of a loving relationship.

It is easy enough to see why the thought of merging should have come to occupy such a prominent position in our shared ideas about love. The yearning of lovers, as Aristophanes rightly depicts, is never to be apart, never to let anything (any distance, any disagreement, anyone else) come between them, and what better way for that to be achieved than to cease to be two distinct identities and instead fuse into one enlarged and wondrous whole? Moreover, a hint of that

---

[76]   Marcel Proust, *Remembrance of Things Past* (3 vols, Harmondsworth, 1983), vol. 1, p. 917.

[77]   Ibid., vol. 3, p. 393.

[78]   Ibid.

[79]   Ibid. For excellent discussions of Proust, see İlham Dilman, *Love and Human Separateness* (Oxford, 1987), pp. 93–108, and Singer, *Modern World*, pp. 159–218.

oneness is found in 'the molten intensity of sexual intimacy',[80] in which, for a while at least, two identities seem to move together in united and ecstatic harmony, the unparalleled pleasure of the sexual act maybe producing an inchoate longing for a more permanent fusion. But to move from these feelings to a full theory of merging is to ignore the context within which lovers' declarations of union arise and have their sense. According to the later Wittgenstein, it is the neglect of such contextual matters – a disregard of what he calls the '*environment* of a way of acting'[81] – that leads to all manner of philosophical confusions. These confusions arise 'when language *goes on holiday*',[82] or 'when language is like an engine idling, not when it is doing work'.[83] In such a manner arise typical philosophical problems concerning (for instance) time and being, and these problems are to be dissolved by attending to the *use* made of the words 'time' and 'being' in their everyday (non-metaphysical) context. This diagnosis can fruitfully be applied to philosophical talk of love as a literal merging, as when Solomon plays with an analogy between the union of two lovers and the fusion of two independent atoms forming a molecule,[84] or when Mark Fisher writes that fused lovers 'perceive, feel and act as a single person',[85] neither party being able to tell each other's feelings and perceptions apart. But when two lovers, over a candlelit dinner or during lovemaking, declare to each other their unified being, their words do not describe a process that may or may not be a possible one, but rather constitute an expression of their love. It is, simply, one of those things that lovers, at certain times, say to one another, and indicates such things as shared goals, a shouldering of each other's joys and burdens, a resolute determination to stand by one another come what may, and so on. To extract the idea of merging from that context and then to raise theoretical questions about how two identities can fuse together, or how two persons can be so conjoined that they experience the same perceptions, is to be led astray ('bewitched', as Wittgenstein says[86]) by language; it leads discussions about love into darkness, mystification and seemingly endless disputes. The kind of context-specific clarity advocated by Wittgenstein might have the same effect on philosophical discussions of love 'as sunlight has on the growth of potato shoots. (In a dark cellar they grow yards long.)'[87]

---

[80] Singer, *Courtly*, p. 392.

[81] Ludwig Wittgenstein, *Remarks on Frazer's Golden Bough* (Retford, 1979), p. 16.

[82] Ludwig Wittgenstein, *Philosophical Investigations* (Oxford, 1953), §38.

[83] Ibid., §132.

[84] Solomon, *About Love*, p. 65.

[85] Mark Fisher, *Personal Love* (London, 1990), p. 28.

[86] See Wittgenstein, *Philosophical Investigations*, §109.

[87] Ludwig Wittgenstein, *Philosophical Grammar* (Oxford, 1974), p. 381. See in the context of this paragraph's discussion Irving Singer's critique of the misleading analogies involved in the idea of merging (see Irving Singer, *The Pursuit of Love* (Baltimore, MD, 1994), pp. 22–30, and Singer, *Philosophy of Love*, pp. 17–20). If oneness is to be spoken of, he says, it should best be seen not as a kind of chemical fusion, as in the

In addition to being a confused notion, the idea of love as merged identity distorts the character of a romantic relationship. One of love's most wonderful features is the fact that a human being, usually occupied with his or her own concerns and well-being, expands that circle of concern to include the well-being of another. Soble refers to this quality of love as 'robust concern': 'x desires for y that which is good for y, x desires this for y's own sake, and x pursues y's good for y's benefit and not for x's (a corollary: sometimes at possible loss to x).'[88] If robust concern for another is indeed definitive of love (and it is reasonable to believe that it is), then such an idea is incompatible with the notion of merged union, since in this latter concept there are no longer two persons and only one. Love of another becomes love of oneself, and this egoistic turn, as Soble remarks, 'must dampen our enthusiasm for love'.[89] İlham Dilman concurs: 'Just as my left hand cannot take what my right hand is giving, or my right hand give it to my left hand, so equally I cannot really love someone with whom I have identified myself to the extent that I do not feel her to have an identity apart from mine.'[90] Insuperable problems therefore attend any attempt to conceive love in terms of a merging of identities and these go far beyond the criticisms of its attainability lodged by the likes of Sartre and Proust. Merging is an entirely confused philosophical notion, springing from a failure to attend to the context of declarations of love, this failure giving rise to unintelligible attempts to explain fused identity (what sense, really, can be made of Fisher's claim that two lovers do not know whose idea it was to go to the cinema, or which of the two perceived that beautiful sunset a few evenings previously?) and it undermines the wondrous reality of a loving relationship, namely that distinct persons come to care so deeply about the happiness of each other. One might go so far as to say that the ideal of fused identity is nothing short of a grotesquery, comparable indeed to Ovid's depiction of the merging of Salmacis and Hermaphroditus, their bodies monstrously amalgamated, 'one body, one face, one pair of arms / And legs, as one might graft branches upon / A tree.'[91] When one thinks about what merging 'literally' means, whether a physical merging or the indistinguishability of mental contents, the grounds for fleeing from this idea of love as 'the development of a single fused individual' multiply.[92]

From the perspective of thinking of love as a palliative, there is a further good reason for dispensing with a conceptualization of love that is at best unattainable and at worst unintelligible. The notion of fused identities has become a prevalent idea of what love really means, but if – as it must – that aim proves impossible,

---

production of salt out of sodium and chloride, but as perhaps akin to a political union such as the United States, in which each state retains its distinct character while also being united with the rest in crucial ways.

[88]   Soble, 'Union', p. 68.
[89]   Ibid., p. 69.
[90]   Dilman, *Love*, pp. 105–6.
[91]   Ovid, *Metamorphoses* (New York, 1958), p. 122.
[92]   Fisher, *Personal*, p. 27.

then people labouring under its misconceptions may come to feel that their love relationship is deficient. Fisher tells me that my beloved and I are so melded that we can no longer distinguish each other's beliefs, tastes, acts and perceptions apart. Must I now worry that we do not truly love one another because I can distinctly remember that it was me (and not her) who walked the dogs earlier in the day? Must a doubt settle over the authenticity of our love due to the fact that our musical tastes do not entirely coincide? Must fights and rows be seen, not as the inevitable consequence of two prickly individuals negotiating a collaborative life together, but as a disastrous failure of coalescence, maybe even a sign that this is not genuine love at all? It is easy to see how fixation on the ideal of merging might thus introduce no small degree of suffering into a person's life were they to fret over those matters, and this would attenuate love's palliative function. Hence, grand sounding but ultimately incomprehensible accounts of love should best be jettisoned and replaced by more modest conceptions. Such conceptions are not hard to find, and indeed constitute the reality of romantic relationships, as opposed to the highfalutin abstractions advanced by the advocates of merging. In the notion of robust concern, for example, or in Singer's replacement of merging with *wedding* (a 'prosaic joining of human interests'[93]), we are brought face to face with the reality of love as we experience it in ourselves and in others: two distinct persons, retaining their identities, and yet joining intimately together in a shared experience of life, each one supporting the other through struggles, false steps and illness, each one celebrating the other's joys and triumphs, each taking pleasure in the other's mental and physical being, and (as Singer puts it) 'in general attend[ing] to the being of a person reciprocally attending to one's own'.[94] A loving relationship, modestly thus conceived, would seem to be both intelligible and attainable, its achievement surely amounting to a considerable fortification against some of life's most keenly felt sufferings.

Overvaluation, Crystallization and Transference: The Illusions of Love

The upbeat tone of the previous paragraph might yet be tempered by the suspicion that love is just as enmeshed in illusions as we earlier saw religion to be and, accordingly, just as worthy of our disdain. In Schopenhauer's account we find just such a suspicion. Love is here reduced to a species-serving biological instinct, for 'all amorousness is rooted in the sexual impulse alone, ... however ethereally it may

---

[93] Singer, *Modern World*, p. 370. In George Eliot's touching formulation, there is no greater thing for two human souls than 'to strengthen each other in all labor, to rest on each other in all sorrow, to minister to each other in all pain' (George Eliot, *Adam Bede* (Chicago, IL, 1888), p. 479).

[94] Ibid., p. 390.

deport itself'.[95] On this view, love is simply the device utilized by the will-to-live of our species in order to get men and women to engage in sexual intercourse, thereby ensuring the reproduction of humankind. Egoism is so deeply ingrained in human beings, Schopenhauer thinks, that it is hard to imagine sufficient numbers willing to make the sacrifices entailed by parenthood and necessary for the propagation of the species (not to mention that rational and ethical considerations would lead to the resolution, born of compassion, that one should not bring more lives into a world as terrible as this one).[96] The species overcomes these anti-reproductive impulses by instilling in individuals feelings of love, which, by way of the desire for physical unity with a loved object, leads ineluctably to the real aim of romantic relations: human reproduction. In making this case, Schopenhauer postulates the same dual identity for the human person that Freud was later to describe, when the latter writes that the 'individual does actually carry on a twofold existence: one to serve his own purposes and the other as a link in a chain, which he serves ... involuntarily', the individual thus being 'the mortal vehicle of a (possibly) immortal substance'.[97] In pursuing an amatory relationship, the individual feels that he or she is chasing something beneficial for him- or herself, but this is a delusion, for it is the interests of the species only that are being furthered. This account, moreover, aims to show how love cannot advance an individual's happiness. Firstly, since the interests of the species are stronger than those of the individual, love not infrequently has catastrophic consequences for a person, ruining their career or reputation, or (at the very least) introducing 'disturbance and confusion' into a hitherto well-regulated life.[98] Secondly, once the species' goal has been achieved, the individual experiences a marked disillusionment and 'finds himself duped; for the delusion by means of which the individual was the dupe of the species has disappeared'.[99] A pair of lovers, each of whom had once meant the world to the other, now lose their intoxicated love and at best live together drearily or at worst they separate with bitterness and in animosity. All is well for the species, however, for it has achieved its desire.

Also worthy of our attention are those accounts that seek to expose the illusory idealizations found in romantic relationships. A good starting point is Stendhal's idea of *crystallization*, by which he means 'a certain fever of the imagination which translates a normally commonplace object into something unrecognizable'.[100] The memorable image provided for crystallization (and the inspiration, indeed, for Stendhal's theory) concerns a natural process occurring in the salt mines in Salzburg: the miners throw a leafless wintry bough into one of the abandoned

---

[95]   Arthur Schopenhauer, *The World as Will and Representation* (2 vols, New York, 1969), vol. 2, p. 533.

[96]   See Arthur Schopenhauer, *Parerga and Paralipomena* (2 vols, Oxford, 1974), vol. 2, p. 300.

[97]   Freud, 'On Narcissism', p. 78; compare Schopenhauer, *World*, vol. 2, p. 538.

[98]   Schopenhauer, *World*, vol. 2, p. 534.

[99]   Ibid., p. 540.

[100] Stendhal, *Love* (London, 2004), pp. 64–5, n. 1.

shafts and when it is drawn out two or three months later it has been, through the effect of the salt-saturated water flowing over it, covered with a shiny deposit of crystals. The original modest twig is now no longer recognizable, having become a thing of crystalline beauty. The analogy Stendhal wishes to draw is clear to see: a beloved person, as he or she is in reality, is like the bough in its previous, unadorned state; the crystals later encrusting the little twig are the beloved's unique and unsurpassable qualities as imagined by the lover. The beloved is, in this sense, entirely a creation of the lover, who, under the influence of passion, fails to see or encounter that person and their objective characteristics: 'from the moment you begin to be interested in a woman, you no longer see her *as she really is*, but as it suits you to see her.'[101] We witness therefore – just as we witness in religion – a marked contrast between a stern reality and a 'wonderful inner vision'[102] projected onto it, that projection being taken (and mistaken) for things as they really are. Nietzsche's words here come to mind: 'Love is the state in which man sees things most of all as they are *not*.'[103] Unlike the beneficent illusions of art, which as we earlier saw are rarely if ever confused with reality, the illusions of both religion and love constitute a confusion of reality with desire-driven falsifications.

Freud refers to this falsification of judgement as *idealization*, connecting it with 'the phenomenon of sexual overvaluation – the fact that the loved object enjoys a certain amount of freedom from criticism, and that all its characteristics are valued more highly than those of people who are not loved, or than its own were at a time when it itself was not loved'.[104] This overvaluation is a familiar enough thing, and we have all experienced it. One's beloved is not simply attractive, smart and at times amusing, but rather the most beautiful person in the world, the most incisively intelligent, and absolutely hilarious, his or her physical features not simply pleasing but perfect, the very product, perhaps, of divine workmanship. To those untouched by the amatory feeling, the lover's evaluation of his or her beloved's qualities will seem exaggerated and mysterious, and if the love fades the lover will be bemused that unexceptional traits and features had for a time proved so utterly captivating. Freud's explanation for this process of overvaluation emphasizes, once again, both the legacy of childhood and those narcissistic and/ or anaclitic tendencies earlier examined. Hence in one place he explains that the loved object 'is being treated in the same way as our own ego, so that when we are in love a considerable amount of narcissistic libido overflows on to the object',[105] overvaluation of the beloved being thus an extension of our own egoistic and self-directed overvaluation. In the anaclitic alternative, the exaggerated idealization of the beloved is rooted in the infant's attachment to its mother: 'The trait of

---

[101] Ibid., p. 287.

[102] Ibid., p. 54.

[103] Friedrich Nietzsche, *Twilight of the Idols and the Anti-Christ* (Harmondsworth, 1968), p. 133.

[104] Freud, *Group Psychology*, p. 112.

[105] Ibid.

overvaluing the loved one, and regarding her as unique and irreplaceable, can be seen to fall just as naturally into the context of the child's experience, for no one possesses more than one mother, and the relation to her is based on an event that is not open to any doubt and cannot be repeated.'[106]

This explanation of idealization can further (and dramatically) be developed by reference to the clinical phenomenon of *transference*. Freud found that his patients typically began to develop erotic feelings towards him (and other analysts reported the same experience, sometimes with catastrophic results). Freud concluded, modestly, that the ubiquity of these patients' amorous feelings was not due to his own overpowering sexual magnetism, but was instead an inevitable outcome of the psychoanalytic situation, that situation in which a therapist listens attentively to the free ranging thoughts and associations of a patient, the former only occasionally interjecting questions and interpretations. What happens, Freud contends, is that feelings, attachments and desires developed in childhood are projected onto the figure of the therapist, who becomes thus a screen upon which memories, fantasies and models of love are projected:

> What are transferences? They are new editions or facsimiles of the impulses and phantasies which are aroused and made conscious during the progress of the analysis; but they have this peculiarity, which is characteristic for their species, that they replace some earlier person by the person of the physician. To put it another way: a whole series of psychological experiences are revived, not as belonging to the past, but as applying to the person of the physician at the present moment.[107]

What the patient is required to realize is that the feelings felt towards the analyst (whether these are feelings either of love or of hatred) are not really to do with the analyst at all, but are feelings directed towards some early love-object and simply resuscitated by the peculiarity of the analytic situation. In an important paper on this subject, Freud accordingly writes that transference-love is a kind of hallucinatory (or fake) love. Disconcertingly, however, he proceeds to blur that very distinction between transference-love and 'normal' or 'real' love:

> It is true that [transference] love consists of new editions of old traits and that it repeats infantile reactions. But this is the essential character of every state of being in love. There is no such state which does not reproduce infantile

---

[106] Sigmund Freud, 'A Special Type', p. 169.

[107] Sigmund Freud, 'Fragment of an Analysis of a Case of Hysteria', S.E. vol. VII, p. 116. Note another definition which brings out the illusory nature of this experience, transference being defined as 'a specific illusion which develops in regard to the other person, one which, unbeknown to the subject, represents in some of its features a repetition of a relationship towards an important figure in the person's past' (Joseph Sandler, Christopher Dare and Alex Holder, *The Patient and the Analyst* (London, 1973), p. 47).

prototypes. It is precisely from this infantile determination that it receives its compulsive character, verging as it does on the pathological.[108]

With this, the promise of love – that 'refinding of an object' – turns sour. Rather than the ecstatic union with a person who complements or completes us, we find instead in love a desperate engagement, not with a person actually present, but with traces of childhood experiences and figures forever lost: not the merging of souls, but instead the merely tangential relation of two 'solitary fantasy systems'.[109] Our lovers are <u>revenants</u>. *(one that comes back after an absence.)*

In terms of the mitigation of unhappiness, there may be some benefit in highlighting these illusory aspects of love. The pain of heartbreak, after all, of being spurned and rejected by a loved person, could well be alleviated by the Proustian thought that

> … this love of ours, in so far as it is a love for one particular creature, is not perhaps a very real thing, since, though associations of pleasant or painful musings can attach it for a time to a woman to the extent of making us believe that it has been inspired by her in a logically necessary way, if on the other hand we detach ourselves deliberately or unconsciously from those associations, this love, as though it were in fact spontaneous and sprang from ourselves alone, will revive in order to bestow itself on another woman.[110]

If what we call our love is really just a solitary fantasy system projected on to a person, then any number of individuals could serve as alternative screens. Comparably, if we become convinced that overvaluations and crystallizations transform an objectively commonplace person into a unique and unsurpassable object, then the pain of unrequited or lost love may be treated by undoing that process of overvaluation, by engaging, in other words, in a process of *de-crystallization*.

Ovid and Lucretius, each a warrior in the struggle against the illusions of love, demonstrate how this de-crystallization may be effectively wielded. Lucretius, first of all, enumerates the falsifications of love's exaggerated judgements, how faults become transformed into delights (a stringy lover is 'lithe as a gazelle', a speech impediment becomes 'a charming lisp', and so on). The process of escape from the pain of love is, accordingly, conducted along precisely the same lines, though this time in reverse. Lucretius thus instructs us to 'concentrate on all the faults of mind or body of her whom you covet and sigh for',[111] and Ovid concurs:

> Decry, as best you can, your girl's attractions

---

[108] Sigmund Freud, 'Observations on Transference-Love (Further Recommendations on the Technique of Psycho-Analysis III)', S.E. vol. XII, p. 168.

[109] Janet Malcolm, *Psychoanalysis: The Impossible Profession* (London, 1982), p. 6.

[110] Proust, *Remembrance*, vol. 1, p. 691.

[111] Lucretius, *On the Nature of the Universe* (Harmondsworth, 1951), p. 166.

And let your judgement fall on the wrong side.
She's buxom, call her fat …
  Her figure's slender, say she's lank and lean …
Then too whatever talent the girl's short of
  Keeping coaxing her to demonstrate its charms.
If she's no voice, insist upon her singing,
  And make her dance if she can't move her arms.
Her accent's bad? Keep her in conversation;
  She hasn't learnt to play? Call for the lyre.
She waddles? Make her walk.[112]

But what if the beloved's features have not been exaggerated by love's falsifying stare? We are given an answer:

[S]uppose her face in fact is all that could be desired and the charm of Venus radiates from her whole body. Even so, there are still others. Even so, we lived without her before. Even so, in her physical nature she is no different, as we well know, from the plainest of her sex.[113]

Illusions of uniqueness and perfection thus dispelled, the lover's suffering is eased.

Regarding these views of love's illusions, two criticisms may briefly be noted. First, it might plausibly be said that though idealization undeniably occurs, it is largely a feature of the condition of *falling in love*, and less of a presence in the more stable, realistic conditions of what might be called *being* in love (or *staying*, *standing*, *persisting* in love). Given the high drama of the heady experience of falling in love, overly idealistic conceptions of the beloved and his or her features naturally arise. When a couple has persisted in love for a great many years, living together and sharing all manner of thoughts, experiences and burdensome domestic chores, illusory overvaluation is harder to maintain. Each becomes perfectly aware of the other's faults and limitations and in such conditions it is harder to say that idealizations predominate (even though love persists). A second criticism contends that idealization is by no means always a thing to be avoided. Solomon, for example, holds that love in part constitutes 'a transcendence and an enrichment of mundane reality',[114] and that idealizing one's beloved (within limits, of course)[115]

---

[112] Ovid, 'The Cures for Love', in *The Love Poems* (Oxford, 1990), pp. 159–60.

[113] Lucretius, *Nature*, p. 167.

[114] Solomon, *About Love*, p. 161.

[115] There is evidently a difference between idealizing (or overvaluing) some real feature of the beloved and having an entirely illusory conception of an adored person's nature. Don Quixote's idea of Dulcinea del Toboso as a noble woman who manifests 'all the impossible and chimerical attributes of beauty' contrasts sharply with Sancho Panza's accurate experience of her as quite simply a 'brawny girl' (Miguel de Cervantes, *Don Quixote* (Harmondsworth, 1950), pp. 100 and 209 respectively). Lacking any connection

is to this end preferable to a purely objective evaluation of that person's qualities. The contrast Singer draws between appraisal and bestowal may here be useful in illuminating these matters. In appraisal, value is *discovered* in things or in people (and if love of another person is viewed in these terms, then the idealizations of that other will be viewed as lacking objectivity and enmeshed in illusions; the valuation of that person will be precisely an *over*valuation); in bestowal, value is *created* by means of a relationship of appreciation that has been established with a person. Appraisive judgements are not absent in amatory relationships (for love is never entirely blind), but bestowal transcends mere appraisal, conferring significance upon a person over and above their objective value. In the notion of bestowal, therefore, we find what is perhaps best regarded as a middle position between purely objective evaluation on the one hand and illusory overvaluation on the other, and this captures something crucial about love, when we engage our own life with that of someone who has taken on an incomparable value for us.[116]

Weighing the Palliative Value of Love

Love occupies such an important position in the lives of human beings that it is frequently portrayed in extravagant fashion. Two such extravagances are the claims that love results in (or at least aims at) a merging or fusion of two hitherto distinct persons and that it possesses a healing power. The faults in the theory of merging have already here been enumerated, and its grandiosity deserves to be replaced by a more modest (and, indeed, more accurate) conception of love as the robust concern of two distinct (that is, unmerged) individuals for one another. In the claim that love heals we find another idea which, though born of exemplary reverence towards love, should best be jettisoned in favour of another, more low-key conception. Nozick advances the extravagant view: 'In the full intimacy of love, the full person is known and cleansed and accepted. And healed.'[117] It is not hard to see where this is headed. When we speak of healing, we generally refer to a process of repair, restoration or cure, so on this view love must constitute a kind of curative treatment taking a person from a damaged, incomplete or afflicted condition to one in which the painful problem has been eradicated. That process is most clearly expressed in Fromm's account of love, in which the central problem of human existence – our separateness – is cured by the establishment of a loving relationship with another person. It is no surprise, then, that the notion of healing is closely allied with that of merging, and subject to the same weaknesses: if healing

---

to the truth of the matter, Don Quixote's conception can properly be regarded as merely illusory. Fortunately, idealizations are rarely so thoroughly divorced from reality.

[116] The contrast between appraisal and bestowal runs throughout Singer's writings on love. For a preliminary discussion, see Singer, *Plato*, pp. 3–22.

[117] Nozick, 'Love's Bond', p. 234.

consists of merging, and merging is unattainable or even unintelligible, then this kind of healing will be abortive.

It is important to note that Freud himself spoke on occasion of love's healing power, but the trajectory of his thoughts on this matter takes us to a very different place than that envisioned by the advocates of merging. In his study of Jensen's short story *Gradiva*, Freud speaks of love as a transformative experience, in which a person's capacity to love is liberated by an amatory relationship with another, thereby producing a reanimation of an individual hitherto languishing. This he links to the goal of psychotherapy, itself pursuing 'a cure by love'.[118] Before we become overly excited by Freud's upbeat tone, two things are to be stressed. First, the concept of cure (and the role of loving relationships in producing such a cure) was focused by Freud (and others[119]) upon the treatment of specific instances of neurotic distress and not upon anything as grand as 'the problem of human existence' itself. Given the multiple problems of that human condition, it is hard even to begin to comprehend what a cure for that might look like. Secondly, it should be remembered that Freud's claims for therapeutic success were tempered by a recognition that the human condition was indeed so profoundly painful that nothing like a complete healing could be expected: the purpose of therapy, he tells us in the *Studies on Hysteria*, is to take a person from a condition of hysterical misery to one of common human unhappiness.[120] We need, moreover, to remind ourselves that our aim here is not to think of love as a cure for human ills, but simply as a palliative, as a non-curative alleviator of suffering, as something with an auxiliary function, stopping a person from entirely collapsing under the weight of life's troubles. Our enquiry, accordingly, retreats from the grandiose question about love's ability to heal and focuses instead upon a more modest one: how effective is love as a palliative?

As we earlier saw in relation to intoxicants, certain painful accompanying effects can attenuate the palliative quality of an auxiliary structure. Something similar might be said of amatory relations. After all, everyone knows the pain love can cause. A number of these painful effects might actually ensue simply from overblown and unattainable expectations, and the ideal of merging was earlier in part dismissed on those grounds. But society has placed such a great weight on love's ability to deliver all that is required for a happy (or at least tolerable) life that it is probably unable to support that burden. As Lisa Appignanesi has observed, romantic relationships are now expected to deliver all 'the goods of earthly paradise ... fulfilling unruly sexual and romantic dreams as well as the

---

[118]   Sigmund Freud, *Delusions and Dreams in Jensen's 'Gradiva'*, S.E. vol. IX, p. 90.

[119]   See, for example, Anthony Storr, 'The Concept of Cure', in Charles Rycroft (ed.), *Psychoanalysis Observed* (London, 1966), pp. 51–84, in which two factors (the adoption of some narrative with which the patient can make sense of his distress, and the establishment of a fruitful personal relationship) are seen as crucial to a recovery from neurotic anguish.

[120]   See Sigmund Freud and Josef Breuer, *Studies on Hysteria*, S.E. vol. II, p. 305.

X not the same as love ?

high callings of friendship and self-realization'.[121] We are led to expect too much from romance – a best friend, domestic tranquillity, invariably great (and frequent) sex, a total 'acceptance and cleansing' of one's own being, and so on – and risk being painfully disappointed. More reasonable expectations should result in less suffering. But this is not to deny that love, even on a moderate conception, is an unalloyed source of happiness and satisfaction: 'reciprocal torture' is how Proust describes it,[122] while the singer Townes Van Zandt, voicing that perennial theme of country and western music, concluded that 'love is just basically heartbreak'.[123] Locating the pains of love within the larger context of the dreariness of life, a person may even see love, in Baudelaire's words, as 'an oasis of horror in a desert of boredom'.[124] While these may all be exaggerations, one cannot ignore the peculiar kinds of pain love engenders.

What a source / or sources

The most extreme of these pains would appear to be the conspicuous disturbance of one's mental stability wrought by love, that feature that has led so many thinkers to describe love as a rather specific kind of madness.[125] Beyond that general state (again, probably best understood as limited to the state of *falling* in love), there are the many particular kinds of pain associated with love. Some of these – such as the specific vulnerability produced by opening ourselves up to another and placing our happiness at their mercy – we have already noted, but more can be added. There is, for example, the experience of jealousy in which a disagreeable emotion such as panic ensues from the understanding or suspicion that one's love object has developed (or is in the process of developing) a romantic attachment to another.[126] Then we have the whole range of small anxieties so brilliantly dissected by Roland Barthes in *A Lover's Discourse*: the rising sense of alarm caused by waiting longer than expected for a phone call or at a rendezvous, for example, or the obsessive attention to pauses and phrases in the object's speech,

---

[121] Lisa Appignanesi, *All About Love: Anatomy of an Unruly Emotion* (London, 2011), p. 172.

[122] Proust, *Remembrance*, vol. 3, p. 105.

[123] Townes Van Zandt, liner notes to 'A Far Cry From Dead', Arista Records, 1999.

[124] Charles Baudelaire, *Les Fleurs du Mal* (New York, 1992), p. 101.

[125] See, for example, Plato's depiction of the lover as a person 'who from the very nature of things is bound to be out of his mind' (Plato, *Phaedrus* (Harmondsworth, 1973), p. 41). See also Stendhal's sustained account of love as a 'disease of the soul', and 'a madness which nevertheless provides man with the greatest pleasures the species can know on earth' (Stendhal, *Love*, pp. 26, 49).

[126] Daniel Farrell's definition of jealousy is precise and brings out well the pain of the experience: 'someone, A, believing that someone else, B, is attached or attracted to them romantically, and wanting B to continue to remain so attached, comes to believe (or at least suspect) that B has begun to become attached (or attracted) to some other person, C, instead, and experiences, because of this belief (or suspicion), one or more of a fairly large number of possible (essentially negative) feelings: panic, for example, or anger, or despair, and so on' (Daniel M. Farrell, 'Jealousy and Desire', in Roger E. Lamb (ed.), *Love Analyzed* (Boulder, CO, 1997), p. 167).

the lover trying to discern whether these indicate a diminution of interest.[127] On the other end of a scale having frenetic anxiety and dreariness as its polarities, one encounters the peculiar pains of domesticity, that setting in which the electrified interaction of two physical beings must, as Balzac noted, 'incessantly contend with a monster which devours everything, that is, familiarity'.[128] The passion that attended the earlier stages of love not infrequently finds it hard to persist in a domestic situation, and this change may bring all kinds of heartache. In thoughts applicable to this matter, Freud contended that a successful romantic relationship is attained by the convergence of two currents – an affectionate current and a sensual current – which must come together 'like the completion of a tunnel which has been driven through a hill from both directions'.[129] Freud's detailing of the failure of these currents to meet occurs during his consideration of impotence and psychanaesthesia (the inability to attain pleasure from sexual intercourse), the separation of these currents in those with such sexual disorders being concisely summarized thus: 'Where they love they do not desire and where they desire they cannot love.'[130] Without exploring further the determinants of such dysfunctions, it might be suggested that the condition of domesticity, despite its many benefits with regard to interpersonal support, may sometimes bring about a de-convergence of the two currents, the affectionate current becoming more dominant while the sensual abates, a degree of tension resulting. Finally, hovering in the background of even the most successful of relationships, there is the gruelling recognition that this love will one day come to an end, when death separates two people who longed so fervently never to part.

We thus can, with Annette Baier, say emphatically that there are no safe loves, romantic relationships commonly bringing emotions harmful both to others (jealousy and hate, for example) and to oneself: 'paralyzing grief or reckless despair at the loss or death of loved ones, retreat into a sort of psychic hibernation when cut off from "news" of them, crippling anxiety when they are in danger, helpless anguish when they are in pain, crushing guilt when one has harmed them, deadly shame when one fails them.'[131] These painful aspects of love are undeniably real, so if love is to function as an effective palliative there had better be pleasurable aspects sufficient to counterbalance or outweigh them. For most people, of course, such things are present in abundance, and barely require enumeration. There are, to begin with, the pleasures of intimate physical and mental contact with another person, and the satisfaction that results from 'being oneself' after all of the guarded interactions with others inevitable in

[127] See Roland Barthes, *A Lover's Discourse* (New York, 1978), especially pp. 37–40.

[128] Honoré de Balzac, *The Physiology of Marriage* (Cirencester, 2005) p. 42.

[129] Freud, *Three Essays*, p. 207.

[130] Sigmund Freud, 'On the Universal Tendency to Debasement in the Sphere of Love (Contributions to the Psychology of Love II)', S.E. vol. XI, p. 183.

[131] Annette Baier, 'Unsafe Loves', in Robert C. Solomon and Kathleen M. Higgins (eds), *The Philosophy of (Erotic) Love* (Lawrence, KS, 1991), pp. 433–4.

our daily lives; and there are the joys of shared plans and shared experiences, pointing out to another a sight or a thought that we might otherwise have had to keep to ourselves. Loving another human being seems also to alter one's overall perception of the world, which appears a better, more congenial place when we love, and often produced is a sense of euphoria that can only elsewhere be found in the state of intoxication.[132] In short, the pleasure, intensity and richness of life found when we love is judged by most to justify the risks inherent in throwing oneself into this vulnerable condition.[133] This is not to say that those who have turned their back on the pursuit of lasting love are in error. As Anthony Storr has argued, we have in recent times underestimated (even stigmatized) the value for many people of a life lived without romantic relationships,[134] while others (such as Frederick Elliston[135]) have highlighted the beneficial quality, not of exclusive and intentionally life-long love, but of a sequence of fleeting sexual relationships. (One might here be reminded of the comedian Bill Hicks' observation that, in order to get through the difficulties of his life, 'it's gonna take one very special woman, you know? Or a bunch of average ones.'[136]) There are still others for whom deep, non-sexual friendships are preferable to romantic love, friendships being more stable and less prone to agitated disturbances. We can accommodate these differences since our project is pluralistic in character: there are many ways that people deal with their troubles, and we pause over romantic love since so many people have opted for that route.

really?

Since we are predominantly concerned with humanity's palliative strategies, it is the role of love in the protection against (and amelioration of) suffering that is crucially to be stressed. As Nozick, in his less extravagant thoughts, had seen, love does indeed 'place a floor' under our well-being. This 'floor' would seem to be achieved both by the presence of another who takes an active role in securing our comfort and by the creation of a secure little world – a home – functioning as a shield against life's troubles, 'an island of coupled safety in a lonely world'.[137] The at-homeness thus experienced contrasts markedly from the cold and sometimes dangerous nature of the world outside and serves as a refuge from it. Beyond that, it may just be – as the attachment theorists duly say – that human beings in the main seek the closeness of another person, such closeness instilling both comfort and a greater happiness in pleasant experiences. Hume's thoughts are here pertinent. Noting that the mind is insufficient for its own entertainment, and that the pleasure of the company of an intimate causes the heart to be elevated, he

---

[132]   See Laurie A. Rudman and Peter Glick, *The Social Psychology of Gender* (New York, 2008), p. 206.

[133]   See Halwani, *Philosophy*, pp. 111–19.

[134]   See Storr, *Solitude*, passim.

[135]   See Frederick Elliston, 'In Defense of Promiscuity', in Robert M. Stewart (ed.), *Philosophical Perspectives on Sex and Love* (Oxford, 1995), pp. 146–58.

[136]   Bill Hicks, *Love All the People* (London, 2004), p. 166.

[137]   Appignanesi, *All*, p. 250.

saw how vital the need for a companion is, in days both happy and sad: 'Every pleasure languishes when enjoy'd a-part from company, and every pain becomes more cruel and intolerable.'[138] Even with (and maybe especially because of) the pessimistic structure of the project of this book, a loving relationship can be regarded as a useful weapon in our fight against the threatening conditions of life, one's beloved now treasured, not simply as a person who shares in our joys, but as a veritable companion in our pain, 'a fellow participant in the suffering of life'.[139] With that participation we will be better armed against all that life will throw at us, and in that participation we find the real value of romantic love, rather than in some grand-sounding though ultimately hollow ideal of healing and merging. One of Freud's many touching letters to his then-fiancée Martha brings this out best of all when he stresses what their living together will bring: 'a being-together throughout all the vicissitudes of life, a quiet contentment that will prevent us from ever having to ask what is the point of living.'[140]

---

[138] David Hume, *A Treatise of Human Nature* (Oxford, 1888), p. 363.

[139] Singer, *Courtly*, p. 463; see also Schopenhauer, *Parerga*, vol. 2, p. 304.

[140] Letter to Martha Bernays (23 October 1883), in Ernst L. Freud (ed.), *Letters of Sigmund Freud* (New York, 1960), p. 71.

Chapter 6
Religion beyond Illusion

The important thing, as Abbé Galiani said to Mme d'Epinay, is not to be cured,
but to live with one's ailments.

Albert Camus

In an earlier (and unremittingly hostile) chapter, the palliative role of religion was
addressed. Accepting the broad outlines of the Freudian and Marxist critiques,
I there presented religion as a desperate response to the defects of existence, a
set of reality-denying, illusory beliefs which are infantile in character and which
undeniably provide consolation but only at the expense of a significant distortion of
reality. It was, however, noted in that chapter that this analysis should not be seen
to apply to *all* instances of religion but only to a very specific, though nonetheless
widespread, variety: namely, to that consoling set of beliefs revolving around the
ideas of a loving and protective divine being, a providential order, and the prospect
of continued existence after death. The judgement that these beliefs are merely
illusions flows from their possession of two suspicion-arousing characteristics: a
lack of evidence in support of their truth (indeed, the fact that they stand in stark
contradiction to what we know of the world), and their correspondence to deeply
held human wishes. The purpose of this concluding chapter is to consider the
possibility of a religious perspective which might retain the auxiliary function of
holding up and supporting human existence but which does this without standing
in denial of the reality of the world as we know it and which is not analysable
purely in terms of wish-fulfilling fantasies. Evidently, one can point to extant
religions consistent with this demand (Theravada Buddhism being an obvious
case in point), but the concern of this chapter is to discern whether aspects of
the Western monotheistic tradition can be salvaged and utilized as the basis for a
mature, non-illusory religious perspective. The motivation informing this chapter,
therefore, is a desire to preserve something both of the legacy of Western religion
(a legacy that has informed and underpinned so much of Western art, thought and
culture) and of the significant role that it has had in aiding people in their lives and
in their sufferings (in other words, its palliative or auxiliary role).

Our task, thus, centres on the possibility of being able to amputate the false
and illusory elements of religion while nonetheless being left with something
recognizably religious and capable still of providing auxiliary support to
individuals struggling with the keenly and painfully felt problems of existence.
We can take some encouragement, and some assurance that this task is not a futile
one, from the lessons gleaned from our previous consideration of humanity's
other palliative measures. In each of these cases, there were seen to be – for want

of better terms – *escapist* and *realistic* implementations or manifestations of the palliative: intoxication is frequently used for escapist purposes of withdrawal from a painful reality, but is also commonly utilized to facilitate more authentic (because less guarded) social interaction with others, and (with a nod to Huxley) maybe even allows an individual to gain a greater degree of self-understanding; art certainly has its escapist and sentimental forms, but great art throws considerable light on the nature of reality and serves to reconcile us to that reality; and few will doubt that romantic love, though so often enmeshed in illusions of transference (Freud) and crystallization (Stendhal), can provide a genuine mitigation of suffering by allowing two distinct individuals, not to merge, but to face life's difficulties together in mutual support and solidarity. Thus far in this book, it is the illusory, escapist dimension of religion that has been the subject of our attention. It now remains to be seen what might be left once religion has been shorn of all escapist characteristics.

True Religion and the Religion of Kitsch

It is to be admitted at the outset that the amputations involved in this process will be extensive. But though very little will be left, what remains may nonetheless be precious. The heart of an artichoke, after all, is rather small, at least when compared with the rest of that vegetable, but it is worth stripping away those unpalatable leaves for the tender prize of what lies within. By the same token, the jewel lying at the heart of religion may be better seen and appreciated once the husk of false and illusory belief has been removed and washed away. We will operate, therefore, with a distinction between true and false religion, a distinction according to which the former is dwarfed by the latter. Echoes of Hume are clearly to be detected here. Hume consistently maintained that his criticisms of religion applied only to a certain type of the phenomenon (which he variously designated as 'corrupt', 'vulgar' or 'popular' religion), and not to 'true religion', the principles of which he claimed to venerate. Falling into the category of the vulgar would appear to be all rituals and all convoluted doctrinal formulae, with true religion constituting something of an inconspicuous remnant, encompassing the simple belief that a deity exists and that one must act on one's moral obligations. In a letter outlining his view, Hume declared his 'Objection both to Devotion & Prayer, & indeed to every thing we commonly call Religion, except the Practice of Morality, & the Assent of the Understanding to the Proposition *that God exists*'.[1] Nor is Hume alone in seeking to strip the least intellectually viable and

---

[1]   Letter to William Mure (30 June 1743), in Raymond Klibansky and Ernest C. Mossner (eds), *New Letters of David Hume* (Oxford, 1954), pp. 12–13. For a detailed discussion of Hume's distinction between 'true' and 'corrupt' religion, see J.C.A. Gaskin, *Hume's Philosophy of Religion* (Basingstoke, 1988), pp. 187–91.

most 'frivolous'[2] elements from religion in order to salvage its most important elements. A great many other thinkers engaged in the task of revisionary theology have sought to expunge from their presentations of religion elements deemed to be outdated, intellectually unacceptable or morally undesirable. Hence, Kant sought to contrast a true religion of moral duty with a 'delusional' and 'counterfeit' faith based on rituals and acceptance of statutory articles. It was, he proclaimed, a 'superstitious delusion to want to become well-pleasing to God through actions that any human being can do without even needing to be a good human being (e.g. by the profession of statutory articles of faith, the observance of ecclesiastical practice and discipline, etc.)'.[3] Once the delusional and extraneous trappings of religion have been expelled, one is left with religion's true heart: inward moral disposition. Likewise, Friedrich Schleiermacher's defence of religion against the criticisms of its 'cultured despisers' consists in downplaying – even dismissing – the literal significance of doctrines, and contrasting these with a conception of religion as a specific kind of *feeling*, namely 'sense and taste for the Infinite'.[4] About Schleiermacher we will later have more to say. As a final example of such revisionary work, we may note the more recent project undertaken by Stewart Sutherland in *God, Jesus and Belief*. There, recognition of the full implications of the problem of evil leads Sutherland to a profound agnosticism about the divine nature and an attendant reigning in of theological pretension and dismissal of the unworkable idea of a personal God. In its place is erected what is found to be the legacy of theism: the preservation of a particular perspective on existence, a view of human affairs *sub specie aeternitatis*.[5]

More important than the specific details of these revisionary projects is a principle at work in such enterprises. That principle is that a viable form of religion can be advanced and defended if certain elements, which, though traditionally present, have been demonstrated to be morally and intellectually indefensible,

---

[2] The charge of frivolity is levelled by Hume in *The Natural History of Religion*: 'It is certain, that, in every religion, however sublime the verbal definition which it gives of its divinity, many of the votaries, perhaps the greatest number, will still seek the divine favour, not by virtue and good morals, which alone can be acceptable to a perfect being, but either by frivolous observances, by intemperate zeal, by rapturous extasies, or by the belief of mysterious and absurd opinions' (David Hume, *The Natural History of Religion* (London, 1956), p. 70.

[3] Immanuel Kant, *Religion Within the Boundaries of Mere Reason*, in *Religion and Rational Theology* (Cambridge, 1996), p. 194.

[4] Friedrich Schleiermacher, *On Religion: Speeches to Its Cultured Despisers* (New York, 1958), p. 39. Schleiermacher's words concerning the revisionary project are here useful. 'Religion', he writes, 'never appears quite pure', and its outward form ('determined by something else') is not to be equated with its 'true nature' (ibid., p. 33). We must learn, then, to look beyond appearances (what might be termed here, adapting Freud's dream terminology, the *manifest content* of religion) to religion's true heart (its *latent* content): 'Did you but know how to read between the lines!' (ibid.).

[5] See Stewart R. Sutherland, *God, Jesus and Belief* (Oxford, 1984).

are excised. The case of Hume is again instructive. Though opinions differ as to the sincerity of his depiction of 'true religion', Hume's strategy can be seen to be an appealing one. A number of features of religion inconsistent with what a supremely perfect divine being would want (frivolous rites, morally-irrelevant 'virtues' such as celibacy and fasting[6]) are to be removed, as are those 'mysterious and absurd' beliefs that are evidentially unsupportable. What is left after the process is a somewhat bare though – and this is what is important – intellectually reputable version of religion: the simple assent to the proposition that there is a God (conceived simply, and without extension, as the cause of order in the universe)[7] and the earnest execution of one's moral responsibilities.

Though in agreement with Hume's strategy of selective excision, I differ with respect to what elements must remain in a variety of religion that is 'true' or, at least, intellectually reputable. Firstly, 'the practice of morality' will not be emphasized in my account since religion has nothing distinctively valuable to offer in this realm. Although there is here insufficient space to explore this in detail, it has for a long time (since the time of Plato indeed) been established that morality depends in no wise upon the existence of a God and has a life independent of religion;[8] since morality ceases thus to be the preserve of religion, a moral perspective cannot be what religion distinctively offers. For that we must look elsewhere. And with regard to the second element of Hume's 'true religion' – namely, assent to the proposition that there is a God – it is precisely beliefs of this nature that are to be jettisoned from our revised account of religion.

It is consistent with the conclusion of this book's earlier chapter on religion to state here that the belief in God – and in particular a loving God, a God having a providential concern for humanity and the world – forms part of a reality-fleeing desire to sugar-coat existence. Here a connection can profitably be made between this wish-driven variety of religious beliefs and the kind of sanitized and sentimental art we previously had reason to consider. As we saw, art of this nature consists of a falsification of reality, a project in which things ugly or disagreeable are erased, and a consoling, idealized version of the world is advanced. We find

---

6   The list of 'monkish virtues' contained in Hume's *Enquiry Concerning the Principles of Morals*, brings this out nicely: 'Celibacy, fasting, penance, mortification, self-denial, humility, silence, solitude, and the whole train of monkish virtues; for what reason are they everywhere rejected by men of sense, but because they serve to no manner of purpose ...?' (David Hume, *Enquiries Concerning Human Understanding and Concerning the Principles of Morals* (Oxford, 1975), p. 270). Kant's censure of 'pious play-acting and nothing-doing' is here also apposite (Kant, *Religion*, p. 192).

7   See David Hume, *Dialogues Concerning Natural Religion* (New York, 1948), p. 94.

8   The question lying at the heart of Plato's *Euthyphro* – aptly adapted by Leibniz as whether what is good and just 'is good and just because God wills it or whether God wills it because it is good and just' (G.W. Leibniz, 'Reflections on the Common Concept of Justice', in *Philosophical Papers and Letters: A Selection* (Dordrecht, 1976), p. 561) – aims to establish that there is no significant informative link between morality and the will of God.

here the exercise of what Milan Kundera referred to as the 'beautifying lie',[9] that characteristic element of all things *kitsch*. Armed with this insight, we might come to see the aforementioned problematic aspects of religion as having a kitsch character, as constituting, in Kundera's terms, an 'absolute denial of shit'.[10] Hence, just as kitsch art shields from us the most unacceptable aspects of reality (those things designated by the word 'shit'), so religious ideas of a wish-driven character negate and distort those self-same troubling elements: the world is not cold and indifferent, but manifests instead a loving, providential order; our existence is not gratuitous or meaningless, but is instead ordained and watched over by the omnipotent ruler of the universe; we do not die and moulder away, but rather our consciousness continues to exist in a blissful hereafter. These pleasant reassurances precisely constitute 'beautifying lies', and it is these elements that will be conspicuously missing in the revised account of religion that follows.[11]

As construed here, religious beliefs of a kitsch nature exhibit two odd characteristics that should arouse a person's suspicions: they conform to how human beings would wish the world to be; and they appear to be cocooned from reality, lacking any significant connection to the world as it is in actuality experienced. With regard to the second characteristic, some aspects of that familiar (though now somewhat neglected) debate concerning falsificationism are here instructive.[12] One of the things brought into prominence by falsificationist critiques of religion was the peculiar resistance of religious beliefs to pieces of empirical evidence patently appearing to disconfirm the truth of those beliefs. So, to take the most obvious and frequently used example,[13] believers will typically contend that God loves human beings as a father loves his children. As with any statement concerning the love of one person for another, however, this contention should be open to testing and possible refutation. In such a manner, for instance, the claim that a particular mother loves her children would (presumably) be falsified by the production of evidence that she consistently belittled them in

---

[9]   Milan Kundera, *The Art of the Novel* (New York, 1988), p. 135.

[10]   Milan Kundera, *The Unbearable Lightness of Being* (New York, 1999), p. 248.

[11]   Pleasant reassurances of this nature are uppermost in Mawson's account of the bounteous extent of God's provision of eternal life: 'If Rachel has a desire to see her sadly deceased pet hamster again, then … it would be less than ideal for Rachel were she to find in Heaven that her hamster had not been brought back to life too … So I see no reason why if there were a God, he would not bring back Rachel's pet hamster for no other reason than that Rachel, as by then a resident of Heaven, wants him to bring it back' (T.J. Mawson, *Belief in God* (Oxford, 2005), p. 102).

[12]   See Brian R. Clack, 'Religious Belief and the Disregard of Reality', in Joseph Carlisle, James C. Carter and Daniel Whistler (eds), *Moral Powers, Fragile Beliefs* (New York, 2011), pp. 261–87.

[13]   See Anthony Flew, 'Theology and Falsification', in Antony Flew and Alasdair MacIntyre (eds), *New Essays in Philosophical Theology* (London, 1955), pp. 98–9, and Michael Martin, *Atheism: A Philosophical Justification* (Philadelphia, PA, 1990), p. 40.

front of other people, thwarted all their plans, inflicted physical harm on them, and so on. We would not understand a person who accepted all of that evidence and yet persisted in claiming that this mother loves her children; indeed, we may suspect that in such a case the word 'love' had been misunderstood, or had lost all of its meaning. Likewise, the theological claim that 'God loves human beings as a father loves his children' would appear to be falsified by the overwhelming data of pervasive human suffering, suffering which an omnipotent loving God would really not permit. And yet this evidence seems to have no impact on the contention that God loves us, which believers persist in proclaiming, even in the face of the most horrific events.[14]

The falsificationist conclusion concerned the cognitive insignificance of religious utterances: since the statement 'God loves us' is compatible with any state of affairs, it asserts nothing and is thus without factual content. I have written elsewhere that the issue of falsifiability (and of verifiability) raises considerable (and as yet unanswered) questions about the meaningfulness of religious assertions.[15] Here, however, my point is of a somewhat more modest nature, namely that the resistance of certain religious beliefs to contrary evidence marks them off as cognitively defective candidates for exclusion from a revised, intellectually reputable version of religion. The criterion for inclusion in this revised version, on the other hand, is that a belief under consideration must be *sensitive to experience*. About this a little more needs to be said.

Cheryl Misak's discussion of David Wiggins' account of the nature of belief will here be our guide. A belief aims at truth: if a person believes x, then that person believes x to be true. But if this is indeed the essence of belief, then the belief that x is true must be sensitive to whether or not x is in fact true; the belief, that is, must be sensitive to 'the ins and outs of some reality or other'.[16] Beliefs must rise and fall, therefore, with experience of that reality: 'the very notion of a belief is such that an inquirer stops believing (i.e. doubts) in the face of a surprising experience that upsets an expectation produced by the belief.'[17] Again: 'Beliefs are such that they automatically resign in the face of recalcitrant experience.'[18] Important things follow from this explication of the persuasive point that a belief must be sensitive to experience:

---

[14]   This is not to deny the considerable energy expended by the theologian in producing defences of God in the face of evil. But even those (notably Basil Mitchell) who have pointed to the theological engagement with the problem of evil as showing that religious believers *do* recognize potentially falsifying evidence have admitted that the believer will not allow anything to count *decisively* against his or her belief in God (see Basil Mitchell, 'Theology and Falsification', in Antony Flew and Alasdair MacIntyre (eds), *New Essays in Philosophical Theology* (London, 1955), p. 103).

[15]   See Clack, 'Religious Belief'.

[16]   David Wiggins, *Needs, Values, Truth* (Oxford, 1998), p. 150.

[17]   C.J. Misak, *Verificationism: Its History and Prospects* (London, 1995), pp. 172–3.

[18]   Ibid., p. 173.

It [a belief] must be in principle sensitive to sensory experience and to experience in diagrammatic, argumentative and theoretical contexts. If an inquirer says that she is going to believe *P*, irrespective of what the evidence is or may turn out to be, she is mistaken in thinking that her propositional attitude is one of belief. There is a distinction between deciding that the evidence favours *P* and thereby believing *P*, and deciding to believe *P*, irrespective of evidence. It is not at all clear that, given what belief is, the latter is possible.[19]

Applying these insights to our earlier, hostile treatment of religion, we might say that such a belief as the one that God loves human beings, since it is inflexible in the face of experience, barely constitutes a belief at all. It is certainly not a reputable belief, and is perhaps better regarded as an imagining, an illusion or even a delusion.[20] Sensitivity to experience is, therefore, our key element in determining whether any putative belief can be admitted into our revisionary account of religion. The consequences of this must now be marked.

Consequences of Sensitivity

It is the problem of evil that most properly sets a limit to religious utterance. Though the problem is a familiar one, it is worth reiterating. There is, at the very least, an apparent contradiction between the existence of God and the presence of suffering in the world. This contradiction is brought to light by elaborating on those divine attributes relevant to the fact of human suffering: God, we are told, is omniscient (so he must know that people suffer); God is omnipotent (so he must be able to put a halt to suffering); and God is all loving (so he must want to put a halt to that suffering). Suffering, however, persists (and to an overwhelming degree), and this must have consequences for belief in a God possessing the aforementioned attributes. The tension between the co-existence of God and evil can be reduced by removing one of the problem-inducing attributes: maybe God is not omniscient and is simply incognizant of suffering; or perhaps he falls short of complete omnipotence, lacking the ability to put an end to suffering; a third possibility is that he does not in fact take a loving interest in human affairs, and is instead indifferent to suffering. This last option (advanced by Hume at the end of the *Dialogues Concerning Natural Religion*) is perhaps the most appealing, given the inherent implausibility of the eternal creator of the universe having a concern for the lives and well-being of tiny and evanescent beings such as ourselves. After all, is there not something irredeemably narcissistic in the notion that my brief and largely insignificant existence should be of concern to a deity? Though sympathetic to the idea of divine indifference, my preferred course of action is simpler. Given

---

[19] Ibid.

[20] On the distinction between belief and delusion, see Gregory Currie and Ian Ravenscroft, *Recreative Minds* (Oxford, 2002), pp. 170–79.

that there is something evidently arbitrary about picking, in the absence of any observational evidence, which attributes God may or may not possess, it seems more economical, in the face of the problem of evil, to deny the existence of God altogether.[21] It is not just the fact of suffering that leads us to this conclusion, of course. The very idea of an immaterial personal being (such as God is contended to be) is precisely the kind of thing that should 'resign in the face of recalcitrant experience': we have no grounds for thinking that an immaterial personal being could exist, as all of our experiences of personal beings are precisely experiences of material beings. These observations, coupled with our prior isolation of the deep wishful desires that generate the idea of God, lead us to a firm denial of the existence of God. The notion of God is not, therefore, to figure in our revised understanding of religion.

It is not just God who needs to be taken down a peg or two. Lofty conceptions of human life and its significance also take a beating when the full implications of the existence of suffering are registered. As we saw in a previous chapter, suffering occupies the place between desire and its fulfilment, signifying the gap between the way one would like life to be and the way it actually turns out. The fact of physical suffering, including the pain of the process of dying, is most strongly indicative of this, and bears witness to the universe's lack of concern for our most fundamental wishes and desires. No person, if they had the power, would write into their destiny the pain and anguish of dying (which, it must be noted, is a very different thing from death itself, something which many would be perfectly happy to accept, particularly when they have grown tired of living). And yet such pain and anguish awaits every one, against our wishes and in denial of them all. The

---

[21]   A formulation of the problem of evil that stresses the contradiction between the existence of God and the presence of suffering is usually referred to as 'the logical problem of evil', since it aims to demonstrate that the propositions 'God exists' and 'Evil exists' are logically inconsistent (see J.L. Mackie, 'Evil and Omnipotence', *Mind*, 64/254 (1955), pp. 200–212). It should not be overlooked that theists have worked hard to resolve this problem, showing that the introduction of some third proposition (concerning, for example, free will or greater goods) can harmonize the apparent inconsistency, thereby dismissing the logical form of the problem of evil (for an example of this strategy, see Alvin Plantinga, *God, Freedom and Evil* (Grand Rapids, MI, 1977), pp. 7–64). The intellectual gymnastics exhibited in such consistency-seeking enterprises arise (in Sutherland's words) 'because the problems of evil and suffering are introduced into the discussion later rather than earlier' (Sutherland, *God*, p. 31). The theologian *starts* with a fully worked-out theology and then has to try – in a rather desperate and 'Procrustean' manner (ibid., p. 25) – to fit that theology to the facts of the world as they present themselves to us. We, on the hand, start from a different place altogether: from the world as we find it, and will not permit anything theological to be said that does not stem from our experience of that world. With Hume, then, we can once again agree that the co-existence of God and evil can be made *compatible*, but the existence of God can certainly not be *inferred* from the facts of the world (of which evil forms such a conspicuous part) (see David Hume, *Dialogues Concerning Natural Religion* (New York, 1948), p. 73; see also Simon Blackburn, *Think* (Oxford, 1999), p. 170).

proper response to this is not the age-old cry of 'Why is this happening to me?', but a due recognition of what such suffering ultimately denotes: that from the point of view of the universe we are as nothing.   *too dramatic*

This conclusion can also be drawn from attention to the significance of that less acute species of suffering considered earlier on in this book: boredom. There is in this phenomenon a similar clash between expectation and fulfilment,[22] though in the case of boredom the expectation (and the desire) is that our lives should be, not painless, but exhilarating. We anticipate that our lives will be thrilling, possibly because we think of ourselves as being central characters in some grand narrative of life. The phenomenon of tedium negates and contradicts that ✓ narcissistic expectation. In this regard, the experience of boredom – far from being of negligible value – shows itself to be of a revelatory character. The importance of boredom in revealing the true nature of life has been noted by many great thinkers, including Pascal and Schopenhauer (the latter of whom saw it as demonstrative of the emptiness of existence),[23] but it has also been explored, with at least equal beauty, by Joseph Brodsky, who urges us not to run away from boredom, but rather to embrace it, since it is a 'window on time's infinity':

> Once this window opens, don't try to shut it; on the contrary, throw it wide open. For boredom speaks the language of time, and it is to teach you the most valuable lesson in your life … the lesson of your utter insignificance. It is valuable to you, as well as to those you are to rub shoulders with. 'You are finite,' time tells you in a voice of boredom, 'and whatever you do is, from my point of view, futile.' As music to your ears, this, of course, may not count; yet the sense of futility, of limited significance even of your best, most ardent actions is better than the *ok* illusion of their consequences and the attendant self-aggrandizement.[24]

Of Brodsky more will be said. What we initially need to gather from this is simply that sensitivity to the implications of suffering and boredom, with regard both to human life and to the existence of God, leads to a judgement about what should properly be excised from a revised religious perspective taking its cue from experience. And the preliminary result is clear. There is to be no place for the notion of a God (for reasons already extensively provided), nor is any place to be found for appeal to a personal immortality (this notion relies upon an untenable

---

[22]   Otto Fenichel detects an element common to all instances of boredom, namely that '*something expected does not occur*' (Otto Fenichel, 'On the Psychology of Boredom', in *The Collected Papers of Otto Fenichel* (2 vols, New York, 1953), vol. 1, p. 301, italicized in the original).

[23]   See Blaise Pascal, *Pensées* (Oxford, 1999), pp. 44–8 (§168), and Arthur Schopenhauer, *Parerga and Paralipomena* (2 vols, Oxford, 1974), vol. 2, pp. 287–8.

[24]   Joseph Brodsky, 'In Praise of Boredom', in *On Grief and Reason* (New York, 1995), p. 109.

confidence in the significance of the human individual, it lacks evidential support, and appears to be generated by the wish for survival).

It has been stated that our revised account of religion is to be sensitive to experience. This requirement has led us, quite drastically, to excise from religion its most comforting elements. But here a second requirement must make itself felt. Throughout this book we have been concerned to explore how certain cultural phenomena are utilized as palliatives (or auxiliaries), providing support, consolation or solace to human beings. Religion, evidently, is to be understood within this framework. It appears hard at first to see how it can function in this capacity once divested of those elements – a loving God, providential care, the promise of an afterlife – which have been its principal appeal and source of strength. In order to maintain an auxiliary role for religion, our revised account will need to show how the unique resources of religion (even in such an austere account as this) can be of value in supporting human beings, and holding us up in the face of the crushing recognition of our insignificance. Its ability to do this, we will now see, must rise and fall with its capacity to reconcile us to that recognition of our nullity.

At Home in the Unhomely

We return, initially, to *The Future of an Illusion*. Freud suggests there that the humanization of nature lies at the root of religion, and that this process of humanization serves the purpose of making impersonal destinies approachable. But now take note of something that results from that humanization. If, Freud says, there are personal supernatural beings at work in the universe and behind nature, 'then we can breathe freely, can feel at home in the uncanny and can deal by psychical means with our senseless anxiety'.[25] *At home in the uncanny*. This rather strange formulation will prove to be of significance in our quest for a form of religion that does something other than propagate illusions, so it is necessary to investigate its various layers of meaning. To this end we must first turn to Freud's essay of 1919, 'The "Uncanny"'.

The 'uncanny' is a species of the frightening; something which evokes fear and dread. The English word 'uncanny' does not, however, fully capture the nuances of the equivalent German word *unheimlich* (literally 'unhomely' or 'unhomelike'). Our investigation must then focus on the peculiarities of this German term, as only this will enable us to understand what Freud means by being at home in the uncanny (*heimisch im Unheimlichen*, literally: 'at home in the unhomely'). Freud's first step is to investigate the definition of *unheimlich*. Its converse – *heimlich* – means 'belonging to the house, not strange, familiar, tame, intimate,

---

[25]   Sigmund Freud, *The Future of an Illusion*, in *The Standard Edition of the Complete Psychological Works of Sigmund Freud* (24 vols, London, 1953–74) (hereafter S.E.), vol. XXI, p. 17.

friendly, etc.'.[26] Given this, we may be 'tempted to conclude that what is "uncanny" is frightening precisely because it is *not* known and familiar'.[27] That would be the thesis regarding the uncanny that had earlier been advanced by Ernst Jentsch: Jentsch had contended that an impression of uncanniness (*Unheimlichkeit*) arises when a person does not feel at ease ('at home') in a situation. The uncanny is thus a by-product of <u>intellectual</u> uncertainty.[28] But Freud is dissatisfied with that, drawing our attention instead to those uses of the word *heimlich* which mean, not simply homely, but, rather, *concealed, kept from sight, secret*; how the 'close walls' of *Heimlichkeit* not only protect and make comfortable, but *hide* things too. He wants to suggest that 'the word "*heimlich*" is not unambiguous, but belongs to two sets of ideas, which, without being contradictory, are yet very different: on the one hand it means what is familiar and agreeable, and on the other, what is concealed and kept out of sight'.[29] Two pieces of evidence Freud draws from Daniel Sanders' *Wörterbuch der Deutschen Sprache* are crucial in drawing this out. First (a quotation from Karl Gutzkow):

> 'The Zecks [a family name] are all "heimlich".' '"Heimlich"? ... What do you understand by "heimlich"?' 'Well, ... they are like a buried spring or a dried-up pond. One cannot walk over it without always having the feeling that water might come up there again.' 'Oh, we call it "unheimlich"; you call it "heimlich". Well, what makes you think that there is something secret and untrustworthy about this family?'[30]

The strange convergence in meaning of *heimlich* and *unheimlich* is here explicit, and *heimlich* may thus be regarded as a word developing 'in the direction of ambivalence'.[31] Even more significant for Freud's investigation, however, is Friedrich Schelling's definition of the uncanny: '*"Unheimlich" is the name for everything that ought to have remained ... secret and hidden but has come to light.*'[32] With these two memorable images – water coming up from a dried spring; hidden things coming to light – it can be seen that the uncanny is fundamentally a *return of the repressed*: 'the uncanny [*unheimlich*] is something which is secretly familiar [*heimlich-heimisch*], which has undergone repression and then returned from it.'[33]

Turning his attention away from definitions and towards those impressions that serve to evoke a sense of the uncanny, Freud produces what Terry Castle has aptly

---

[26]   Sigmund Freud, 'The "Uncanny"', S.E. vol. XVII, p. 222.

[27]   Ibid., p. 220.

[28]   Ernst Jentsch, 'On the Psychology of the Uncanny (1906)', *Angelaki*, 2/1 (1995), pp. 7–16.

[29]   Freud, 'Uncanny', pp. 224–5.

[30]   Ibid., p. 223.

[31]   Ibid., p. 226.

[32]   Ibid., p. 224, italics in the original.

[33]   Ibid., p. 245.

dubbed a 'theme-index: an obsessional inventory of eerie fantasies, motifs, and effects, an itemized tropology of the weird'.[34] The list includes such phenomena as: hauntings and haunted houses; the feeling of déjà vu; curious coincidences (the reappearance during the day of a certain number or name, say); the idea of being buried alive; dismemberment; certain dolls and mechanical figures. Freud traces some of these impressions back to the experiences and anxieties of childhood. For example, the weird feeling aroused in us by dolls which seem peculiarly animated has just such a source: in the fact that children treat their dolls as though they are alive or wish that they may become so animated. In certain of these experiences we find, then, infantile beliefs, beliefs that have long since in the adult been forgotten. Just as the uncanny element appears when repressed childhood complexes and impressions are revived, so too the appearance of modes of thought, once habitual but now surmounted by civilized human beings, gives rise to this odd and frightening feeling. There is for Freud an overlap here – for ontogeny recapitulates phylogeny – so the child's belief in its living dolls mirrors the animistic beliefs of primitives, who were seen by Freud and others to occupy a position in the development of humanity characterized as 'the childhood of the species'. Freud summarizes thus: 'an uncanny experience occurs either when infantile complexes which have been repressed are once more revived by some impression, or when primitive beliefs which have been surmounted seem once more to be confirmed.'[35]

Of these primitive beliefs, the two most notable concern the omnipotence of thoughts and the return of the dead. The former is a feature of magical thinking, a mode of thought that has been surmounted and left behind by the forward advance of the human intellect. Sometimes, however, things occur – a person who we bring to mind after a long absence of thought suddenly calls us; or we secretly wish for the death of a person and their demise is reported to us – and the magical view no longer appears superannuated. And here the uncanny arises, for the apparently outdated omnipotence of thoughts has returned.[36] A comparable explanation can also be provided for the effect of what is perhaps the most uncanny thing of all: 'death and dead bodies, … the return of the dead, … spirits and ghosts';[37] indeed, the equivalent German term for our 'haunted house' is '*unheimlich Haus*'. With regard to death, Freud contends, our thoughts and feelings are scarcely different from those of our earliest ancestors. Hence Freud's words: 'Since almost all of us still think as savages do on this topic, it is no matter for surprise that the primitive fear of the dead is still so strong within us and always ready to come to the surface

---

[34] Terry Castle, *The Female Thermometer: Eighteenth-Century Culture and the Invention of the Uncanny* (Oxford, 1995), p. 4.

[35] Freud, 'Uncanny', p. 249.

[36] For more on the omnipotence of thoughts, see Brian R. Clack, '"At home in the uncanny": Freud's Account of *das Unheimliche* in the Context of His Theory of Religious Belief', *Religion*, 38/3 (2008), pp. 252–3.

[37] Ibid., p. 241.

on any provocation.'[38] It is this atavistic element of our personality which accounts for our uneasiness when hearing tales of ghosts and the supernatural, hastening past a house deemed to be haunted, and being troubled by creaking noises in an old house at night, even though we have ostensibly passed beyond the belief that the dead return to haunt us.

The significance of these thoughts on the reconfirmation of the surmounted is that they suggest to us that 'the uncanny' is, culturally speaking, a *borderline experience*. It is a liminal condition, existing on the boundary between the animistic and the scientific worldviews. Note Freud's words concerning the return of the dead and the omnipotence of wishes:

> We – or our primitive forefathers – once believed that these possibilities were realities, and were convinced that they actually happened. Nowadays we no longer believe in them, we have *surmounted* these modes of thought; but we do not feel quite sure of our new beliefs, and the old ones still exist within us ready to seize upon any confirmation. As soon as something *actually happens* in our lives which seems to confirm the old, discarded beliefs we get a feeling of the uncanny; it is as though we were making a judgement something like this: 'So, after all, it is *true* that one can kill a person by the mere wish!' or, 'So the dead *do* live on and appear on the scene of their former activities!' and so on. Conversely, anyone who has completely and finally rid himself of animistic beliefs will be insensible to this type of the uncanny.[39]

The animist does not feel a sense of the uncanny (for there is nothing surmounted to return). Nor does the opposite type – the completely rational person of science who has entirely embraced the rationalist assumption of the inviolability of natural laws – for the 'most remarkable coincidences of wish and fulfilment, the most mysterious repetition of similar experiences in a particular place or on a particular date, the most deceptive sights and suspicious noises – none of these things will disconcert him or raise the kind of fear which can be described as "a fear of something uncanny"'.[40] But such a completely rational person is rare. Most of us are insecure in our rejection of the supernatural, and uncanniness has its roots precisely in that insecurity.

Armed with these thoughts, we may begin to explore what it might mean to say that religious ideas serve to make a person feel 'at home in the uncanny'. The full force of his remark becomes clear in the original German ('*heimisch im Unheimlichen*'[41]), with its play on the homely and the unhomely: religious ideas make the believer feel at home in the unhomely. We can begin with two straightforward readings. Given what has been said about the borderline nature of

---

[38] Ibid., p. 242.
[39] Ibid., pp. 247–8.
[40] Ibid., p. 248.
[41] Sigmund Freud, *Die Zukunft einer Illusion* (Frankfurt, 1967), p. 97.

the uncanny, we might simply contend that for the religious believer *there is no uncanny*, nothing unhomely to experience. What Freud says concerning the world of fairy tales is here apposite:

> In fairy tales … the world of reality is left behind from the very start, and the animistic system of beliefs is frankly adopted. Wish-fulfilments, secret powers, omnipotence of thoughts, animation of inanimate objects, all the elements so common in fairy stories, can exert no uncanny influence here; for, as we have learnt, that feeling cannot arise unless there is a conflict of judgement as to whether things which have been 'surmounted' and are regarded as incredible may not, after all, be possible; and this problem is eliminated from the outset by the postulates of the world of fairy tales.[42]

Religion – for Freud a fundamentally antique and animism-embracing phenomenon – would share this feature of fairy tales. For the believer, nothing has been 'surmounted', and there is therefore nothing to return. The world lacks uncanniness for the religious believer just as it does for the pure rationalist. As we earlier noted, it is only outside the realms of these different certainties – religion and full naturalistic rationalism – that we can experience the 'trembling of belief' characteristic of the uncanny.[43]

A second reading is related to this. The religious believer evades the strange uncertainties of an unhomely world by embracing dogmatic assumptions by means of which everything makes perfect sense. Hence Freud's sardonic words in *Moses and Monotheism*:

> How enviable, to those of us who are poor in faith, do those enquirers seem who are convinced of the existence of a Supreme Being! … How comprehensive, how exhaustive and how definitive are the doctrines of believers compared with the laborious, paltry and fragmentary attempts at explanation which are the most we are able to achieve![44]

Evidently, these two readings cohere perfectly with Freud's criticisms of religion as explored in an earlier chapter: religion is a superannuated system of thought; it stands in stark contrast with what science tells us of the world; and the completeness of its doctrines is due to its fantastical and delusional nature (recall the diagnosis of amentia).

Though Freud may have meant nothing more than this when he wrote that religious ideas make one 'feel at home in the uncanny', there is perhaps something more that we can draw out of this comment, something that will help to frame a

---

[42]   Freud, 'Uncanny', p. 250.
[43]   This excellent description of the uncanny as a 'trembling of belief' is offered by Nicholas Royle (Nicholas Royle, *The Uncanny* (London, 2003), p. 35).
[44]   Sigmund Freud, *Moses and Monotheism: Three Essays*, S.E. vol. XXIII, p. 122.

conception of religion as an auxiliary structure of a non-illusory character. For Freud's comment is not simply a remark about what religion does (*it makes us feel at home*); it is also a remark about our human condition (*we are not at home*), and it is this uncanny condition of unhomeliness that we try, by one means or another, to address and to ease.

Martin Heidegger will prove to be a helpful ally here. Especially useful are his thoughts regarding the nature of anxiety (and recall here that, alongside the task of making one feel at home in the uncanny, religion, according to Freud, ameliorates humanity's 'senseless anxiety'). Heidegger – for whom, '[a]t bottom, the ordinary is not ordinary; it is extra-ordinary, uncanny'[45] – roots uncanniness in the nature of what he calls 'Dasein' (literally 'being-there', the being of man). The specific being of Dasein (existing in a state of 'care') is defined as 'ahead-of-itself-Being-already-in-(the-world) as Being-alongside (entities encountered within-the-world)'.[46] This formula encompasses the essentially temporal and triadic nature of Dasein, that it is oriented towards past, present and future. Being 'ahead-of-itself' involves the future, in resoluteness (or authenticity) running ahead to death; while 'being-alongside-entities-encountered-within-the-world' encompasses our present involvement with things (we are always engaged in some task). For our purposes, though, it is the third of these elements – the one directed towards the past ('being-already-in-the-world') – that is of principal concern. Dasein has been 'thrown' into the world. As such, we are in a condition of 'facticity': we are 'always already' in a specific situation that determines our possibilities (my own set of beliefs, attitudes, aesthetic tastes – and so on – are determined by the fact that I was born in England in the latter half of the twentieth century, for example). Thrown-ness is revealed by a mood such as anxiety, which is past-directed. Crucially, Heidegger writes: 'Anxiety is anxious about naked Dasein as something that has been thrown into uncanniness.'[47] Hence:

> In anxiety one feels '*uncanny*' [*In der Angst ist einem 'unheimlich*'] … But here 'uncanniness' also means 'not-being-at-home' [*das Nicht-zuhause-sein*]. In our first indication of the phenomenal character of Dasein's basic state, Being-in was defined as 'residing alongside …', 'Being familiar with …' This character of Being-in was then brought to view more concretely through the everyday publicness of the 'they', which brings tranquillized self-assurance – 'Being-at-home', with all its obviousness – into the average everydayness of Dasein. On the other hand, as Dasein falls, anxiety brings it back from absorption in the 'world'. Everyday familiarity collapses. Dasein has been individualized, but individualized *as* Being-in-the-world. Being-in enters into the existential 'mode' of the '*not-at-home*'. Nothing else is meant by our talk about 'uncanniness'.[48]

---

[45]   Martin Heidegger, *Poetry, Language, Thought* (New York, 1975), p. 54.

[46]   Martin Heidegger, *Being and Time* (Oxford, 1962), p. 237.

[47]   Ibid., pp. 393–4.

[48]   Ibid., p. 233.

Despite their very different modes of expression, it might well be suggested that
Heidegger's thoughts on uncanniness march closely with those of Freud. Uncanny
anxiety results when the familiarity of the everyday collapses and becomes strange.
The state of 'being-at-home' gives way to the condition of 'not-at-homeness'; the
familiar turns on us and becomes unfamiliar.

In Hubert Dreyfus' interpretation of Heidegger, the human condition is one of
radical unhomeliness and estrangement: we are so fundamentally unsettled that we
can never be at home in the world. But we do not (can not) rest content with this,
and instead 'plunge into trying to make ourselves at home and secure'.[49] Religion
would count among the strategies for feeling at home in this unhomeliness. It
may of course be that religion has something inauthentic, conformist and escapist
about it, a strategy which provides merely 'tranquillized self-assurance': comfort
and consolation in a world of alien strangeness, a kind of regression either to
a primitive stage of enchantment or to that much missed period of infantile
dependence upon protective parents. This may well be all that Freud means when
he writes of the believer's home in the uncanny. It may even be that this catches
something of the essence of the religious attitude. And yet it would be overly hasty
to ignore other possibilities. Consider, for example, how William James describes
a particular kind of religious sensibility in which – before conversion – the world
'looks remote, strange, sinister, *uncanny*':[50]

> Now there are some subjects whom all this leaves a prey to the profoundest
> astonishment. The strangeness is wrong. The unreality cannot be. A mystery
> is concealed, and a metaphysical solution must exist. If the natural world is
> so double-faced and *unhomelike*, what world, what thing is real? An urgent
> wondering and questioning is set up, a poring theoretic activity, and in the
> desperate effort to get into right relations with the matter, the sufferer is often
> led to what becomes for him a satisfying religious solution.[51]

Considered in this manner, religion may be seen as an attempt to come to terms
with a world which presents itself to us as in some sense *wrong*, a world in which
we *should* feel at home but *don't*. Our attention must now turn to ways in which
religion might successfully achieve this goal without its solution being simply that
of withdrawal into a blissful hallucinatory confusion.

[49] Hubert Dreyfus, *Being-in-the-World* (Cambridge, MA, 1991), p. 37.
[50] William James, *The Varieties of Religious Experience* (London, 1960), p. 158
(emphasis added).
[51] Ibid., p. 159 (emphasis added).

The Transient Individual Against the Backdrop of Eternity

The account of the religious life to follow draws its inspiration from three under-utilized sources in philosophical discussions of religion: John Stuart Mill's depiction of a 'religion of humanity', found in his *Three Essays on Religion*; Michael Oakeshott's thoughts on the distinctive gifts of religious faith; and Freud's own musings on the implications of transience.

Mill's views provide an appropriate starting point for us, since (just as we ourselves have earlier done) he articulates strident denunciations of the wishful thinking involved in much religious belief before elaborating his own (divergent) view of faith. Mill speaks of 'the tendency of the human mind to believe what is agreeable to it',[52] warning the theologian that 'it is not legitimate to assume that in the order of the Universe, whatever is desirable is true'.[53] One might have a desire that there should be some loving power governing the universe, but a belief of that kind must resign in the face of an accurate recognition of the world as it really is:

> Nature impales men, breaks them as if on the wheel, casts them to be devoured by wild beasts, burns them to death, crushes them with stones like the first christian martyr, starves them with hunger, freezes them with cold, poisons them by the quick or slow venom of her exhalations, and has hundreds of other hideous deaths in reserve, such as the ingenious cruelty of a Nabis or a Domitian never surpassed.[54]

Given the appalling character of the natural world into which we have each been thrown, it is not credible that the author of all things should have an omnibenevolent character, and the conclusions of natural theology must therefore be minimal: we perhaps arrive at the conception of a very powerful being, but 'any idea of God more captivating than this comes only from human wishes'.[55] Though critical of the common form of faith, Mill recognizes that religion serves an important purpose in human life, functioning as 'a source of personal satisfaction and of elevated feelings', and meeting our 'craving for higher things'.[56] He denies, however, that one must 'travel beyond the boundaries of the world which we inhabit'[57] in order to have these needs met: 'the idealization of our earthly life, the cultivation of a high conception of what *it* may be made' can provide all the materials required for our religious impulses, even when 'the short duration, the smallness and insignificance of life' is fully recognized and accepted.[58] There is no belief in heaven here, no

---

[52] John Stuart Mill, *Three Essays on Religion* (London, 1874), p. 166.
[53] Ibid., p. 165.
[54] Ibid., p. 29.
[55] Ibid., pp. 194–5.
[56] Ibid., p. 104.
[57] Ibid.
[58] Ibid., p. 105.

confident expectation of personal immortality; but though our individual lives are short, the life of our species is long, and by taking our moral duties seriously – and by feeling a sense of the significance of life through the hold those duties have on us – maybe we can 'live ideally in the life of those who are to follow [us]'.[59]

Though Mill's preferred picture of the religious life differs somewhat from the view to be elaborated in the remainder of this chapter – we have no room for belief in God (even in Mill's austere, unsentimental formulation) and will place little emphasis upon moral duties – there is in what he says much to be admired and built upon. The dismissal of merely wish-driven elements is evidently a common element, but the truly positive thing that Mill contributes is an understanding that the consoling satisfaction brought by religion might lie in something other than illusory assurances concerning the individual's own abiding importance (such assurances as might typically be provided by the ideas of immortality and a personal relationship with a concerned God).[60] These sources of consolation are replaced by earthly and unselfish ideals, the consolation of a personally fulfilling hereafter giving ground to the more elevated satisfaction deriving from co-operative efforts to leave for future generations of humanity a society more harmonious and a world better understood. In enacting this change of perspective from narrow self-concern (*I must continue to live; the universe must care about me!*) to an expansive concern for the well-being of those who will follow us, the individual relativizes her own significance, recognizes the very smallness of her own life in relation to the vastness of the whole,

---

[59]   Ibid., p. 119.

[60]   Some elements of Mill's thoughts regarding immortality are worthy of note, particularly as they pertain to the palliative function of such a belief. Mill notes that the hope for immortality seems to derive from a person's dissatisfaction with the character and content of their life, detecting that those whose lives have been full seem less desirous of post-mortem existence than those who have found themselves disappointed: 'They who have had their happiness can bear to part with existence: but it is hard to die without ever having lived' (ibid., p. 119; see also Theodor Adorno, *Negative Dialectics* (New York, 1973), p. 370). Accordingly (and in optimistic mode), Mill conjectures that as the living conditions of humanity improve and life becomes more fulfilling for people, the desire for immortality should wane. He also suggests a great limitation attending immortality's consolations: after a long while, most people will 'have had enough of existence' (Mill, *Three Essays*, p. 119). This suggests that, far from being a compensatory remedy for the sufferings endured during life, the condition of immortality would ultimately supply a person only with that other deeply unsatisfactory experience previously explored, namely boredom. (See also in this context Bernard Williams' classic paper 'The Makropulos Case', in *Problems of the Self* (Cambridge, 1976), pp. 82–100.) It would appear, therefore, that the palliative quality of immortality has been severely overestimated. What Wittgenstein had concluded about the relation of immortality to the meaning of life might thus be used by us with regard to its role as an effective palliative: 'The temporal immortality of the soul of man, that is to say, its eternal survival also after death, is not only in no way guaranteed, but this assumption in the first place will not do for us what we always tried to make it do' (Ludwig Wittgenstein, *Tractatus Logico-Philosophicus* (London, 1922), 6.4312 (p. 185).

and adjusts her focus and consolations accordingly. Encountered in this adjustment is an element that will subsequently be brought to prominence, though more work must be done in order to turn this into a recognizably religious perspective.[61] To this end we may turn to Oakeshott.

In a short (and quite beautiful) section of his book *On Human Conduct*, Oakeshott locates the value of religious faith in its power to address and to reconcile us to 'the unavoidable dissonances of a human condition',[62] dissonances which include 'disease, urgent wants unsatisfied, the pain of disappointed expectations, the suffering of frustrated purposes, the impositions of hostile circumstances, the sorrows of unwanted partings, burdens, ills, disasters, calamities of all sorts, and death itself, the emblem here of all such sufferings'.[63] The role religion plays in relation to these dissonances, and in relation to a recognition of an aspect of the human condition still more disconcerting – namely, 'the hollowness, the futility of that condition'[64] – would thus appear to be of an auxiliary nature (as earlier defined in this book), but Oakeshott adds enormously to our understanding of the multilayered nature of religion in this regard by explicating the range of ways in which religious faith might perform this task. The obvious first way takes the form of a 'somewhat prosaic consolation',[65] consisting in the hope of afterlife compensation for sufferings endured; a variation on this theme being that our earthly woes are sent merely to try us, so that the act of enduring them functions as our 'passport to future happiness'.[66] Such a system of consolation evidently falls within the realm of those wish-driven illusions we have throughout been concerned to expose and censure. More interesting are those religious strategies which neither console nor compensate but rather generate 'a reconciliation to nothingness',[67] 'a serene acquiescence in mortality and a graceful acceptance of the *rerum mortalia*, joys and sorrows alike transformed'.[68] It is important to emphasize this possibility. Hitherto, we have spoken of religious ideas as constituting a flight from the least agreeable aspects of reality. Oakeshott alerts our attention to the fact that religion need not always do this, that it has within it the resources to allow a person to come to terms with his or her ultimate nullity, and that it can do this without denying the disturbing truth of our fundamental nothingness.

---

[61]   If one agrees with John Hick that at the heart of religion lies a particular movement – a 'transformation of human existence from self-centredness to Reality-centredness' (John Hick, *An Interpretation of Religion* (Basingstoke, 1989), p. 367) – then the perspective just outlined would not appear to be at all alien to the essential nature of religion.

[62]   Michael Oakeshott, *On Human Conduct* (Oxford, 1975), p. 81.

[63]   Ibid.

[64]   Ibid., p. 83.

[65]   Ibid., p. 82.

[66]   Ibid.

[67]   Ibid., p. 84.

[68]   Ibid., p. 86.

The details of this religious reconciliation to nothingness require some exploration, but before we address this we should turn once more to Freud. The reason for this is straightforward. Oakeshott highlights how it is the evanescent quality of our little lives that most clearly reveals their nihility ('no more than "un voyage au bout de la nuit"'[69]), and he is concerned with investigating the differing ways in which the religious imagination confronts and processes that evanescence. Freud likewise addresses this issue in his haunting paper 'On Transience', which we have already had reason to mention in a previous chapter. Freud here recounts a summer walk he took in the Dolomites 'in the company of a taciturn friend and of a young but already famous poet',[70] now plausibly identified as Lou Andreas-Salome and Rainer Maria Rilke respectively.[71] The poet, though appreciating the striking beauty of the landscape, could find no joy in it, and was instead disturbed by the thought that its beauty would vanish, be extinguished, when winter came: 'All that he would otherwise have loved and admired seemed to him to be shorn of its worth by the transience which was its doom.'[72] Freud sees in this attitude one of a number of possible responses to the inevitable decay and disappearance of all things beautiful and perfect. Here, recognition of the indisputable transience of all things leads to a reduction in a person's ability to detect any worth in the world. How, after all, can any thing be of value when it is doomed to dust?[73] We can see this 'aching despondency' operating in the work of another poet, Padraic Pearse:

> The beauty of the world hath made me sad,
> This beauty that will pass;
> Sometimes my heart hath shaken with great joy
> To see a leaping squirrel in a tree,
> Or a red lady-bird upon a stalk,
> Or little rabbits in a field at evening,
> Lit by a slanting sun,
> Or some green hill where shadows drifted by
> Some quiet hill where mountainy man hath sown
> And soon would reap; near to the gate of Heaven;
> Or children with bare feet upon the sands
> Of some ebbed sea, or playing on the streets
> Of little towns in Connacht,
> Things young and happy.
> And then my heart hath told me:
> These will pass,

---

[69]   Ibid., p. 83.

[70]   Sigmund Freud, 'On Transience', S.E. vol. XIV, p. 305.

[71]   See Matthew von Unwerth, *Freud's Requiem* (New York, 2005), pp. 3–5.

[72]   Freud, 'On Transience', p. 305.

[73]   With these thoughts we are returned to the theme of Leopardi's poem 'On the Portrait of a Beautiful Lady', as discussed in the opening chapter of this book.

nice link w/ repetition

Will pass and change, will die and be no more,
Things bright and green, things young and happy;
word ending And I have gone on my way
Sorrowful.[74]

In such thoroughly pessimistic responses as these, the fact of transience entails a *why?* diminution in the value of all things, and possibly even reveals their entire futility and worthlessness.

What of the other possible responses? One alternative consists in a rebellion against transience, a denial that beauty is doomed to destruction.[75] This demand for persistence and immortality would appear to manifest itself in a variety of forms, not only in the idea of continued personal consciousness beyond the grave, but in the theological and philosophical construction of an eternal, changeless realm standing in contradistinction to earthly, mutable life. In this latter camp we find the Platonic conception of unchanging Forms, as well as the classical theistic doctrine of divine immutability, which in the Christian imagination emerges as the hope that there should exist some power able to console us, and to rescue us, indeed, from the inexorable process of decay:

Swift to its close ebbs out life's little day;
Earth's joys grow dim, its glories pass away;
Change and decay in all around I see;
O Thou, Who changest not, abide with me.[76]

This movement – from recognition of evanescence to desire for the immutable or immortal – is dismissed by Freud as being a mere product of wishes: transience is undeniable, while the belief in things immortal is an unjustified illusion.

Freud himself advocates a third response. Both the religious and the despondent reactions operate upon a basis that finds in the fact of transience a problematic dimension of existence, something that requires an immutable corrective or else entails a loss in the worth of being. Freud emphatically disagrees with those diagnoses, holding that transience actually guarantees an *increase* in worth:

Transience value is scarcity value in time. Limitation in the possibility of an *Supply &* enjoyment raises the value of the enjoyment … The beauty of the human form *demand?* and face vanish for ever in the course of our own lives, but their evanescence

---

[74]   Padraic Pearse, 'The Wayfarer', in *Selected Poems* (Dublin, 1993), p. 29.
[75]   Oakeshott refers to such an attitude as 'a contemptuous defiance of this common and continuous destiny' (Oakeshott, *On Human Conduct*, p. 85).
[76]   'Abide With Me' (words by H.F. Lyte), in Sydney Nicholson (ed.), *Hymns Ancient and Modern* (London, 1916), p. 17.

only lends them a fresh charm. A flower that blossoms only for a single night does not seem to us on that account less lovely.[77]

Here we find Freud at his least downbeat, and the view he advances is both persuasive and potentially salubrious. It certainly seems correct to maintain that the fleeting nature of a pleasant experience enhances a person's enjoyment of it. Consider the reactions a sunset rarely fails to generate. Gasps of delight are elicited from its observers, who eye with rapt attention every alteration in the constantly changing sky until night draws down its curtain upon the fugitive show. It is the ephemeral nature of the event that produces these elated responses; few would doubt that people would be held entranced by a sunset's colours if the sky always looked that way. And much the same can be said for many if not all of life's ephemeral pleasures. Festivals, holidays, concerts and – yes, indeed, Freud's own examples – flowers and faces: were they to be always present, always unchanging and forever fresh, it is not unlikely that we would barely notice them, still less relish them as we do. Were such a Freudian love of transience to be instilled in us, instead of a contempt for it and a corresponding yearning for the persistent, one source of suffering might be removed, or at least lessened, and we might come to love our life for what it is, and to live it briefly and yet brightly, 'like a star / That shoots and is gone'.[78] Positively embracing transience might thus be beneficial, even healthy, for a person, and it might in addition produce welcome results in our relations with others. This is a point that Brodsky wishes to impress upon us. Recognition of finitude puts, he says, our existence into perspective. Instead of engaging in self-aggrandizing actions and projects, to realize our transient condition is to embrace humility: 'The more you learn about your own size, the more humble and the more compassionate you become to your likes.'[79]

Freud evidently sees the acceptance of transience as an *alternative* to the religious response, and incompatible with it. What I wish to suggest here, however, is that a reconciliation to our transient condition might be aided by an engagement with (carefully selected) aspects of a religious tradition, such aspects as might serve to effect a fuller adjustment to the more troubling dimensions of that condition. There is, after all, something rather roseate about the examples of value-enhancing transience that we have considered. The fleeting presence of a rose or a sunset need not inspire melancholy since there will be others to follow in their wake. As Freud himself notes with regard to the beauty of the natural world, it is comforting to know that 'each time it is destroyed by winter it comes again next year'.[80] On the other hand, the transience of one's *own* life (and of the lives of those we love) might not be so blithely embraceable, for there is inevitably some disquiet felt when it is realized that our existence is but a fleeting and inconsequential episode in the life of

---

[77] Freud, 'On Transience', pp. 305–6.
[78] Edward Thomas, 'Roads', in *The Work of Edward Thomas* (Ware, 1994), p. 163.
[79] Brodsky, 'In Praise', p. 109.
[80] Freud, 'On Transience', p. 305.

the universe, that this brief candle will be extinguished and never again be relit: our ✓ life will not 'come again next year'. The point to be drawn is not that recognition of evanescence must lead to the despondency felt by the likes of Rilke and Pearce, but that there is ambivalence in our reaction to transience: it adds both fascinated appreciation and aching distress. Freud's paean to transience may not entirely help a person struggling to come to terms with his or her impermanence; at the very least, it might require a supplement. Certain religious resources, I suggest, might be ~~ok~~ valuable precisely in this respect.

Returning initially to Oakeshott, we see in his exploration of the religious response to nothingness possible ways in which some degree of (what we might provisionally term) *eternal significance* might co-exist with a person's irreducibly ephemeral nature. One such way might be detected in the peculiar qualities of human agency, particularly when a person's actions are recognized as 'self-enactments' and understood in terms of the sentiments motivating them. An action motivated by loyalty, or simply by duty, seems to be 'released from the transitory arbitrament of substantive inconclusion'.[81] Since moral values have an eternal ✗ significance (for one does not speak of 'a time to be good'), a life characterized by dutiful adherence to those values rises above the fleeting and potentially trivial nature of a human life and assumes a kind of immortal dimension.[82] Though there are problematic aspects in such a view (even a self-enactment cannot, for instance, be divorced from the passing satisfactions and disappointments of an agent's life), the great quality exhibited by a religion lies in its bolstering of this sense of an action's significance, in 'the intrepidity of its acknowledgement of [the mutability of] this human condition' and in its invitation to live 'so far as is possible as an immortal'.[83] The nature of this invitation lies in its provision of a framework in terms of which life is enacted and evaluated:

> Religious faith is the evocation of a sentiment ... to be added to all others as the motive of all motives in terms of which the fugitive adventures of human conduct, without being released from their mortal and their moral conditions, are graced with an intimation of immortality: the sharpness of death and the deadliness of doing overcome, and the transitory sweetness of a mortal affection, the tumult of a grief and the passing beauty of a May morning recognized neither as merely evanescent adventures nor as emblems of better things to come, but as *aventures*, themselves encounters with eternity.[84]

---

[81] Oakeshott, *On Human Conduct*, p. 84.

[82] For a view of this kind, see Stewart R. Sutherland, 'What Happens after Death?', *Scottish Journal of Theology*, 22/4 (1969), pp. 404–18. See also Peter Byrne, 'F.R. Leavis and the Religious Dimension in Literature', *Modern Theology*, 1/2 (1985), pp. 119–30, and D.Z. Phillips, *Death and Immortality* (London, 1970), pp. 41–60.

[83] Oakeshott, *On Human Conduct*, p. 86.

[84] Ibid., p. 85.

The success of this framework of thought is grounded in the ubiquitous meditations on the interplay of evanescence and immutability found within the image-repertoire of religion, and the promise of religion in this regard would appear to be that its rich resources can be utilized to place our transient lives against the backdrop of eternity, and by means of that setting to gain some kind of reconciliation to our condition, and thereby some more than illusory consolation.

Before proceeding further, it should be asserted that with this talk of 'eternity', I am not smuggling in unwarranted and previously eschewed metaphysical speculation but want, rather, to operate with what may be called a mitigated conception of the eternal. There are a number of ways in which a person might experience an engagement with something eternal, without that experience being tied up with the idea of a God or of an unchanging realm of Platonic ideas. As previously indicated, the binding sense of moral responsibility might (at least for some people) assume this character. And Freud has a mitigated conception of eternity in mind when he says of Nature that 'in relation to the length of our lives it can in fact be regarded as eternal'.[85] There are certain things – the universe, the natural world, the life of our species, and so on – that in relation to our own tiny and transient lives have an eternal quality and by us are experienced as such. What Mill constructs as the centrepiece of his religion of humanity – the renunciation of shrill calls for personal compensation in favour of an engagement with the larger (and future) needs of our species – similarly appeals to a larger context in which the transient individual can be located and by engagement with which the individual can find some degree of satisfaction. This mitigated sense of the eternal now in place, the perspective offered by religion can be seen to constitute precisely that (properly qualified) 'sense and taste for the Infinite' spoken of by Schleiermacher, an endeavour to live 'a life in the infinite nature of the Whole',[86] 'to return into the Whole, and to exist for oneself at the same time'.[87]

As I earlier suggested, in the resources of the Western religious tradition we are fortunate to have an inheritance of imaginative brilliance to draw upon, resources which constitute a part of our cultural legacy and which can be utilized to develop the kind of reconciliation to our transient condition that we are here seeking. The traditional ceremonial life of Christianity may be regarded as one such resource. To attend a church service (for example, the structured tranquillity of evensong) is, first of all, to suspend for a short time the commotion of one's daily commerce and to lose oneself in liturgy and reflection; it is also (crucially) to immerse oneself in an ongoing traditional form of life which both pre-dates and will outlive the participant. Roger Scruton's description of the nature of a tradition can here be applied to fruitful effect: 'When a man acts from tradition he sees what he *now* does as belonging to a pattern that transcends the focus of

---

[85]   Freud, 'On Transience', p. 305.

[86]   Schleiermacher, *On Religion*, p. 36.

[87]   Ibid., pp. 42–3.

his present interest.'[88] To stand thus 'in the current of some common life'[89] is to bring about that desired two-stage reconciliation I have here indicated to be the jewel at the heart of the religious perspective: the smallness of one's life is duly recognized, one's centrality and importance now banished; and then, in spite of this recognition, a sense of peace and consolation is gained by reflecting upon that thing of greater significance within which one's life is situated.

The Bible, too, can be mined as a repository of reflections on our ephemeral state and its location within an infinitely larger whole. In comparison with the eternal being of God, we are mere 'grasshoppers',[90] our 'days are as grass',[91] and a person's very life no more permanent than a flower of the field: 'For the wind passeth over it, and it is gone; and the place thereof shall know it no more.'[92] The theme of humankind's dust-bound life persists throughout – 'for dust thou art, and unto dust shalt thou return'[93] – while perennial anxieties regarding the significance of life are given perfect expression in the genius of the book of Ecclesiastes. The vanity of life is there expressed in a hail of memorable images: 'There is no remembrance of former things';[94] the lives of men and beasts can be no different since 'all are of the dust, and all turn to dust again';[95] nor do the wise have an advantage over fools: 'how dieth the wise man? as the fool'.[96] Alongside the impermanence, vanity and vexations of all human endeavour, however, the author of Ecclesiastes gives us glimpses both of a higher order of things and of the (even if only fleeting) projects and satisfactions that can mitigate the sense of futility that threatens to overwhelm a person. Accepting that there is 'a time to every purpose under the heaven',[97] and that there is something beyond us that eternally abides ('whatsoever God doeth, it shall be for ever: nothing can be ... taken from it'[98]), one may become reconciled to one's own transient lot and find significance in ventures undeniably fleeting yet beautiful nonetheless:

> Go thy way, eat thy bread with joy, and drink thy wine with a merry heart; for God now accepteth thy works. Let thy garments be always white; and let thy head lack no ointment. Live joyfully with the wife whom thou lovest all the days of the life of thy vanity, which he hath given thee under the sun, all the days of thy vanity: for that is thy portion in this life, and in thy labour which thou takest

---

88 Roger Scruton, *The Meaning of Conservatism* (London, 1984), p. 42.
89 Ibid., p. 21.
90 Isaiah 40:22.
91 Psalms 103:15.
92 Psalms 103:16.
93 Genesis 3:19.
94 Ecclesiastes 1:11.
95 Ecclesiastes 3:20.
96 Ecclesiastes 2:16.
97 Ecclesiastes 3:1.
98 Ecclesiastes 3:14.

under the sun. Whatsoever thy hand findeth to do, do it with thy might: for there is no work, nor device, nor knowledge, nor wisdom, in the grave, whither thou goest.[99]

With such a perspective in place, a person may both find some joy in the pleasures and projects of a human life, and at the same time find their passage eased into a calm acceptance of transience and personal annihilation.

Conclusion: Not Only Is There No God …

It is not hard to anticipate criticisms that might be levelled at the account of religion just articulated. These would inevitably focus upon the perceived reductionist quality of that account, and might thus complain that the view of religion it offers up lacks some of the essential characteristics of that phenomenon. For a start, it might be felt that there is something disingenuous in engaging in a religious ceremony once the beliefs in God, providence and immortality have been relinquished. Such a criticism has little force. Ritual and ceremonial acts occupy a central place in the life of a society, and rarely require any metaphysical commitments from a participant (think about such commonly performed acts as dressing a home with Christmas decorations or singing 'Happy Birthday', as well as weddings, funerals, and such state ceremonies as presidential inaugurations, trooping the colour and laying wreaths on war memorials). In the face of such examples, it seems somewhat arbitrary to insist that a religious ceremony should have a metaphysical entrance requirement. Another set of concerns could focus on what might be felt to be the insincere employment of the idea of God sometimes at work in this account: what, after all, can be the justification for including any reference to God after so conclusively dismissing the possibility of his existence? To this I can only respond that talk of God has occupied a significant place in humanity's reflections on existence, constituting (in Leslie Stevenson's words) 'a scheme of interpretation that many people from biblical times down to the present day have found helpful, useful, or illuminating in the effort to understand and express their experience of life – its ups and downs, its delights and disasters, its loves and hates, its moral failures, its illuminations, and its new possibilities',[100] and that the store of images it contains has an application in the reconciliation to transience we have here been exploring. Given that so many problems attend thinking of God as an actually existing being, to conceive of 'God' as something of a portmanteau term for this collection of interpretative devices and reconciliatory images might just be the best one can do.

---

[99]   Ecclesiastes 9:7–10.

[100]   Leslie Stevenson, David L. Haberman and Peter Matthews Wright, *Twelve Theories of Human Nature* (Oxford, 2013), p. 121.

One might be more swayed by the criticisms that Freud himself would make of the kind of revisionary exercise just undertaken. Having condemned the religion of the common man as 'patently infantile' and 'foreign to reality', Freud turns his fire on those philosophers who try to rescue the religious life by replacing the God of religion with 'an impersonal, shadowy and abstract principle'. Such revisionary exercises are contemptuously dismissed as 'pitiful rearguard actions'.[101] On this view, the attempt to salvage something from the wreckage of religion is driven by something akin to misplaced nostalgia or sentimental loyalty and exhibits a kind of intellectual dishonesty. While registering the force of this criticism, I can only respond by repeating that my desire has been to extract from religion something precious lying at its heart but generally obscured by illusory elements. This core, as we have seen, concerns the relation of transient individual lives to eternity. But even here (indeed, especially here) Freud is dismissive:

> Critics persist in describing as 'deeply religious' anyone who admits to a sense of man's insignificance or impotence in the face of the universe, although what constitutes the essence of the religious attitude is not this feeling but only the next step after it, the reaction to it which seeks a remedy for it. The man who goes no further, but humbly acquiesces in the small part which human beings play in the great world – such a man is, on the contrary, irreligious in the truest sense of the word.[102]

Freud may have a point, but it is possible that an overly restrictive conception of religion stops him from seeing other, non-compensatory possibilities in religious ideas and practices, that range of possibilities that we have here extracted from Oakeshott and found potentially fruitful.

None of this is to suggest that the religious perspective (even in this mitigated form) would be of use or appeal to all people in their navigations through the difficulties of life. But this doesn't matter. In our view concerning humanity's palliatives, one takes whatever works, and Freud's words on that matter accordingly deserve our acceptance: 'There is no golden rule which applies to everyone: every man must find out for himself in what particular fashion he can be saved.'[103] The range of palliative measures we have surveyed in this book gives a sampling of the ways in which a person can be 'saved', but here three caveats must be noted. Firstly, out of a commitment to intellectual responsibility one should avoid embracing a palliative measure of a thoroughly illusory nature. Secondly, those who are wise should probably seek to draw from the widest range of acceptable palliatives, so as not

---

[101] Sigmund Freud, *Civilization and Its Discontents*, S.E. vol. XXI, p. 74.

[102] Freud, *Future*, pp. 32–3.

[103] Freud, *Civilization*, p. 83. Freud's allusion is to a saying attributed to Frederick the Great regarding his policy of religious toleration: 'Let every man be saved after his own fashion.'

to place too strong a weight on one source of auxiliary support alone.[104] And thirdly, it is to be stressed that the palliatives surveyed hitherto should not be regarded as an entirely exhaustive list, and that, in particular, the category of 'powerful deflections' can be seen to include certain strategies not heretofore given sustained attention in this book. A word about this is in order.

Freud provides as examples of such deflections scientific activity and 'cultivating one's garden' (referring in this context to work of some kind). Evidently, the satisfactions to be gained from scientific activity cannot be regarded as an auxiliary structure open to the vast mass of people, though one might more feasibly point to work as a source of fulfilment. About even this, however, one should be circumspect. It is no doubt true that many people gain satisfaction and a sense of purpose from the work they undertake, but it is at least doubtful that this is the case for the vast majority of workers. As the Marxist tradition correctly sees, work in capitalist society has largely been reduced to a series of repetitive and monotonous actions, producing nothing more than a sense of alienation and frustration in the worker, who has become merely 'an appendix to the machine or to the bureaucratic organization'.[105] While a person may count him- or herself fortunate to have a rewarding and meaningful job, without a radical change in the structure of contemporary society one should not expect work to be a source of fulfilment for many. Indeed, work is more than likely to be just another source of pain, itself contributing to a life requiring palliation. More therefore than a job, it may be a person's chosen (and perhaps to others seemingly trifling) occupations and projects that provide satisfaction and contribute to a sense of well-being and purpose. A great deal of a person's life may be taken up with such pursuits (gardening, surfing, collecting,[106] to name but a few of these personal projects) and it would be wrong to ignore the extent of the happiness that people find therein. One might scoff haughtily at the perceived insignificance of such activities (recall Woody Allen's contempt for sports mentioned earlier), but in a world recognized as fleeting and insubstantial there may be little justification for praising one person's lifelong engagement with (for example) the philosophy of Heidegger or the plays of Shakespeare while laughing at another's preoccupation with baseball or cricket statistics. Any of these projects, lovingly and enthusiastically undertaken, might just constitute the difference between a full and an empty life. The words of Ecclesiastes once more come to mind, and remind us of the value of fully engaging

---

[104] 'Just as a cautious business-man avoids tying up all his capital in one concern, so, perhaps, worldly wisdom will advise us not to look for the whole of our satisfaction from a single aspiration' (ibid., p. 84).

[105] Erich Fromm, *The Art of Loving* (New York, 2006), p. 17.

[106] I recall here Bruce Chatwin's novel *Utz* (London, 1988), in which the eponymous central character's collection of Meissen porcelains makes up the very centre of his world and provides him with a refuge from the oppressive political climate in mid-twentieth-century Czechoslovakia.

with a personally rewarding task: *Whatsoever thy hand findeth to do, do it with thy might.* For the rest, as Hamlet says, is silence.

Freud writes of these powerful deflections that they cause us to make light of our misery, and it is in this context worth noting one further strategy that can effectively be utilized to evade suffering. This strategy may be referred to as the development of a humorous attitude towards existence, and Freud explores the nature and technique of this attitude both in *Jokes and Their Relation to the Unconscious* and in his later paper on 'Humour'.[107] Humour is regarded by Freud as a defensive process, one in which a person adopts a rebellious, rather than a resigned, attitude towards those aspects of reality which are set to cause them pain. A situation expected to produce distress is met, not with anger, fear or despair, but rather with a jest, and pleasure results from this unexpected development. As an example, Freud recounts the story of a criminal who was being led out to execution on a Monday and who remarked: 'Well, the week's beginning nicely.'[108] The remark deflates and makes nothing of the seriousness of the situation, thereby producing a sense of satisfied pleasure, both in the speaker and in his listeners. Freud explains that in instances of humour such as this, a person's ego 'refuses to be distressed by the provocations of reality, to let itself be compelled to suffer. It insists that it cannot be affected by the traumas of the external world; it shows, in fact, that such traumas are no more than occasions for it to gain pleasure.'[109] This humorous attitude also gains illumination from the fears and anxieties of childhood, fears and anxieties at which we now, as adults, can smile. The humorous attitude replicates this retrospective relief, for it is as though we are saying with regard to the sufferings of the world, 'I am too big (too fine) to be distressed by these things',[110] and that attitude might well be encapsulated in a victorious air of dismissal towards those things (death, pain, frustration and meaninglessness) which threaten the human person with so much distress. With the exercise of humour it is as if one were declaring, 'Look! here is the world, which seems so dangerous! It is nothing but a game for children – just worth making a jest about!'[111]

Given what was earlier concluded about the infantile character of the traditional religious attitude, we might see the perspective of humour as providing a viable alternative to the yearning for a protective father. To recall, in the response of the religious believer, we see a repetition of the child's fear of a threatening world, wherein a person runs for comfort to an illusory father, in whose narcotic embrace the terrors of the world are dampened and denied. No such denial occurs in the

---

[107] Freud even places the exercise of humour 'among the great series of methods which the human mind has constructed in order to evade the compulsion to suffer', thereby explicitly linking it with the palliatives we have had as our focus throughout this book (Sigmund Freud, 'Humour', S.E. vol. XXI, p. 163).

[108] Ibid., p. 161.

[109] Ibid., p. 162.

[110] Sigmund Freud, *Jokes and Their Relation to the Unconscious*, S.E. vol. VIII, p. 234.

[111] Freud, 'Humour', p. 166.

humorous attitude. We look at the world and at our own transience, we register and process those things, and then find a way to live through it all by reducing its crushing weight and refusing to be beaten down by it. This is achieved by what Freud calls 'broken' humour – 'the humour that smiles through tears'.[112] A one-liner from Woody Allen exhibits this attitude well: 'Not only is there no God, but try getting a plumber on weekends.'[113] The effectiveness of this line lies in part in its subversion of the expectations one has regarding a sentence of the form 'Not only ... but also ...'. Typically, the second part of that sentence frame will serve to introduce a piece of information of greater magnitude ('Not only did I fall asleep on the train and miss my stop, but I left my wallet and passport behind when I got out'), so we expect 'Not only is there no God ...' to be followed by: '... but there is no immortality also', or '... but life is also completely meaningless'. In Allen's one-liner, on the other hand, the issue of apparently greater significance (the godless universe) is reduced to having lesser weight than the minor inconvenience of a plumber's unavailability. The ridiculousness of our metaphysical anxieties is thus seen, and we laugh, both at the vexations and irritations of modern life and at the abiding troubles of our human condition, our sense of abandonment and our ephemerality. These, too, are just games for children.

The development of a humorous attitude may well then constitute a further bulwark against the pains and troubles of our shared human condition, and deserves to take its place alongside those other methods of palliation we have in this book surveyed. As we have seen, none of these measures is to be regarded as entirely effective, each having its limitations and negative side effects. Yet it is hard to deny that this strange, sad human condition may be alleviated considerably by a combination of such prizes as the appreciation of artistic production, evenings with friends in which both the conversation and the wine flow freely, loving relations with those who share our light moments and comfort us through the darker ones, and throughout it all an appreciation of the vastness of all things compared with our own smallness, and a corresponding recognition that we might, in some positive way or another, contribute a brief verse to the ongoing drama.[114] And amidst all of that, we have recourse to those treasured though oft-overlooked moments, disclosures and quotidian resources alluded to by Fontane in his articulation of auxiliary structures, an articulation that exerted such a profound influence upon Freud:

---

[112]   Freud, *Jokes*, p. 232.

[113]   Woody Allen, *Getting Even* (New York, 1971), p. 33.

[114]   The allusion, of course, is to the response provided by Walt Whitman in 'O Me! O Life!' to the question of whether there is, amid all its foolishness and sadness, any good at all in life. The answer: 'That you are here – that life exists and identity, / That the powerful play goes on, and you may contribute a verse' (Walt Whitman, *Leaves of Grass* (New York, 1992), p. 410).

'Show me someone who isn't depressed. Someone who doesn't say to himself every day, "A very questionable business, when you think about it." … Stand in the breach and hold the line till you fall, that's the best thing. And before you go, get as much as possible out of the small things of life, the smallest of all. Don't miss the violets in bloom, or the flowers coming out round the Luise Monument, or the little girls in high-laced boots jumping over their skipping-ropes … There's *Sardanapalus* or *Coppélia* with dell'Era, and after that's over there's Siechen's beer-restaurant. Not to be sneezed at. Three small beers always do the trick.'[115]

Things of this nature – and all the other auxiliary structures we have enumerated in this book – unquestionably serve to palliate the most overwhelmingly painful aspects of our lives. But more than that, they maybe even allow us to look back over our lives and hopefully, at the very end, to say, *Yes, that was worthwhile. That was good.*

---

[115] Theodor Fontane, *Effi Briest* (London, 2000), p. 212. It is hard here not to be reminded of Woody Allen's *Manhattan*, in which the character of Isaac (played by Allen) lists some personally specific things that make life worth living: 'For me, ooh, I would say, what, Groucho Marx to name one thing, and Willie Mays, and the second movement of the Jupiter Symphony, and Louis Armstrong's recording of "Potato Head Blues", Swedish movies, naturally, *Sentimental Education* by Flaubert, Marlon Brando, Frank Sinatra, those incredible Apples and Pears by Cézanne, the crabs at Sam Wo's, Tracy's face …'. It is to be noted how small-scale and personal all these things are, encompassing art, music, food, laughter and romantic relationships. What makes life worth living, on this view, is not some grand cosmic purpose, but a collection of little things that make a person think – contra Schopenhauer and Silenus – 'Yes, it was better to have been born!'

Bibliography

Adorno, Theodor, *Negative Dialectics* (New York: Continuum, 1973).

Allen, Woody, *Getting Even* (New York: Random House, 1971).

Appignanesi, Lisa, *All About Love: Anatomy of an Unruly Emotion* (London: Virago, 2011).

Bacon, Francis, *The New Organon* (Cambridge: Cambridge University Press, 2000).

Baier, Annette, 'Unsafe Loves', in Robert C. Solomon and Kathleen M. Higgins (eds), *The Philosophy of (Erotic) Love* (Lawrence, KS: University Press of Kansas, 1991), pp. 433–50.

Balzac, Honoré de, *The Physiology of Marriage* (Cirencester: Echo Library, 2005).

Barthes, Roland, *A Lover's Discourse* (New York: Hill & Wang, 1978).

Baudelaire, Charles, *Les Fleurs du Mal* (New York: Dover, 1992).

Beauvoir, Simone de, *The Second Sex* (Harmondsworth: Penguin, 1972).

Bentham, Jeremy, 'The Rationale of Reward', in *The Works of Jeremy Bentham* (11 vols, Edinburgh: William Tait, 1843), vol. 2, pp. 189–266.

——, *Memoirs and Correspondence*, in *The Works of Jeremy Bentham* (11 vols, Edinburgh: William Tait, 1843), vol. 10.

——, *An Introduction to the Principles of Morals and Legislation* (Amherst, NY: Prometheus Books, 1988).

Bergmann, Martin, *The Anatomy of Loving* (New York: Columbia University Press, 1987).

Björkman, Stig, *Woody Allen on Woody Allen* (New York: Grove Press, 1995).

Blackburn, Simon, *Think* (Oxford: Oxford University Press, 1999).

Bonaparte, Napoleon, *Aphorisms and Thoughts* (Richmond, Surrey: Oneworld, 2008).

Bowlby, John, *Attachment* (Harmondsworth: Penguin, 1971).

——, *Loss* (London: Penguin, 1991).

Bowman, Wayne D., *Philosophical Perspectives on Music* (New York: Oxford University Press, 1998).

Brodsky, Joseph, 'In Praise of Boredom', in *On Grief and Reason* (New York: Farrar Strauss Giroux, 1995), pp. 104–13.

Brontë, Emily, *Wuthering Heights* (Harmondsworth: Penguin, 1965).

Buckley, William F., Kurt Schmoke, Joseph D. McNamara and Robert W. Sweet, 'The War on Drugs Is Lost', in Hugh LaFollette (ed.), *Ethics in Practice* (Oxford: Blackwell, 2002), pp. 300–306.

Burton, Robert, *The Anatomy of Melancholy* (New York: Tudor, 1948).

Butler, Christopher, *Pleasure and the Arts* (Oxford: Oxford University Press, 2004).

Byrne, Peter, 'F.R. Leavis and the Religious Dimension in Literature', *Modern Theology*, 1/2 (1985): 119–30.

Camus, Albert, *The Myth of Sisyphus* (Harmondsworth: Penguin, 1975).

Castle, Terry, *The Female Thermometer: Eighteenth-Century Culture and the Invention of the Uncanny* (Oxford: Oxford University Press, 1995).

Cervantes, Miguel de, *Don Quixote* (Harmondsworth: Penguin, 1950).

Chatwin, Bruce, *Utz* (London: Jonathan Cape, 1988).

Cioffi, Frank, 'Explanation and Biography: A Conversation', in *Freud and the Question of Pseudoscience* (Chicago, IL: Open Court, 1998), pp. 265–79.

Cioran, E.M., *Tears and Saints* (Chicago, IL: University of Chicago Press, 1998).

Clack, Beverley and Brian R. Clack, *The Philosophy of Religion: A Critical Introduction* (Oxford: Polity Press, 2008).

Clack, Brian R., '"At home in the uncanny": Freud's Account of *das Unheimliche* in the Context of His Theory of Religious Belief', *Religion*, 38/3 (2008): 250–58.

——, 'Cannabis and the Human Condition', in Dale Jacquette (ed.), *Cannabis* (Oxford: Blackwell, 2010), pp. 90–99.

——, 'Religious Belief and the Disregard of Reality', in Joseph Carlisle, James C. Carter and Daniel Whistler (eds), *Moral Powers, Fragile Beliefs* (New York: Continuum, 2011), pp. 261–87.

Clifford, W.K., *The Ethics of Belief and Other Essays* (London: Watts & Co., 1947).

Conrad, Mark T., 'God, Suicide, and the Meaning of Life in the Films of Woody Allen', in Mark T. Conrad and Aeon J. Skoble (eds), *Woody Allen and Philosophy* (Chicago, IL: Open Court, 2004), pp. 7–23.

Currie, Gregory and Ian Ravenscroft, *Recreative Minds* (Oxford: Oxford University Press, 2002).

Dawkins, Richard, *River Out of Eden* (New York: Basic Books, 1995).

Dekkers, Midas, *The Way of All Flesh* (London: Harvill Press, 2000).

DiCenso, James J., *The Other Freud: Religion, Culture and Psychoanalysis* (London: Routledge, 1999).

Dickens, Charles, *Hard Times* (Harmondsworth: Penguin, 1969).

Dienstag, Joshua Foa, *Pessimism: Philosophy, Ethic, Spirit* (Princeton, NJ: Princeton University Press, 2006).

Dilman, İlham, *Love and Human Separateness* (Oxford: Basil Blackwell, 1987).

Dormandy, Thomas, *The Worst of Evils: The Fight Against Pain* (New Haven, CT: Yale University Press, 2006).

Doyle, Arthur Conan, *The Sign of Four* (London: Penguin, 2001).

Doyle, Derek, Geoffrey Hanks and Neil MacDonald, 'Introduction', in Derek Doyle, Geoffrey Hanks and Neil MacDonald (eds), *The Oxford Textbook of Palliative Medicine* (Oxford: Oxford University Press, 1999), pp. 3–10.

Dreyfus, Hubert, *Being-in-the-World* (Cambridge, MA: MIT Press, 1991).

Eco, Umberto, *On Ugliness* (London: Harvill Secker, 2007).

Edmundson, Mark, *The Death of Sigmund Freud* (New York: Bloomsbury, 2007).

Elliston, Frederick, 'In Defense of Promiscuity', in Robert M. Stewart (ed.), *Philosophical Perspectives on Sex and Love* (Oxford: Oxford University Press, 1995), pp. 146–58.

Eliot, George, *Adam Bede* (Chicago, IL: Belford, Clarke & Co., 1888).

Emmanuel, Linda L., 'Comprehensive Assessment', in Linda L. Emmanuel and S. Lawrence Librach (eds), *Palliative Care* (Philadelphia, PA: Saunders, 2007), pp. 27–41.

Engelmann, Paul, *Letters from Ludwig Wittgenstein with a Memoir* (Oxford: Basil Blackwell, 1967).

Engels, Friedrich, 'Ludwig Feuerbach and the End of Classical German Philosophy', in Karl Marx and Friedrich Engels, *On Religion* (Moscow: Progress Publishers, 1957), pp. 187–234.

——, 'On the History of Early Christianity', in Karl Marx and Friedrich Engels, *On Religion* (Moscow: Progress Publishers, 1957), pp. 275–300.

Epicurus, 'The Principal Doctrines', in J.C.A. Gaskin (ed.), *The Epicurean Philosophers* (London: J.M. Dent, 1995), pp. 5–11.

Farrell, Daniel M., 'Jealousy and Desire', in Roger E. Lamb (ed.), *Love Analyzed* (Boulder, CO: Westview Press, 1997), pp. 165–88.

Faull, Christina, 'The History and Principles of Palliative Care', in Christina Faull, Yvonne Carter and Richard Woof (eds), *Handbook of Palliative Care* (Oxford: Blackwell, 1998), pp. 1–12.

Faupel, Charles, Alan Horowitz and Greg Weaver, *The Sociology of American Drug Use* (Oxford: Oxford University Press, 2010).

Fenichel, Otto, 'On the Psychology of Boredom', in *The Collected Papers of Otto Fenichel* (2 vols, New York: W.W. Norton, 1953), vol. 1, pp. 292–302.

——, *The Psychoanalytic Theory of Neurosis* (London: Routledge & Kegan Paul, 1955).

Feuerbach, Ludwig, *Lectures on the Essence of Religion* (New York: Harper & Row, 1967).

——, *The Essence of Religion* (Amherst, NY: Prometheus Books, 2004).

——, *The Essence of Christianity* (New York: Dover, 2008).

Finger, Anja, 'The Pains and Pleasures of Opium, Religion, and Modernity: A New View of Robert Owen', in Michael R. Ott (ed.), *The Future of Religion* (Leiden: Brill, 2007), pp. 147–64.

Fischer, Ernst, *The Necessity of Art* (Harmondsworth: Penguin, 1986).

Fisher, Mark, *Personal Love* (London: Duckworth, 1990).

Flew, Anthony, 'Theology and Falsification', in Anthony Flew and Alasdair MacIntyre (eds), *New Essays in Philosophical Theology* (London: SCM Press, 1955), pp. 96–9.

Fontane, Theodor, *Effi Briest* (London: Penguin, 2000).

Forbes, Karen and Christina Faull, 'The Principles of Pain Management', in Christina Faull, Yvonne Carter and Richard Woof (eds), *Handbook of Palliative Care* (Oxford: Blackwell, 1998), pp. 99–133.

Frazer, J.G., *The Belief in Immortality and the Worship of the Dead* (London: Macmillan, 1913).

Freud, Anna, *Normality and Pathology in Childhood* (London: Hogarth Press, 1973).

Freud, Ernst L. (ed.), *Letters of Sigmund Freud* (New York: Basic Books, 1960).

—— (ed.), *The Letters of Sigmund Freud and Arnold Zweig* (New York: Harcourt Brace Jovanovich, 1970).

Freud, Sigmund, 'Project for a Scientific Psychology', in *The Standard Edition of the Complete Psychological Works of Sigmund Freud* (24 vols, London: Hogarth Press, 1953–74) (hereafter S.E., followed by volume number and date of original publication), S.E. I, pp. 281–397 (1895).

Freud, Sigmund, and Josef Breuer, *Studies on Hysteria*, S.E. II (1893–95).

Freud, Sigmund, 'Sexuality in the Aetiology of Neuroses', S.E. III, pp. 259–85 (1898).

——, *The Interpretation of Dreams* (First Part), S.E. IV (1900).

——, *The Interpretation of Dreams* (Second Part), S.E. V, pp. 339–627 (1900).

——, *On Dreams*, S.E. V, pp. 629–86 (1901).

——, 'Fragment of an Analysis of a Case of Hysteria', S.E. VII, pp. 1–122 (1905).

——, *Three Essays on the Theory of Sexuality*, S.E. VII, pp. 123–243 (1905).

——, *Jokes and Their Relation to the Unconscious*, S.E. VIII (1905).

——, *Delusions and Dreams in Jensen's 'Gradiva'*, S.E. IX, pp. 1–95 (1907).

——, 'Obsessive Actions and Religious Practices', S.E. IX, pp. 115–27 (1907).

——, 'Creative Writers and Day-Dreaming', S.E. IX, pp. 141–53 (1908).

——, *Five Lectures on Psycho-Analysis*, S.E. XI, pp. 1–55 (1910).

——, 'A Special Type of Choice of Object Made by Men (Contributions to the Psychology of Love I)', S.E. XI, pp. 163–75 (1910).

——, 'The Psycho-Analytic View of Psychogenic Disturbance of Vision', S.E. XI, pp. 209–18 (1910).

——, 'On the Universal Tendency to Debasement in the Sphere of Love (Contributions to the Psychology of Love II)', S.E. XI, pp. 177–90 (1912).

——, 'Formulations on the Two Principles of Mental Functioning', S.E. XII, pp. 213–26 (1911).

——, *Totem and Taboo*, S.E. XIII, pp. 1–161 (1913).

——, 'On Narcissism: An Introduction', S.E. XIV, pp. 67–102 (1914).

——, 'Observations on Transference-Love (Further Recommendations on the Technique of Psycho-Analysis III)', S.E. XII, pp. 157–71 (1915).

——, 'Instincts and Their Vicissitudes', S.E. XIV, pp. 109–40 (1915).

——, 'On Transience', S.E. XIV, pp. 303–7 (1916).

——, 'A Metapsychological Supplement to the Theory of Dreams', S.E. XIV, pp. 217–35 (1917).

——, 'Mourning and Melancholia', S.E. XIV, pp. 237–58 (1917).

——, *Introductory Lectures on Psycho-Analysis* (Part III), S.E. XVI (1916–17).

——, *From the History of an Infantile Neurosis*, S.E. XVII, pp. 1–122 (1918).

——, 'The "Uncanny"', S.E. XVII, pp. 217–56 (1919).

——, *Beyond the Pleasure Principle*, S.E. XVIII, pp. 1–64 (1920).

——, *Group Psychology and the Analysis of the Ego*, S.E. XVIII, pp. 65–143 (1921).

——, *The Ego and the Id*, S.E. XIX, pp. 1–59 (1923).

——, 'The Economic Problem of Masochism', S.E. XIX, pp. 155–70 (1924).

——, *An Autobiographical Study*, S.E. XX, pp. 1–74 (1925).

——, *Inhibitions, Symptoms and Anxiety*, S.E. XX, pp. 75–172 (1926).

——, *The Question of Lay Analysis: Conversations with an Impartial Person*, S.E. XX, pp. 177–258 (1926).

——, *The Future of an Illusion*, S.E. XXI, pp. 1–56 (1927).

——, 'Humour', S.E. XXI, pp. 159–66 (1927).

——, 'Dostoevsky and Parricide', S.E. XXI, pp. 173–94 (1928).

——, *Civilization and Its Discontents*, S.E. XXI, pp. 57–145 (1930).

——, *Civilization and Its Discontents* (translated by Joan Riviere) (London: Hogarth Press, 1930).

——, *New Introductory Lectures on Psycho-Analysis*, S.E. XXII, pp. 1–182 (1933).

——, 'Analysis Terminable and Interminable', S.E. XXIII, pp. 209–53 (1937).

——, 'Constructions in Analysis', S.E. XXIII, pp. 255–69 (1937).

——, *Moses and Monotheism: Three Essays*, S.E. XXIII, pp. 1–137 (1939).

——, *An Outline of Psycho-Analysis*, S.E. XXIII, pp. 139–207 (1940).

——, *Die Zukunft einer Illusion* (Frankfurt: Fischer Taschenbach Verlag, 1967).

——, 'Über Coca', in *Cocaine Papers* (New York: Stonehill, 1974), pp. 47–73.

——, 'On the General Effect of Cocaine', in *Cocaine Papers* (New York: Stonehill, 1974), pp. 111–18.

Fromm, Erich, *The Art of Loving* (New York: HarperCollins, 2006).

Gansberg, Martin, 'Moral Cowardice', in Louis Pojman and Lewis Vaughn (eds), *The Moral Life* (New York: Oxford University Press, 2011), pp. 487–91.

Gaskin, J.C.A., *Hume's Philosophy of Religion* (Basingstoke: Macmillan, 1988).

Gay, Peter, *Freud: A Life for Our Time* (New York: W.W. Norton, 1998).

Goodstein, Elizabeth, *Experience Without Qualities: Boredom and Modernity* (Stanford, CA: Stanford University Press, 2005).

Guntrip, Harry, *Personality Structure and Human Interaction* (London: Hogarth Press, 1968).

Halwani, Raja, *Philosophy of Love, Sex, and Marriage* (New York: Routledge, 2010).

Hardy, Thomas, *Two on a Tower* (London: Penguin, 1999).

——, *Jude the Obscure* (Oxford: Oxford University Press, 2002).

——, *Tess of the d'Urbervilles* (Oxford: Oxford University Press, 2005).

Harlow, Harry F., *Learning to Love* (New York: Jason Aronson, 1974).

Hart, Melissa, 'Spiritual Care', in Linda L. Emmanuel and S. Lawrence Librach (eds), *Palliative Care* (Philadelphia, PA: Saunders, 2007), pp. 524–39.

Healy, Seán Desmond, *Boredom, Self, and Culture* (London: Associated Universities Presses, 1984).

Hegel, Georg Wilhelm Friedrich, *Introductory Lectures on Aesthetics* (London: Penguin, 1993).

Heidegger, Martin, *Being and Time* (Oxford: Basil Blackwell, 1962).
——, *Poetry, Language, Thought* (New York: Harper & Row, 1975).
Hick, John, *Evil and the God of Love* (London: Macmillan, 1966).
——, *Death and Eternal Life* (London: Collins, 1976).
——, *An Interpretation of Religion* (Basingstoke: Macmillan, 1989).
Hicks, Bill, *Love All the People* (London: Constable, 2004).
Holbach, Paul Henri Thiry, Baron d', *Good Sense* (Amherst, NY: Prometheus Books, 2004).
Homer, *The Odyssey* (Oxford: Oxford University Press, 1980).
Huemer, Michael, 'America's Unjust Drug War', in James Rachels and Stuart Rachels (eds), *The Right Thing To Do* (Boston, MA: McGraw Hill, 2010), pp. 223–36.
Hume, David, *A Treatise of Human Nature* (Oxford: Clarendon Press, 1888).
——, *Dialogues Concerning Natural Religion* (New York: Hafner, 1948).
——, *The Natural History of Religion* (London: Adam & Charles Black, 1956).
——, *Enquiries Concerning Human Understanding and Concerning the Principles of Morals* (Oxford: Clarendon Press, 1975).
——, 'Of Polygamy and Divorces', in *Essays: Moral, Political, and Literary* (Indianapolis, IN: Liberty Fund, 1985), pp. 181–90.
——, 'Of Suicide', in *Essays: Moral, Political, and Literary* (Indianapolis, IN: Liberty Fund, 1985), pp. 577–89.
Husak, Douglas, *Legalize This! The Case for Decriminalizing Drugs* (London: Verso, 2002).
Huxley, Aldous, *Island* (New York: HarperCollins, 1962).
——, *Brave New World* (London: Granada, 1977).
——, *The Doors of Perception and Heaven and Hell* (London: Vintage, 2004).
Iverson, Leslie, *Drugs: A Very Short Introduction* (Oxford: Oxford University Press, 2001).
James, William, *Pragmatism* (New York: Longmans, Green, & Co., 1907).
——, *The Varieties of Religious Experience* (London: Collins, 1960).
Jentsch, Ernst, 'On the Psychology of the Uncanny (1906)', *Angelaki*, 2/1 (1995): 7–16.
Johnson, Samuel, *Consolation in the Face of Death* (London: Penguin, 2009).
Jones, Ernest, *Sigmund Freud: Life and Work* (3 vols, London: Hogarth Press, 1953–57).
Kant, Immanuel, *Critique of Judgement* (Oxford: Oxford University Press, 1952).
——, *Lectures on Ethics* (New York: Harper & Row, 1963).
——, *Religion Within the Boundaries of Mere Reason*, in *Religion and Rational Theology* (Cambridge: Cambridge University Press, 1996), pp. 39–215.
——, *Anthropology from a Pragmatic Point of View* (Cambridge: Cambridge University Press, 2006).
Klein, Richard, *Cigarettes Are Sublime* (London: Picador, 1995).
Klibansky, Raymond and Ernest C. Mossner (eds), *New Letters of David Hume* (Oxford: Oxford University Press, 1954).

Kuhn, Cynthia, Scott Swartzwelder and Wilkie Wilson, *Buzzed* (New York: W.W. Norton, 2003).

Kundera, Milan, *The Art of the Novel* (New York: Grove Press, 1988).

——, *The Unbearable Lightness of Being* (New York: HarperCollins, 1999).

Küng, Hans, *Freud and the Problem of God* (New Haven, CT: Yale University Press, 1979).

Laplanche, Jean and Jean-Bertrand Pontalis, *The Language of Psychoanalysis* (London: Karnac, 1973).

Leibniz, G.W., 'Reflections on the Common Concept of Justice', in *Philosophical Papers and Letters: A Selection* (Dordrecht: Reidel, 1976), pp. 561–73.

Lenin, V.I., 'Socialism and Religion', in *Collected Works*, vol. 10 (Moscow: Progress Publishers, 1965), pp. 83–7.

——, 'The Attitude of the Workers' Party to Religion', in *Collected Works*, vol. 15 (Moscow: Progress Publishers, 1973), pp. 402–13.

Leopardi, Giacomo, *Selected Prose and Poetry* (London: Oxford University Press, 1966).

Lewin, Louis, *Phantastica* (Rochester, VT: Park Street Press, 1998).

Lewis, C.S., *The Four Loves* (London: Geoffrey Bles, 1960).

Lichtenberg, Georg Christoph, *Aphorisms* (London: Penguin, 1990).

Lucretius, *On the Nature of the Universe* (Harmondsworth: Penguin, 1951).

Mackie, J.L., 'Evil and Omnipotence', *Mind*, 64/254 (1955): 200–212.

Malcolm, Janet, *Psychoanalysis: The Impossible Profession* (London: Picador, 1982).

Markel, Howard, *An Anatomy of Addiction: Sigmund Freud, William Halsted, and the Miracle Drug Cocaine* (New York: Pantheon, 2011).

Martin, Michael, *Atheism: A Philosophical Justification* (Philadelphia, PA: Temple University Press, 1990).

Marx, Karl, 'Contribution to the Critique of Hegel's Philosophy of Law', in Karl Marx and Friedrich Engels, *On Religion* (Moscow: Progress Publishers, 1957), pp. 39–52.

——, 'On the Jewish Question', in David McLellan (ed.), *Karl Marx: Selected Writings* (Oxford: Oxford University Press, 1977), pp. 39–62.

Masson, J.M. (ed.), *The Complete Letters of Sigmund Freud to Wilhelm Fliess 1887–1904* (Cambridge, MA: The Belknap Press of Harvard University Press, 1985).

Mawson, T.J., *Belief in God: An Introduction to the Philosophy of Religion* (Oxford: Oxford University Press, 2005).

McLellan, David, *The Young Hegelians and Karl Marx* (London: Macmillan, 1969).

——, *Marxism and Religion* (London: Macmillan, 1987).

Mill, John Stuart, *Utilitarianism* (London: Longman, Green, Longman, Roberts, & Green, 1864).

——, *Three Essays on Religion* (London: Longmans, Green, Reader, & Dyer, 1874).

——, *On Liberty* (Oxford: Oxford University Press, 1991).

Misak, C.J., *Verificationism: Its History and Prospects* (London: Routledge, 1995).

Mitchell, Basil, 'Theology and Falsification', in Anthony Flew and Alasdair MacIntyre (eds), *New Essays in Philosophical Theology* (London: SCM Press, 1955), pp. 103–5.

Nicholson, Sydney (ed.), *Hymns Ancient and Modern* (London: William Clowes and Sons, 1916).

Nielsen, Kai, 'Is Religion the Opium of the People? Marxianism and Religion', in D.Z. Phillips (ed.), *Can Religion Be Explained Away?* (Basingstoke: Macmillan, 1996), pp. 177–223.

Nietzsche, Friedrich, *Thus Spoke Zarathustra* (Harmondsworth: Penguin, 1961).

——, *Twilight of the Idols and the Anti-Christ* (Harmondsworth: Penguin, 1968).

——, *Human, All Too Human* (Cambridge: Cambridge University Press, 1986).

——, 'On the Uses and Disadvantages of History for Life', in *Untimely Meditations* (Cambridge: Cambridge University Press, 1997), pp. 57–123.

Nozick, Robert, 'Love's Bond', in Robert M. Stewart (ed.), *Philosophical Perspectives on Sex and Love* (Oxford: Oxford University Press, 1995), pp. 231–40.

Nuttall, A.D., *Why Does Tragedy Give Pleasure?* (Oxford: Oxford University Press, 1996).

Oakeshott, Michael, *On Human Conduct* (Oxford: Clarendon Press, 1975).

Ovid, *Metamorphoses* (New York: Viking, 1958).

——, *The Love Poems* (Oxford: Oxford University Press, 1990).

Paley, William, *Natural Theology* (London: Scott, Webster & Geary, 1838).

Palmer, Michael, *Freud and Jung on Religion* (London: Routledge, 1997).

Pascal, Blaise, *Pensées* (Oxford: Oxford University Press, 1999).

Pearse, Padraic, *Selected Poems* (Dublin: New Island Books, 1993).

Pessoa, Fernando, *The Book of Disquiet* (London: Penguin, 2002).

Phillips, D.Z., *Death and Immortality* (London: Macmillan, 1970).

Plantinga, Alvin, *God, Freedom and Evil* (Grand Rapids, MI: William B. Eerdmans, 1977).

——, *Warranted Christian Belief* (New York: Oxford University Press, 2000).

Plato, *The Symposium* (Harmondsworth: Penguin, 1951).

——, *The Republic* (Harmondsworth: Penguin, 1955).

——, *Phaedrus* (Harmondsworth: Penguin, 1973).

Proust, Marcel, *Remembrance of Things Past* (3 vols, Harmondsworth: Penguin, 1983).

Pugmire, David, 'Sentimentality and Truthfulness', in Alex Neill and Aaron Ridley (eds), *Arguing About Art* (London: Routledge, 2008), pp. 354–8.

Randall, Fiona and R.S. Downie, *The Philosophy of Palliative Care: Critique and Reconstruction* (Oxford: Oxford University Press, 2006).

Raposa, Michael, *Boredom and the Religious Imagination* (Charlottesville, VA: University Press of Virginia, 1999).

Reynolds, Graham, *Constable's England* (New York: Metropolitan Museum of Art, 1983).

Rhees, Rush, 'Postscript', in Rush Rhees (ed.), *Recollections of Wittgenstein* (Oxford: Oxford University Press, 1984), pp. 172–209.

Richards, I.A., *Practical Criticism* (New York: Harcourt Brace Jovanovich, 1929).

Rousseau, Jean-Jacques, *Reveries of the Solitary Walker* (Harmondsworth: Penguin, 1979).

——, 'Discourse on the Origin and Foundations of Inequality Among Men', in *The Basic Political Writings* (Indianapolis, IN: Hackett, 1987), pp. 23–109.

——, 'Preface to *Narcissus*', in *The Discourses and Other Early Political Writings* (Cambridge: Cambridge University Press, 1997), pp. 92–106.

Royle, Nicholas, *The Uncanny*, London: Routledge, 2003.

Rudgley, Richard, *The Encyclopedia of Psychoactive Substances* (London: Little, Brown and Company, 1998).

Rudman, Laurie A. and Peter Glick, *The Social Psychology of Gender* (New York: Guilford, 2008).

Russell, Bertrand, 'A Free Man's Worship', in *Mysticism and Logic* (New York: Dover, 2004), pp. 36–44.

Sandler, Joseph, Christopher Dare and Alex Holder, *The Patient and the Analyst* (London: Karnac, 1973).

Sartre, Jean-Paul, *Being and Nothingness* (New York: Philosophical Library, 1956).

Savile, Anthony, 'Sentimentality', in Alex Neill and Aaron Ridley (eds), *Arguing About Art* (London: Routledge, 2008), pp. 337–41.

Schermer, M.H.N., '*Brave New World* versus *Island*: Utopian and Dystopian Views of Psychopharmacology', *Medicine, Health Care, and Philosophy*, 10/2 (2007): 119–28.

Schleiermacher, Friedrich, *On Religion: Speeches to Its Cultured Despisers* (New York: Harper & Row, 1958).

Schopenhauer, Arthur, *Studies in Pessimism* (London: Swan Sonnenschein & Co., 1893).

——, *The World as Will and Representation* (2 vols, New York: Dover, 1969).

——, *Essays and Aphorisms* (Harmondsworth: Penguin, 1970).

——, *Parerga and Paralipomena* (2 vols, Oxford: Oxford University Press, 1974).

——, *On the Basis of Morality* (Oxford: Berghahn Books, 1995).

Schur, Max, *Freud: Living and Dying* (New York: International Universities Press, 1972).

Scruton, Roger, *The Meaning of Conservatism* (London: Macmillan, 1984).

——, 'The Aesthetic Endeavour Today', *Philosophy*, 71/277 (1996): 331–50.

Shakespeare, William, *Hamlet* (London: Penguin, 1996).

Sharpe, R.A., 'Solid Joys or Fading Pleasures', in Eva Schaper (ed.), *Pleasure, Preference and Value* (Cambridge: Cambridge University Press, 1983), pp. 86–98.

Siegel, Ronald, *Intoxication* (Rochester, VT: Park Street Press, 2005).

Singer, Irving, *The Nature of Love: The Modern World* (Chicago, IL: University of Chicago Press, 1987).

——, *The Pursuit of Love* (Baltimore, MD: The Johns Hopkins University Press, 1994).

——, *Philosophy of Love: A Partial Summing-Up* (Cambridge, MA: MIT Press, 2009).

——, *The Nature of Love: Courtly and Romantic* (Cambridge, MA: MIT Press, 2009).

——, *The Nature of Love: Plato to Luther* (Cambridge, MA: MIT Press, 2009).

Soble, Alan, *The Structure of Love* (New Haven, CT: Yale University Press, 1990).

——, 'Union, Autonomy and Concern', in Roger E. Lamb (ed.), *Love Analyzed* (Boulder, CO: Westview Press, 1997), pp. 65–92.

Solomon, Robert C., 'The Virtue of (Erotic) Love', in Robert C. Solomon and Kathleen M. Higgins (eds), *The Philosophy of (Erotic) Love* (Lawrence, KS: University Press of Kansas, 1991), pp. 492–518.

——, *About Love: Reinventing Romance for Our Times* (Indianapolis, IN: Hackett, 2006).

Spacks, Patricia Meyer, *Boredom: The Literary History of a State of Mind* (Chicago, IL: University of Chicago Press, 1995).

Stendhal, *Love* (London: Penguin, 2004).

Stevenson, Leslie, David L. Haberman and Peter Matthews Wright, *Twelve Theories of Human Nature* (Oxford: Oxford University Press, 2013).

Storr, Anthony, 'The Concept of Cure', in Charles Rycroft (ed.), *Psychoanalysis Observed* (London: Constable & Co., 1966), pp. 51–84.

——, *The Dynamics of Creation* (London: Secker & Warburg, 1972).

——, *Music and the Mind* (London: HarperCollins, 1997).

——, *Solitude* (London: HarperCollins, 1997).

Sullum, Jacob, *Saying Yes: In Defense of Drug Use* (New York: Penguin, 2004).

Sutherland, Stewart R., 'What Happens after Death?', *Scottish Journal of Theology*, 22/4 (1969): 404–18.

——, *God, Jesus and Belief* (Oxford: Basil Blackwell, 1984).

Svendson, Lars, *A Philosophy of Boredom* (London: Reaktion, 2005).

Swinburne, Richard, *The Existence of God* (Oxford: Oxford University Press, 1979).

Tanner, Michael, 'Sentimentality', *Proceedings of the Aristotelian Society*, 77 (1976–77): 127–47.

Taylor, Richard, 'Arthur Schopenhauer', in Ninian Smart, John Clayton, Patrick Sherry and Steven T. Katz (eds), *Nineteenth Century Religious Thought in the West* (3 vols, Cambridge: Cambridge University Press, 1985), vol. 1, pp. 157–80.

Thomas, Edward, *The Works of Edward Thomas* (Ware: Wordsworth, 1994).

Tolstoy, Leo, 'Why Do Men Stupefy Themselves?', in *Essays and Letters* (London: Oxford University Press, 1911), pp. 16–35.

——, *What Is Art?* (New York: Oxford University Press, 1962).

Trilling, Lionel, *The Liberal Imagination* (New York: New York Review Books, 1950).

Trotsky, Leon, 'Vodka, the Church, and the Cinema', in *Problems of Everyday Life* (New York: Pathfinder Press, 1973), pp. 38–43.

Unwerth, Matthew von, *Freud's Requiem* (New York: Riverhead Books, 2005).

Voltaire, *Candide* (Bloomington, IN: Indiana University Press, 1961).

Weil, Andrew, *The Natural Mind* (New York: Mariner, 2004).

Weiss, Robert S., 'Attachment in Adult Life', in Colin Murray Parkes and Joan Stevenson-Hyde (eds), *The Place of Attachment in Human Behavior* (New York: Basic Books, 1982), pp. 171–84.

Whitman, Walt, *Leaves of Grass* (New York: Library of America, 1992).

Wiggins, David, *Needs, Values, Truth* (Oxford: Oxford University Press, 1998).

Wilde, Oscar, *De Profundis and Other Writings* (Harmondsworth: Penguin, 1986).

Williams, Bernard, 'The Makropulos Case', in *Problems of the Self* (Cambridge: Cambridge University Press, 1976), pp. 82–100.

Williams, Tennessee, 'The Timeless World of a Play', in *New Selected Essays: Where I Live* (New York: New Directions, 2009), pp. 59–62.

Wilson, James Q., 'Against the Legalization of Drugs', in Hugh LaFollette (ed.), *Ethics in Practice* (Oxford: Blackwell, 2002), pp. 295–9.

Wittgenstein, Ludwig, *Tractatus Logico-Philosophicus* (London: Kegan Paul, Trench, Trubner & Co., 1922).

——, *Philosophical Investigations* (Oxford: Basil Blackwell, 1953).

——, *Philosophical Grammar* (Oxford: Basil Blackwell, 1974).

——, *Remarks on Frazer's Golden Bough* (Retford: Brynmill Press, 1979).

Zagzebski, Linda Trinkaus, *Philosophy of Religion: An Historical Introduction* (Oxford: Blackwell, 2007).

Index